FROM WHERE I SIT...

To Chris,
all the Best-

Anthony Mann

FROM WHERE
I SIT...

ANTHONY MANN

TROUSER PRESS

© Anthony Mann 1990-
Cover design by Jill Wadsworth

Published by Trouser Press

First published 1990

British Library Cataloguing in Publication Data
1. England. Social life biographies
   I. Title
   942–0858092

   ISBN 978 095165 010 3

First reprint 2002 by Haynes, Somerset.
Second reprint 2009 by J F Print Ltd, Sparkford, Somerset.

Dedication

This book is dedicated to all those who buy it, in the hope that it will raise enough money to send our youngest to private school. This would mean he wouldn't have to mix with Council House children unlike our 16 year old, who despite enjoying a high ranking in English and Geography still cannot spell properly and hasn't the faintest inkling that Bradford could be in Yorkshire. She knows every street of the way to Nelson Mandela's house. Mind you, living in the home-counties, she hasn't had the benefit of learning traditional childrens songs in Urdu.

Pity

The original and genuine

This re-print contains as many spelling & grammatical errors as the original.

Time (and money!!) were saved by merely not bothering to do anything!

Unfortunately, there are no prizes for the person who spots the highest number. After all no one likes a Smart-Arse!

January

It's the 5th January 1989 and I'm already sick to death of the name Eddie Edwards. Everyone's supposed to be famous for fifteen minutes in their lifetime, well there's going to be a lot of disappointed people around because he has taken up several hours – so far. The year began badly when having lost at Trivial Pursuit at the in-laws, we drove home from Putney where a wind-down over the remainder of the evening was eagerly awaited. Now our video is one of the things I can safely say my wife is efficient at – well reasonably efficient. So on came the update of the Walton sextuplets. The story reached a point where the family visited a Safari Park – There was Edwards. Twenty-five years of Top of the Pops; there he was again. Yesterday, he broke his collar bone; pity it wasn't his neck. That piece of publicity took up four columns of news space in 'Today'. He's got a good agent, I'll say that for him, his mother says he wants to 'beat the sport' – sounds like having cancer.

I've just opened the post. Two letters, one enclosing my Trade Plate Licence and the other an advert for blinds. Our postman's good value. During last summer either my wife or I would often meet him coming down the lane. He would openly pronounce before handing over the card that so-and-so were enjoying themselves on their holiday and doesn't Disneyworld look fun. He always tells me before my advancing hand can clutch the mail, that there is a nasty one, as it has 'Her Majesty's' franking on it. This assumption being that it must contain bad news concerning money. He did this today. I took hold and explained that it was also franked 'DVLC' and that it would be my Trade Plate Licence. Think it upset him slightly. On Christmas Eve he came round in full

Father Christmas outfit. He did this last year and the kids loved it.

Business is bad at the moment. The interest rates have pushed the acquisition of a second hand car well down the pecking order. I haven't bought anything so far this year. Luckily we had a good weekend over the New Year. We sold four. Two have physically gone, so I'm off to pick up the money for them this afternoon, and the other two should be gone by the weekend. That is one of the beauty's of working from home. Even if I get up late, I can still be in the office by 9 am! It's quite a good relationship that I have with a trader in Bracknell. He is very much into the restoration of vintage motors as well as selling used cars. I supply the cars, between us we have any mechanical and bodywork repairs carried out and he sells them in the Thames Valley Trader. One aspect I do not enjoy is dealing with the public who respond to ads. Some are genuinely interested in a vehicle when they ring and turn up when they say they are going to. Whether they buy the car or not is a different matter, but at least they turn up. It's when you make an appointment, avoid going out and there's not even the courtesy of a phone call saying they're not coming that bugs me.

Unfortunately the Used Car Salesman is generally perceived to be a caricature of 'Arfur Daley', out to suck blood and defraud. Also unfortunate – and not just concerning the motor industry – is the fact that the public are often over-protected by consumer rights. Now don't get me wrong, I'm all in favour of knowing exactly what's in our food and actual weight being shown on goods etc, but I do get the feeling we are cushioned or wrapped-up whereby you don't have to use your judgement, if something goes wrong you fall back on Trading Standards, over the slightest thing. With regard to selling used cars, the easiest customer are those who have over £2,000 to spend. In fact if they have £4,000–£5,000 they tend to be extremely satisfied customers, who know the score and play the white man. It's the ones who have £500 and want £5,000 worth of car that cause the trouble. Whilst I fully accept that £300–£500 has probably been saved just as hard, if not harder than that by the more expensive car buyer, the law gives them the same rights. I couldn't cope with people complaining that the alternator has failed after three weeks on an Alpine costing, say £400. Tough, that's life. It should be a case of buyer beware. Legislation seems to be very one-sided. Anyway that's why my friend in Berkshire sells to retail customers and I trade to dealers or garages and private customers recommended by previous purchasers. I'll tell you an amusing story of the one we called 'fly-me' and her Sunbeam later, but first something to eat and time to pick up the money for the Fiesta and Ital, to the Bank and back home.

I'm back. Here's a good one you'll like this. The other half has just returned from shopping in beautiful downtown Aldershot. Obviously wanted to get the feeling of being a council house tenant as she's been shopping in the Co-op. When I say shopping it was actually 17p worth of Opal Fruits, but it's the principal that counts. It's at times like this that you realise why you shop at Safeways (Yes, we do spend more there). The difference in the quality of the staff is a world apart. Because my wife did not have a shopping basket for her one item, the lady behind thought that my wife was with the previous customer who was just leaving the checkout. She asked for a carrier bag and the 'assistant' rang up 4p. My wife asked if she could pay for the Opal Fruits, which threw the cashier completely. 'Can you pay for the carrier bag' she said and asked the lady behind for 4p. 'What if she wants to pay for her goods by cheque?' retorted my wife. 'Why don't you keep the 17p and ring it up afterwards' She countered 'I can't do that' she replied 'Well add 13p to 4p and you'll get the correct total'. No it wasn't to be. She added a 17p to get a total of 21p so my wife paid her money and left, no doubt causing much confusion to the brainless wonder working at the checkout.

I genuinely do not know where they get these people from. Recently we were in Bejams (Aldershot again) at the checkout. This chap in front had a couple of items and two cases of beer. The spotty youth rang up a total of £36 something. The customer queried this and proffered his estimate of around £18. Said youth calls Supervisor, two years or so older but as inane. 'Yeah that's right' She agrees

'£36 whatever'. 'Doesn't sound right to me' complains the customer again, rubbing his chin. Oik and Oikess are not pleased – nothing worse than a customer who won't agree to being taken for a ride. They add up each item again. Oh yes it's £19.56. Surprise, Surprise. Endless queue has now formed. No second till open. No apologies. Customer packs goods and leaves. I cannot believe it. I find it terribly frustrating that he did not ask to see the manager. If customers do not say anything, bad service thrives, and so do the third rate staff who work in these places.

During the Xmas sales, Maureen my wife, went to Debenhams (Guildford) with my mother and our fifteen year old daughter, Deborah. Sitting in their café they noticed a frustrated customer asking why his order for two rounds of toasted sandwiches had not been delivered in what he assumed was a reasonable period of time. Having received the stock answer that they were on the way a further period elapsed and again he asked the waitress. Her answer (unheard) not being satisfactory, he asked to see the Supervisor. She arrived and when asked why people who came in after him were being served and they were still waiting, she replied 'Well if you think you can do any better, you should try working here'. Exit, smartly Supervisor, without the poor customer getting his next four pennyworth. But they didn't do anything. They just sat there and waited. Amazing isn't it?

This eggs business looks suspicious. You know, life has not been the same since the showing of the very first 'Yes Minister'. I find I am unable to read or watch a political story without musing over the role played by a 'Sir Humphrey'. Now Edwina Currie is not one of my favourite people. I formed an opinion long ago, that politics for her are one long ego trip – see no puns about eggs – and this is the first time I have concurred with her opinion. Not because I know anything technical or have suffered from poisoning, but from the feeling that with a profit conscious government, such as we have, the lengths that the food industry will go to so as to reduce costs, and the fact that at the end of the day we cannot prove or disprove what is in our food, I submit that this argument will continue unresolved for some time. We actually only buy free

4

range eggs on principle. I feel disgusted that in this day and age we still allow battery farms – I use the word loosely, to operate. I've never belonged to any animal rights movement but I cannot see any justification for treating any animal in this way. The argument that eggs would be twice as dear, or more is irrelevant. Don't eat so many eggs. If it means more unemployment, tough. There can be no justification for treating chickens in the way that these so called farmers continue to do.

Talking of animals, I remember just before Christmas reading of the impending departure of the Japanese whaling fleet on its way to kill 300 minke whales. Why oh why just for once do we not have someone in Parliament who will stand up and say that as Japan has broken the agreement signed two years ago stopping these unnecessary deaths we will take trading reprisals. I remember now – we want the next car factory to be in this country not in Europe (No, I do not consider we are Europeans). We continually kow-tow to Japan – but then money speaks.

The other two cars have now been delivered so we can bank the cheques and hopefully find some more stock in the right price range. This is my eighth year of being self-employed, and I've never seen the market so bad. I've spoken to other traders, some of whom seem to be worse off than me – insofar, as they have vehicles adding up to some £40,000–£50,000 with no customers. I deliberately did not buy so much just before Christmas, as the stock that will sell is very thin on the ground. Why couldn't more be done to counter inflation and get to the heart of the consumer spending boom – which is a farce – by declaring war on those buying on credit. The poor individual who pays cash and only buys when he or she can afford it is being hit by the increased mortgage rate, while the credit merchants are still buying on the never-never. It's no good saying that consumer spending has hit a new all time high when so much credit is being thrown at you. There are so many people taken in by ads promising them the financial earth who will certainly be in trouble very soon, joining the swelling ranks of those seeking advice. We never had that when I was young. If you couldn't afford it, you didn't buy it – you saved. In this grabbing society we live in now that's not the case. Values have changed in a relatively short time. Still, with Government, City and Banking institutes being inhabited by the same type of people and in so many cases the *same* people, what chance have we got.

I cannot understand the mentality. There's a chap in Fleet who loses his licence in 1981 for 20 years. He wins an appeal to get it back and then refuses a blood test when stopped only months after he resumes driving. Magistrates ban him for thirty years, he's fined £700 and he says 'This has taken away my livelihood. I'm ever so pleased he did not injure or kill anyone. Because if I were the father of a child anguishing after a court case and he said that I would not be best pleased, to put it mildly.

Our eldest son (Glyn) has just sent off for his provisional licence – he was seventeen in September and we have offered to pay for his first ten lessons. Any after that are down to him. He is a bit worried as he suffered from a slight heart murmur when he was a child and he has obviously disclosed this fact on the application form. Swansea will probably need medical evidence that he is OK to drive so we're keeping our fingers crossed.

Having mentioned the two eldest children, I think it is probably time to complete the family and introduce the name William to the proceedings, he is six years of age and is an absolute toe-rag. He was the product of two – was it three? – minutes of passion after a party. The one time we did not take precautions and while I was waiting to go into Farnham Hospital to have the 'snip'.

I remember being terribly moral at the Health Centre in Ash Vale. When asked if I wanted to pay and have it done straight away or wait and have it done on the National Health, I boldly stated my commitment to the NHS and said I was prepared to wait the six weeks or so. Maureen, if my memory serves me correctly was not getting on too well with the dutch cap or dust cap or whatever it is so we swopped over to the durex. The term condom had fallen into some decline at the time, bearing in mind Aids/Mates/Branson etc were not so well known to the general public then.

I mean it wouldn't be the most romantic comment Maureen had ever made if she asked about 'protective measures' at the very moment I'm transporting her to the very peaks of sexual fulfilment (my assumption, not her verdict). If I remember correctly it's the one time I didn't have to compete with 'Life at Crossroads No 33' – so that's why she's been complaining of double-vision, must have been a good party.

Despite all the frolics, if not the fun, William was conceived and we were both subjected to the obvious comments from friends, that we rather shut the stable door after the horse had bolted. I remember being driven by Maureen to Farnham Hospital, and I must confess to a morsel of nervousness on entering. Having been quickly whisked away to a small anteroom where a pretty nurse said I had to shave myself I knew my luck was at a rather low ebb. Having got this over with I was taken to the operating room, where, resplendent in my green gown I lay on my back expecting the worst. The surgeon was a square-faced man wearing a Colditz barbed wire tie. I always felt this to be somewhat of an irony. A nurse sat next to me and held my hand – I liked that bit. A small injection on either side of the groin, and after a short while and a bit of snipping, I was waiting to leave. That evening I didn't know what all the fuss was about. People had been telling me about how sore it was and how they could not walk. I was to learn what they meant within twenty-four hours. I tried to do a days work by travelling to London, collecting a car and taking it to a garage in Richmond. I remember there being a profit of £300 in the car. I had to give a back-hander to the Sales Manager of £50. The transaction being completed, I drove to Richmond where the chap I had talked to about the car looked around it and agreed with the description. I made out the invoice, he drove the car round the block and I waited for my cheque. About ten minutes later he reappeared genuinely apologising, stating that the car should have had a five speed gear box not four, to be worth what we had agreed. Looking again in the bible, Glasses Guide, I realised I had overlooked the introduction of the new gearbox and that four speed Renault 18s were worth considerably less as they were an older model. After a lot of haggling I was faced with taking the car away or accepting his offer of £300 less. Thinking that the long term view was to take his money and look forward to more business, I agreed to this option. Someone took me to Richmond Station, where clasping my much reduced cheque I made my way home.

Maureen picked me up from Ash Vale Station. I had walked up and down so many steps my balls were blue. I was looking forward to showing them off to the family and neighbours, but Maureen said it wasn't very nice. Anyway, nett result was a great deal of pain, a complete day of required rest wasted, a car sold for the same price as I had paid, and the cost of public transport and petrol down the drain. The only winner being the Sales Manager in London who was fifty pounds better off. Ah well you live and learn.

In all seriousness, we did not plan another child and with the other two at ten and eight we discussed the problems of space, starting all over again and the difficulties that it pro-duces, how the other two would react, and how we would feel in ten years time when we would be in our mid to late forties.

Our six years with William have provided us with the complete range of emotions from despair to amazed laughter. Whether it has anything to do with him being younger and smaller than everyone else in the family I do not know, but he certainly has made his mark on life. He was the most active of the three children before he was born, and shortly after birth, having been hosed down etc and returned to the cot by Maureen's bedside, we noticed his head moving from side to side. The nurse said he had very good muscle tone and the proverbial good set of lungs. He was a very unhappy baby, again different from the other two. He was very demanding and often would not settle for ages.

We were in the process of finding another home when my Mother and Father were both taken ill. I would have been given good odds against either of them going into hospital – but both in wards next to each other at the same time was unthinkable. My Mother stayed in the longest and Dad came to stay with us, during January 1983.

We had been married in September 1969 and after living in a flat in Brudenell Road, Tooting for two years, saving up the obligatory deposit, we moved to Ash Vale near Aldershot. or Aldershit as they chant at the football ground, in mid 1971, when Maureen was expecting Glyn. That was to be our only move until March 1983. From Summer 1982 to January 1983 we had looked at a number of houses and had a number of people look at ours. We finally captured a Welsh couple with a daughter, who after the usual legal procedures purchased our home. We in the meantime had found a little cottage about 100 years old still in Ash Vale, in a little unadopted lane which had been purchased from an elderly owner by a developer who obtained planning permission to build three houses next to it. The cottage received a lick of paint and a modicum of remedial work before being sold off. Opposite the cottage and the newly planned houses was a triangle of land backing onto a railway line. The developer had proposed to build on here also but had been refused. A couple in a neighbouring street offered him the asking price for the cottage if he would throw in the land opposite, which he did. They were there about eighteen months I think before putting the cottage back on the market. In the meantime they had built an extension and added leaded double glazed windows which enhanced the building immensely.

I remember telling Maureen that although the cottage was a lot smaller than our home, being two bedrooms only, we could convert the loft and put in velux windows, add another extension and build a garage across the road on the wasteland – which was all it was at that time. We later had the opportunity of meeting the daughter of the elderly owner who sold the property in the first place, shortly after we had completed major alterations. She seemed pleased at the new lease of life and we arranged to meet again with a view to seeing her photographs. They were taken in the forties and fifties when she was young and the whole garden was laid out and an orchard grew where the wasteland now lay. We had repainted the rendering, which covered all the brickwork, white, with the sills, bargeboards, gable ends, porches etc, in dark red. Ironically the few coloured photographs taken in the fifties, confirmed this colour scheme to be the same as ours some thirty years later.

9

Almost a social comment, I suppose, but the railway line was protected by wooden, three bar, fencing that you could sit on, all those years ago. Now there is the standard BR metal mesh fencing with three strands of barbed wire straddling the top between concrete posts, reminiscent of the army barracks that are such a feature of Aldershot.

Moving in was miserable. It was cold, Dad, my cousin Simon and a friend, Den, helped all day loading and unloading the hired Luton van which travelled back and forth on several occasions, as well as two estate cars. The new houses had not been finished so we were completely alone when we moved in and for several months afterwards.

One of the last items to be moved out of our old house, was the three piece suite. During our time there we had built a hall leading into the living room. It was about 2 pm and the purchasers had been up to see us twice as they were ready to move in at 11 am, bearing in mind completion of contract was only affected at about the same time. How do people manage to be so organised when moving? Anyway, all permutations ended with the settee being locked in between the door frame. The only solution was to take it out of the dining room window. This was affected hurriedly but *without* breaking the glass – clever huh! I rang the Welsh couple to say they could take possession (about 4 pm in the afternoon – they were not best pleased) and cringing pathetically told them that we had left the window glass out so as they could move their settee in without difficulty, adding that we had also left a new tin of putty. End of conversation – end of relationship.

That first night Maureen cried. (She cried a lot at that time) 'What have we done' she said. 'We had a house with shelves and a kitchen with cupboards not to mention a garage' 'I know' I replied 'But it's the potential isn't it?' She was fed up with my use of the word 'potential' within a very short time. True, we did not have any cupboards, there was furniture and books, and books, and books everywhere, I kept telling her that once the extension and garage were built we wouldn't know what to do with the space. Slight exaggeration, but the work was put in hand as soon as we were ensconced and within a year we had our own dressing room and shower room, the kids had their own bathroom, a kitchen, not fitted, but inhabited by pine dressers and cupboards, and two loft converted bedrooms and double garage (for the model railway) expanding the area considerably.

It's Friday evening, Friday 13th, and we're going out to friends this evening for a drink and a snack so I'll end here – beside which my hand is aching.

Back again, I read in the local paper over the weekend – as depressing as usual – the Managing Director of a Company that owns the Wellington Centre in Aldershot is explaining its unexpected sale to another property company and describing Aldershot as a 'growth town' with massive potential! From that one can deduce an ever increasing number of unoccupied office blocks, boring red brick flats and more one-way systems.

They cannot leave a field alone can they? Eversley is a nice village. In the same issue there are pictures of villagers and supporters protesting outside Hart Council Offices. Bryant Homes wish to build 2500 houses on 429 acres outside Eversley. The proposal is three 'village style' clusters (estates) with community facilities (which often fail to materialise). They could also promise road improvements – If they did not build the houses, the roads would not need improving in a lot of cases. Development companies always sound as if they are doing us a favour. Recently Charles Church were given permission to build on one of last remaining open spaces in Ash Vale. The local Council did not want the development to proceed and there was an inquiry. I seem to remember the local Councillor severely criticizing the local population for a low turnout but does that not indicate the level of faith ratepayers have in the ability of those entrusted to look after their area to actually work on behalf of those who live there? The number of Councillors who genuinely care are very small. It would be interesting to see how many of these schemes were passed because of bulky brown envelopes being handed out. After permission was granted for the Charles Church scheme the builders wrote to the local paper telling them how glad they were to be able to help the people of this

11

area by making available low cost homes. Decent chaps aren't they?

These companies know they are destroying the very villages they set out to develop, but the rape is merciless. To be fair to local councils, central Government sets out quotas for housing in certain areas, and the local authority is powerless. But then with a Government that has someone as arrogant, bombastic and downright rude as Mr Ridley running the Environment Ministry, what hope have we got.

It will be interesting to see how many are built, 'cause get built they will. They never learn. Yateley, Blackwater, Camberley, Farnborough have all disappeared under sprawls of concrete, be it on a smaller or larger scale. Yateley shopping centre is typical two storey, low pitch, inner city sprawl — but without a lot of graffiti, which will come. Blackwater has been submerged by major roadworks on the A30 with quick access to the M3 across what were some lovely fields with real cows. Now they're busily expanding the 'Business Park' in an area where before the war you could buy a return ticket from Waterloo and travel to Frimley to connect with a miniature railway, grandly titled the Camberley and Surrey Border Railway, and travel from their own station at Frimley to Watchetts Park and on to Camberley. People picnicked where now they work.

Camberley has emerged with successive building into one of the ugliest and most typical of shopping centres with its slab concrete steps, dirty tiled walkways (complete with graffiti) and ensuing traffic problems. You can't park anywhere, and when you do it costs an arm and a leg.

Farnborough is a complete joke. You've got the worst of both worlds. On one hand a typical planners blight of the late sixties/early seventies when they shiplapped two storey buildings, painted them white and gave them flat roofs. On the other we have futuristic glass buildings with gaudy colour schemes while the main entrance to Kingsmead (the shopping centre) in surrounded by vertical black painted wooden slats giving the impression of boarded up shops but actually hiding a local Company's car park. It looks terrible. The entrance to Kingsmead is almost hidden. The open 'Mall' area, Queensmead, is again dirty and scruffy with small shops, takeaways and unimaginative multi-storey car parks.

Thank God for Farnham. Even the new buildings are brick with sympathetic design and roofing in keeping with existing houses and shops.

I'm depressed just writing about it, so I'll leave Aldershot and my 'beloved' Ash Vale till later. I expect you, the reader, can only take so much anyway.

Here's another thing that surprised me. There's a vicar that is going to be re-licenced as Priest in charge of some Berkshire parishes. He apparently left the area some few years ago, having been charged with criminal damage with intent to endanger the life of someone who rejected his advances. He started a vendetta against his alleged love by cutting brake cables and committing burglary. Yes burglary not buggery. That's the interesting part of the story. He was actually in love with a woman. Unusual for a priest really it's generally men or boys we hear about.

It's been a week since Hirohito died and the papers are full of guessing games concerning who will represent Britain. Although having been born after the war I still feel contempt for Japan. I can't even begin to imagine how an ex-POW must feel. If we do attend the funeral there will be a lot of patriotic British citizens feeling very bitter, and rightly so. Amazingly there appears to be a school of thought which suggests he was not party to the atrocities. How modern trading practices demand a change of views about a Country. If we were not saddled by the lack of ability to produce our cars, electrical goods and high-tech equipment competitively, I wonder if our 'gentleness and concern' would raise its soft head then. I think not. Ironically about a week ago I read of a German who was taken prisoner in Normandy and sent to Somerset where he spent eighteen months in a POW camp. He fell in love with an English girl and asked to stay here. He will shortly be coming up for retirement, but has lived here ever since and is currently a security guard for EMI, at the same place he was held all those years ago. We have all heard of others that stayed after the cessation of war. I wonder how many, if any, British

13

Soldiers stayed in Germany and Japan. It would be interesting to know.

It was sometime last year after returning from Germany, where they had been to support a concert given by a Welsh Male Voice Choir, that my parents told me how a German had come up to the organiser at the end and introduced himself and his family. He said how much he had enjoyed the concert and that they lived some 150 miles away but he had been a POW in Carmarthanshire in the forties and he had enjoyed Welsh singing. Dad said that his enthusiasm was enormous, and his wife added that her husband had always been keen for her to hear a Welsh choir, and how welcome they had been made to feel. Personally I still don't trust the bastards.

I was going to tell you about the one we called 'fly-me', wasn't I. Our William goes to a small primary school about four miles away on the 'right side' of the Hogs Back as the good snobs of Puttenham and Sands like to call it. The school only has about forty children. I won't divulge its name in case Surrey County Council get to hear about it and decide to close it. Anyway, the school secretary asked Maureen if she passed near a particular road as there was a mother who wanted to share the responsibility of a school run. This was agreed and both women took it it turns. It didn't matter to us, but it was helpful to 'fly-me' who worked as an air stewardess on an 'as required' basis. This meant short notice was given, but to be fair she always did her share. They were living in Ash at the time but were moving to the next road from us. This arrangement was started during the Summer of '87 and about November she asked me to find a little car for her. I produced a gold Sunbeam that I had bought from a local garage. I had actually bought the car and sold it about two years previously and it still looked to be in good condition. The MOT was short and I said I would get a new one for her. She took delivery and used it daily. Bearing in mind that my son is being driven in the car every other day I am hardly likely to sell her something that isn't safe am I? Come April and a few thousand miles later she rings up and complains bitterly, because, having felt a pull on the brakes she takes the car to the local Peugeot/Talbot dealer who advise her that because some welding is required

14

on the chassis they will not allow her to drive it home. This of course was the only day I had virtually lost my voice through a cold and could not answer, well only with difficulty, the tirade of abuse that was penetrating through my ears. She was absolutely hysterical. 'You said it had some welding done, I thought I could trust you, they've quoted me £400 to put in right, the MOT was obviously bent!' At this point I rasped annoyance. I have never had a 'bent' MOT done in my life. Frankly I would not know where to go to obtain one. Having received no satisfaction from me she said that as soon as her husband came in she would get him to call me. This he did. The strange thing is that out of the two of them I always imagined him to by the 'snidy' one. He is a bit of an ageing yuppie, but turned out to be perfectly reasonable. No raised voices and an agreement that nothing could be done until the MOT people had seen the car. He did say that he thought I had sold the car in good faith, but the MOT people were at fault. Consequently he would have to sue me, who in turn could sue the MOT station. In between having spoken to me and seeing her husband, she had contacted the Police, AA and Trading standards and no doubt a support group as well. All of whom had considered her case first class on the one sided 'evidence' she had produced.

I rang the garage she had taken the car to and asked to speak to the Service Manager. He confirmed his view about the cars unroadworthiness and told me that in his opinion the car should not have passed the MOT. I mentioned the fact that the MOT is only good on the day it was done. He asked when it was tested and I told him last December, he explained that she had spoken as if it were in the last few days. I added the fact that she wanted her money back or me to get the car repaired at my own cost. The Service Manager agreed that if I rang the MOT station, he would willingly allow them to look over the car there and we could have a chat then.

This was arranged for the following day and the husband had been advised of this. She, by the way, no longer wanted to speak to me.

One point I did make to the husband was that when they took the car, I did specify that they were buying it as seen and they were only too happy to go along with it then. His answer was that it wasn't me he was getting at but the MOT people. I tried to tell him that I didn't need all the hassle of being sued and then suing again – not for a £50 profit I could have made in the trade. I thought I was doing them a favour. Anyway, both proprietor and tester came the next day, armed with the original fail sheet which showed some welding that needed doing and the subsequent pass certificates and comments showing the work to have been done.

'What about the cracks in the chassis' I asked 'They weren't there when the MOT was done' said the tester. The proprietor stood by the claims of his man. Not a youngster, but a man in his late fifties, early sixties who had been the station's main tester for years. 'Between December, and now she could have curbed it, hit a block or anything' He said. 'Does she drive far' asked someone 'To the airport and back about three times a week, plus school runs, shopping etc' I replied. 'How much did she pay?' Asked the proprietor, sarcastically, 'About £3000?' 'No.' I said '£500'. Much mirth, 'I don't know what some people want for their money' someone said. 'Well I'm satisfied that you checked and passed the vehicle properly' said the Service Manager. 'Great' I said 'So if I asked them to phone you, you'll stand by that and tell them?' 'Yes, of course. Now I've got all the story.' I rang the Trading Standards people myself when I got back home. 'I did not advertise the car for sale' I said, 'They asked me if I could find them a cheap car as a runaround. I let them borrow it for three days to make sure they liked it and to get a mechanic of their own to come and look at it if they wanted to.' 'So they had the car for four months, travelled a couple of thousand miles and paid £500?' 'Yes!' 'Well we are not totally unrealistic' said the Trading Standards lady. 'It's unusual to have a trader on to us, but I think in this case you have been fair if not fairer than many dealers and if you want to take my name and get them to ring me, I'll willingly tell them the facts of life concerning cheap cars. Yes they do have the same rights under the Sale of Goods act as someone paying £5000, but we do take into account wear and tear, age and purchase price.'

Armed with the information I rang the ageing yuppie and told him of the Service Managers change of view and that I had rung the Trading Standards who were quite willing to talk to them. 'At the end of the day' I said 'The thing that really annoys me is that you renaged on the deal, I lent you the car to try, I didn't sell it to you – you wanted to buy it, and I said that as far as I'm concerned the warranty is to the end of the drive (about 30'). I don't expect anyone to come back four or five months later and complain even if the engine falls out. You are white and over 21". No further correspondence. We take William everyday ourselves now, and they send their youngster to a private school! It just confirmed what I generally thought about air-hostesses! They're very snobby and consider themselves to be above most people. Only socialise with those whose names they can drop and help boost their egos. Must be something to do with the uniform – but I'll come to that later, I think a little gloat is now in order.

Heard a good one the other day. Poor cowboy goes into Sheriff's office and asks if there's any work. The Sheriff says the only job going is as a bounty hunter. 'OK' he says 'who's your most wanted man?' 'The Brown Paper Kid' replies the Sheriff. 'The Brown Paper Kid?' 'Yes, the Brown Paper Kid' 'Have you a photo' 'No, but I do have description, He wears a brown paper hat, and sits on a brown paper saddle, wearing brown paper spats and a brown paper neckerchief. He's got a brown paper shirt and a brown paper waistcoat and his gun is in a brown paper holster' How much is he worth?' '$10,000' 'What's he wanted for?' 'Rustling' All right, all right, I found it funny.

Getting back to private schools. Some years ago when we were more affluent than we are now (the reason for which I will discuss in August) we sent our two eldest to a small independent school locally. Nice uniform and an emphasis on manners, traditional teaching methods and teachers who looked like teachers and not out of work academics appealed to us. The headmistress was the very epitome of everything we as parents saw as necessary to a good education. Hair greyed, tied back in a bun, well spoken, firm but humorous. She wore tweeds and brogues. Starting time was announced by a hand held bell. The fees were not excessive, although like everything they continued to rise every term. And that was another thing. Terms were called Michaelmas and Trinity, etc.

We ended up believing we were paying through the nose. The founder had died suddenly and it soon became apparent that the emphasis on standards was becoming second to profit. The headmistress had marital problems and had started drinking! Deborah went on a school trip to North Wales and the said headmistress was heard crashing about outside the chalets at night asking occupants to find her abode.

We went to see her at the end of term for the usual report. 'How is Glyn getting on in English' I asked 'I don't take him for English' She replied. Maureen and I look at each other – Silence. 'Hang on, Yes I do' She swayed. the smell of gin hung lazily on the air.

It was shortly after that we took them away. It's back to the old adage – you get what you pay for. Just wish we could send them (too late for Glyn – he's now at Sixth Form College) to Private Schools again, we may have better luck next time.

Glyn and Deborah both went to the same secondary school from the age of twelve in Farnborough, large sprawling extended porta-cabin type. Holds about seven hundred pupils I believe.

The previous Headmaster was very weak and we looked forward in anticipation to a new emphasis on discipline, homework etc. Now he's a very nice chap, the new one, but I remember receiving his first newsletter saying how pleased he was with the standard of turnout and the neatness of the school uniform. I brought this up at the next open evening. I suggested that he should have been savaged by his guide dog. He further commented that rumours had been spread, suggesting he was about to introduce boaters for girls. 'Why not?' I asked. There is in my book nothing nicer than schoolchildren looking smart in identical uniform. I don't suggest that boys are made to wear caps as in my day, but the variations on a very loose theme are commonplace. I asked the Headmaster if he had sat outside, as I do regularly to pick them up, and looked at their plimsolls, hobble skirts, short skirts, earrings, all manner of jackets – no school blazers. A lot of pupils are

18

smoking. I pointed this out also commenting that 'when I was young' bus drivers and local residents pointed offenders out to the teachers and you were made to pay dearly. The new Head replied that they have no powers to interfere once children are out of school. How standards have changed! I went to Spencer Park Secondary Modern in Wandsworth. One thousand boys. There was the odd undesirable, but without looking through rose-coloured glasses, there was very little trouble and uniforms were part and parcel of the school process. But that was what life was like back in the early sixties. You didn't carry knives, sniff glue, take drugs or concern yourselves in any other unsocial act that seems to be part of everyday Britain today – and not only in inner cities. Halcyon days. I seem to remember that an amusing thing we did outside school was to get the Emanual boys in trouble if we could. Bearing in mind that the nineteen bus from Tooting passed our school first, it then collected the boys from Emanual Grammar on its way down to Clapham, wending its way around Wandsworth Common to get there. We often walked down past Emanual and would get on a bus hoping some of their pupils would be sitting on the bench seats nearest the platform – All London buses were proper buses in those days with driver and conductor. Boarding the bus and walking in single file, the first one would drop a sweet bag containing stink bombs, and the second would tread on it as we made our way to the front. Passengers on the other bench and immediate seats would make faces and sometimes complain. Occasionally if we were really lucky the Emanual boys would be thrown off despite their protests that it couldn't possibly have been them. Good clean fun eh!

We used to pull a few strokes at Clapham Junction Station. There were two forms of access to the platforms. A subway that connected both entrances and all seventeen platforms, and a footbridge connecting the platforms only. Platform 1 was unused except during the rush-hour when a shuttle service to Kensington Olympia was in operation for post office workers.

Sunday evenings were quiet on the bridge and uninterrupted could be had via Platform 1. In those days, when carriages were cleaned regularly, we would take up position by an open or broken window on the bridge above the sidings and fire CROW-SCARIERS via catapults at the cleaners standing by the side of the coaches. It was a real hoot to see them jump as the banger exploded nearby. If we hit the target, i.e. a backside, it was a real bonus.

Mind you, if my lads did that now . . .

Getting back to Hirohito. I wouldn't have put money on Terry Dicks (Tory MP) and Ron Brown (Labour MP) ever finding a matter on which to agree, but both found it 'wrong' and 'insulting' for Britain to be represented. Their view, I am glad to say is shared by a number of MP's on both sides of the house. I see that the Queen has sent a letter of condolence to the new Emperor on behalf of herself and the British people. Well she didn't do it on my behalf.

A friend of ours rang us last week and asked if we would like to come to a surprise party for her husband who will be 50. Adding that there was to be a strippogram at 10 pm, we arranged with mutual friends to be there about 9.15 pm. What do you get a chap who is an Aircraft Flight Engineer, into gadgets but no real hobbies.

We hunted around Aldershot and came up with a book for fifty year olds – what you can and cannot do during your senile years, that sort of thing – a fiftieth Birthday badge, something else was needed – but what? We couldn't think of anything appropriate. Brainwave. I went into Concorde Models in Aldershot and asked if they had a model of a Boeing 737. They had, and in B.A. colours. It was one of those clip-fit types. We boxed it up and wrote a note saying that when we bought it, it only had one engine, but we'd managed to find another in Chicago. Didn't know how he was going to take it, but no matter. By the time we'd arrived he was quite well oiled anyway and was last seen holding said model aloft flying around the room making aircraft noises.

What's more the Strippogram was early and we witnessed her departure as we pulled up – Ahh well!

Well that's great isn't it. What a cop out. The Queen instructs Prince Phillip to represent Britain at Hirohito's funeral. The Burma Star Association has quite rightly been against any representation by a Royal, but now that their Patron is to go, Vice-Chairman, Lieutenant Colonel Brooking says that as it is so long ago, they no longer feel it has anything to do with them. Why don't they stand up and say what they mean, they're bloody disappointed. Australia has the right attitude. Bob Hawke said that he never had any intention of going. Japan aren't going to stop trading with them or us if we stand up for ourselves for once. Why do we let the rest of the world walk all over us?

We're nearing the end of January and business has never been worse. My financial year starts in December, when I always loose money, leaving the next two months to bring in a few shillings so that by the end of the quarter I have broken even. December however, was a record loss which has just carried on through January. There is no money about for second-hand cars.

Our local Fiat dealer is doing well on the 0% finance scheme, but people don't realise the repayments are great because they have to pay back within 1 year. There are several garages offering the £99 down on new cars, but again the repayments are severe because of the short loan period. Usually the two or three weekends after Christmas we do well out of the papers, but not this year.

We keep hearing about a consumer spending boom, but it's only because so much plastic is used. I refuse to use credit cards. If the Midland Bank can't afford it on our overdraft, we don't buy it. But seriously, whenever I shop the chances of the customer in front paying by cash are not good. It's not just confined to large items only. I was buying the paper the other morning, and the woman in front bought forty cigarettes, two birthday cards and a daily paper and paid by Visa. The frustration is made all the more intense when you wait for the forms to be filled out – especially in petrol stations – where you're waiting to tender a £5 note or whatever. It's not *real* money they're handing over, it's a convenience for card carrying customers, providing they pay within a certain period of course, otherwise it would be cheaper to have an overdraft. The only winners at the end of the day are the Banks and stores who issue the cards, at rates regarded by most analysts as excessively high. The 'we're taking the waiting out of wanting' campaign sounds more like a moral crusade. The question of whether the card holder actually has the means to pay or will have the means in a few months time is I am sure only considered up to the point where the customer signs on the dotted line. They sound as ingratiating as the developers trying to convey they're doing you a favour. Only a couple of weeks ago a magistrate let off a woman who owed Harrods £1900 on her store card because he considered their greedy action deserved no compensation whatsoever.

Went down to Salisbury a couple of days ago. A friend of mine has been a salesman at a dealership there for about sixteen months now. I used to work with him ten years ago when employed by a British Car Auctions subsidiary. That's the difference between working for a Company with money and being self-employed and working on an overdraft. You don't have to worry about ringing the bank manager when an expensive deal comes along. Geoff was a good salesman and to be fair, I hadn't a clue. On more than one occasion I became tongue-tied when asked specific questions to which I did not have ready answers, he never got annoyed, helping me out continually. It was a good set-up, the boss, secretary, buyer, seller and me. Because trade was booming, bearing in mind this is mid 1978, they needed to have a rep out on the road drumming up new business. The buyer was literally spending all day travelling between the various major rental companies buying fleets of cars and Geoff was spending all day plugging details of the latest purchases to would-be-buyers, such as Geoffrey Davis, Curries, Wadham Stringers etc. The system was good. The money was there and more business could be had. There were very few companies or individuals who had the know-how or guts to buy say £60,000 of cars, phone in the details and start another deal half an our later.

I started working for this company at Easter 1978 having just finished a milk round. I applied for the position of car salesman in a showroom in Farnham. Got the job and was there about five months when I was asked if I fancied changing from retail sales to wholesale. The difference was immense. It was during

22

this period I realised I had little patience with punters, but dealing with people who knew what they wanted was very invigorating. The first two weeks were a hard slog. I would come back of an evening having visited a lot of garages and talked myself into the ground but with no results. On the Tuesday of the third week I called into a garage in Wallington in between calls at Epsom and Croydon. At Epsom in the morning I had reached the depths of despair. Here I was trying to interest garages in a service that my colleagues could sell easily over the phone but I found immensely difficult in person. Perhaps it was me? Perhaps! I knew it was. In the garage in Epsom I meant to say to the bemused Sales Manager who was unable to get a word in edgeways 'This means that you can put fully prepared cars on your front forecourt'. It came out thus 'This means that you can put fully prepared cars on your fore frontcunt'. I skulked away and we never heard anymore from him. It might have been, on reflection, that I felt that when you're on the bottom, things can only get better, as I do not remember seeking dutch courage but in the afternoon when I visited the aforementioned garage in Wallington my patter was more relaxed, I took breath between sentences etc. When I returned to base in Frimley, the Sales Manager had already driven down from Wallington and purchased two transporter loads of cars. Did I celebrate that evening? It all came together after that.

We acquired a Fiat franchise and moved to Reading. Then we took over a little garage in Sandhurst and this and our Farnham branch became Talbot dealers. Did we sell some cars? It was a pity when it folded as it was nothing to do with losing money, but a clash of personalities at a higher level. It would have been easy to go and work as a Used Car Sales Manager at a large concern, but I felt it right to go out by myself. Despite everything, I'm still glad I did. I keep in touch with one or two of the other members of staff, but it's Geoff I do the most business with. Another ex-colleague now works for a prestigious car dealership and he has tried to get me in to buy cars, but the Sales Manager is slightly less than honest to say the least. On several occasions he has rung me and described a car which I have liked, but the car ended up going to another trader who has bid less, sometimes substantially so. By the sounds of it, one very greedy Sales Manager. Still with Geoff it's a case of come and see it and if you want it, and we agree money, it's yours. I normally buy on his description over the phone. When we both worked for the same company, his marriage went through a very sticky patch and he started drinking a lot. He left the marital home and stayed for a while in a club near Crowthorne, drowning his sorrows into the small hours. Despite everything his work hardly suffered, but he was putting on a lot of weight and looking particularly puffy around the eyes. A close friend of his introduced him to a lady who had either just been through or was just going through the tribulation of divorce. Both of them had three children. I liked Geoff's wife but I must confess she was a bit odd. Used to go away for the occasional weekend and meditate with the monks somewhere near Reading. Anyway, it was our bosses birthday, and he was taking staff and friends to a posh restaurant in Ascot for a meal. Geoff was in the embryo stages of his reinstatement as a member of the human race but had arrived already in a state of inebriation. Picture the scene. Jack our boss, is with his girlfriend Samantha – being separated from his wife Melissa, who is our secretary! – outside the restaurant to welcome guests. Geoff and Pat arrive. Jack has never met Pat. Geoff with glazed eyes introduces Pat saying 'Hello Jack, hello Samantha, I'd like you to meet Pat who fucks well!' Silence. Jack takes Pat by the hand and shakes it warmly with a face exuding embarrassment. Geoff is kept in order, and the rest of the evening goes off well and without further incident. The following morning, his comment was the talk of the office. The classic line came from Melissa who said 'I know it was a bit embarrassing, but it's not half as bad as if he'd said – 'This is Pat who doesn't fuck well'. I'd be really annoyed about that'. I liked Melissa.

Anyway Pat managed to curb his excesses and they moved in due course. Geoff's children living with his ex-wife, who has since moved to Dorset and Pat's children living with them, plus one they had together, in Christchurch.

It was during this period of employment that I remember our boss telling the story of a pilot friend of his – cocky

24

sod actually – and his wife who were visiting a couple for dinner. The female being a friend of his wife's, he not knowing either person. As the door opened, pilot in his usual state of intoxication, congratulated the hostess on her clitoris when he meant clematis. Happy days.

February

I've just been in touch with the architect who has drawn up plans for a house across the road on the wasteland. It was late 1987 that I rang Guildford Borough Council and asked if I was likely to be granted planning permission. Bearing in mind that the builder who originally developed the lane was refused, the planning officer was doubtful but did not reject the idea. Basically he suggested that if I didn't try I wouldn't find out. A thumb through Yellow Pages and a chap from Fleet came over and surveyed the area, proposing a chalet bungalow. Outline planning permission was sought. Various people from GBC, Surrey CC and British Railways came and measured, chatted, measured and chatted again. Eventually in January 1988 Maureen and I sat in the public gallery for what seemed an interminable period before the Chairman of the planning committee announced our application number adding' The recommendation is approved' all ayes, no nays. Childishly I raised both my hands in the air as if witnessing Aldershot scoring a winning goal – it wasn't that rare but I was elated. We went for a celebratory drink and discussed all the really important things like what sort of plant tubs we should have on the patio.

Life settled down for a while, I carried on working and Maureen found herself a part-time job as a secretary. During the summer, I contacted the architect again and full plans were drawn up. After various alterations to the building, plans were submitted in November and on 21st January this year we were finally given consent. I was on the phone to our man in Fleet the following day to give him the news and ask him about drawing up the building regulations. My call today was just a follow up to see how things were progressing. Apparently we have to wait for a structural engineer to calculate various loadings etc. All very technical stuff. Anyway, we should have the completed plans by the end of the month.

Being an only child, what we would like to do is move into the new house and sell the cottage to my parents. They live in Hackbridge, sorry Wallington, and own a 'semi' in a small cul-de-sac which backs onto the river Wardle. Nice quiet area, pity about the chap on the left hand side as you enter the road. He owns one of those enormous American Sedans in white which pokes its chrome nose out onto the pavement. It must devalue every house by £10,000. What an eyesore. The sad thing is that he obviously thinks its got style. Typical manual worker, his hall is probably decorated with the obligatory ducks and a picture of an oriental girl crying. I suppose they do own the house and it's not council?

Anyway, that's what we'd like to do, so if the quotes for building are in the region of £45,000–£50,000, we can afford to sell to my parents at below market value, they can sell theirs for about £90,000 and have a bit in reserve to live on.

Mum still works despite being well over retirement age. She's employed by an engineering company in Mitcham as a bookkeeper/telephonist. I have met her boss and some of the chaps who work there. She's very well respected, one of the old school. Everybody's birthday is marked by a cake, her favourites get preference when it comes to a choice of biscuits. You know the sort. Mind you, I never know it's her when she rings from work, she puts on her telephone voice. Not that she speaks badly anyway, but her tone is quieter and softer and her words measured.

It's not a bloody competition. Oh yes it is.

One of the chaps who works with her bought a Cortina from me nearly six years ago and he is now giving it to his son, as he has recently passed his test. We discussed various replacements on the phone the other day and he has plumped for a 1800cc Sierra. Hopefully we can find a nice one for him. A satisfied customer eh! We ought to have him stuffed and mounted. Which reminds me, isn't Emma Samms a cracker! I digress, Mums also recommended me to a chap who has a carpet shop in Battersea. He is looking for an automatic

27

hatchback, and I think I know where there is a Maestro Auto. May fit the bill, will have to wait and see.

Still no clues as to who's right in the salmonella debate.

We went to dinner last night with some friends and during the evening the conversation having skated lightly over several subjects landed on the general deterioration of this Country. It's one of my favourite hobbyhorses as I cannot find many avenues for optimism. Personally I do not feel you can put down the loutish behaviour of many of our youngsters to one cause. Certainly not the red herring used by the tussle-haired, badge endowed, scruffy trendies, ensconced in an office in nuclear free Brent who blame bad housing, cuts in education and everything else on the government. Now I don't believe for one moment that this is a caring government. As I said earlier, I totally abhor the profit motivated principles that forge ahead unhindered but that is to a very large extent down to the lack of opposition. I wish it were better, be it labour or SDLP. But it is so ineffective, and until the SDLP can get their act together the name of Dr Owen will be tied to their legs like a ball and chain. In the case of labour, after ten years of this dreadful government, they should be winning by-elections hands down with thumping majorities and head the various opinion polls. But no. Until they decide which defensive path to follow so that the electorate has a *clear* idea of their policies and everyone knows for definite one way or another whether they would re-nationalise the utilities, replace recent trade union legislation etc I cannot see this government being toppled. I do feel however that it is pursuing more unpopular policies at a time when a shrewd move to grab opposition supporters would not be amiss. I remember M.T. saying years ago that she was not against referendums. Ten years have passed. Why do the government not make use of this facility. Are they so sure that they are carrying out the wishes of the people, or is it an exclusive club. I know I'm not the only one who has felt that referendums on non-political issues such as capital punishment, immigration, The Channel Tunnel and the EEC would be a good test. Now I do not condone terrorism at all, but if someone could only blow up the tunnel without harming anyone and cause it to be beyond uneconomic repair I would be truly happy. We will no longer be an island if it succeeds. Why is there this great exodus of 'touring lemmings every year. You see the photos, of tired and dispirited parents and children waiting at airports for days on end. They sit there for hours on a boat with their car unaware that their P & O ship used to be a Townsend Thorensen one but that's marketing for you. What is the great attraction about abroad. I have lots of relatives in Belgium. In this case its nice people shame about the place. As opposed to Scotland where it's the other way round. Could you live with that accent? My mother-in-law is from a place called Fauldhouse, between Edinburgh and Glasgow. I always know it's her when the phone rings. I give our number and I hear 'eerrr, is that you . . . why do the Scots always start with 'eerrr'. Are they unable to commence a sentence with a word from the O.E.D., there's enough of them.

Mind you. I was with some people the other day and I remember commenting that of all the places you could have been born in the world, London was not the worst. I could have been an Eskimo, a Red Indian, a Jamaican. But someone in his wisdom – yes *his* – decided to make me a Londoner. Now appreciating that there are a few miles in the world, London is bloody close to Birmingham. Imagine having the misfortune to be born there with that accent. I think I prefer to be a Red Indian. I love listening to Brumies when I'm feeling depressed. There's no better pick me up than the realisation that you don't sound like them. My kids always say that if they could have any accent it would be Geordie. I must confess to finding it attractive. But then that's part of why Britain is a super place to have a holiday. We are always pleased so many people go to Spain and France, because they are not where we are, they probably wouldn't be our types anyway. You know, all those forty plus year olds trying to relive their youth on some grotty hotels dance floor clicking fingers and wriggling their bums to Viva Espania whilst eagerly awaiting the following mornings sunrise so that they can fend off any pushy German for the one remaining place on the beach where they can continue attracting the rays that at best will make their skin baggy and loose, and at worst will give them cancer. But as long as they're brown they're happy.

29

It makes you glad when you think of our unpredictable weather. If we had a summer like theirs on the continent, we would have the Germans over here, plus the plebs who go abroad would stay at home. Nasty thought.

We went for a long weekend in the Yorkshire Dales with a couple we're friendly with last June. We stayed in a beautiful little village and toured some lovely countryside. Still with new legislation regarding water privatisation being passed through, the land we travelled across owned by the water authorities will probably have a leisure dome with a business park next time we visit the area. Still every utility must make a profit for its shareholders.

I don't know about you, but I'm sick and tired of the gas and electricity ads. We all have to use either or both of these services. So why advertise. I'm not interested in knowing that 'they're always there' every time half time in a cup final comes along to boost the output so we can have a cup of tea. Or, come to that 'cook ability – that's the beauty of Gas' means you can burn the milk pan quicker. I expect most housewives have sussed out that gas hobs are quicker than electric ones – save the new and expensive halogen ovens.

It's 11.30 am and I've got to go up to London to have a look at a few cars. Let you know how I get on later.

Well that was a waste of time, only two cars worth buying and they were too dear. OK if I'd got customers for them, but better to leave it out. The old maxim applies. If you hesitate over the price it's too dear. Always the way, I'm still looking out for the two retail customers, one of whom wants the medium sized automatic and the other an 1800cc Sierra. They're always thin on the ground when you want one and you've always got them coming out of your ears when you don't. The automatic Maestro still hasn't come in yet, but I've kept in contact with both parties, so they shouldn't be going anywhere else just yet.

I'm sitting down and having a cup of tea. It's the 7th February and I have still not bought any cars this month. Mind you, I haven't sold anything either, but there's still a fair way to go yet. Bulldog spirit required, what! Here we are again. In the local paper, the good residents of Odiham are about to battle to save the grounds of a Grade II listed building – The Priory – from being built on with houses and a car park. They want twenty-four houses and sixty-two car spaces. I used to use a phrase to describe Americans – 'They know the price of everything and the value of nothing'. Was it Oscar Wilde who said that? Anyway, it's becoming more and more true of more and more companies. Back to the greed element. Look at the number of estate agencies owned by banks, building societies and solicitors. They are all jumping on the band wagon. I see in a recent survey, estate agencies are the most disliked of businesses – even below the motor trade – things are looking up. Anyway I wish the Odiham Society the best of luck in their battle to keep Odiham as near to a being a pleasant village as they can.

You know, the September before last Maureen and I went on a long weekend to Southwold and stayed at what used to be the Railway Hotel. The Southwold Railway closed in 1929 but lay dormant until the War Department requisitioned all metal for melting down. Efforts were made in the early sixties to save the odd wagon body found in fields and any reference, be it signboard, nameplate etc, are on public display in Southwold Museum. Anyway, the weekend was pleasurable – no kids for a start. It was like going back fifty years. Peace, tranquillity and Adams prized ale. If only the railway were still there. We toured several beautiful villages and small towns, but there was one fault that was common to most – the number of times council estates typically fifties and sixties style houses – which had been built either as you approached the centre or sprawling all along the main drag into the place. Lavenham was one I remember in particular, full of black and white – see, I'm not prejudice, I put black first – buildings picturesquely situated on a hill with a large square, and lanes running down from it just begging you to explore. And round the back? We could have been in Billericy. There had been no attempt to disguise the fact that they were council at all. It couldn't have been more plain if they'd put up a bloody great banner. The cheapest bricks, plainest windows, flush doors that look tatty. I can image all the children with names like Emma, Rebecca, Tristan and Sam inhabiting the

31

black and white, while all the Waynes, Darrens and newly born Kylies vye with equally commonly named peers for the tea of fish fingers and chips. Now it's not that I'm against council houses or their tenants, but I do feel annoyed that they get such a good view of the countryside. All council houses should be built in high density areas. In the case of East Anglia there's Basildon, Harlow, Brentwood, Chelmsford and of course Billericay. Actually, I was discussing with someone the other day the comments made that the problems caused by the ozone layer breaking up would lay waste under floods many areas of Britain, especially East Anglia. It's not so bad if you think that if they play their cards right and started work now, they could dig inlets so that the above plus Milton Keynes and everywhere south of the line from Chingford to Brentwood to the coast would be submerged. If you want to go the whole hog of course, you can come South of the Thames and include the area known as the North Downs. These towns are the pits, aren't they? Just before Christmas I travelled by train from Gillingham to Victoria. I've never been so pleased to be back in Surrey in all my life. Going through Belgiums bad, but hard as I tried, I could not hold my breath long enough during that awful journey through Chatham, Gravesend and Dartford. How do people live there? They must be terribly miserable. Estate after estate. Quarry after quarry. When you watch holiday programmes and they visit German or French towns, there are always shots of clean well-kept civic buildings and old fashioned shopping centres. Whilst I appreciate that there are down-market squalid areas the world over, it seems to me that Europe especially has taken the view that a place with old world charm and character, and those with historical connections can be left aside from development and reap the benefits of tourism. We seem to have lost our way in this country. To me, despite all the stately homes and other priceless buildings lost in the 1950's, legalised vandalism commenced with the destruction of Euston station and the beautiful doric arch. I have read many letters and reports about the whereabouts of the blocks used in its construction, and the general consensus of opinion seems to be that they were used for breakwater construction and for the marble DIY fireplaces that were very much in vogue at the time. I am led to believe that the demolition contractors offered to number the blocks so that they could be rebuilt in a public area again, but British Railways were not sympathetic. Since then so many fine buildings the country over have been destroyed. I hate to say this, but we seem to have learned nothing, still money talks and the unrelenting destruction of our commercial and industrial heritage goes unabated. As I said earlier, Western European countries seem to have stepped back to survey their towns. Obviously they have built modern monstrosities the same as we have but they do appear to have accepted the need to leave well alone.

I don't know, but is governmental interference in local politics less in Europe? Local authorities in this country are forever having to meet targets for housing set by the government. We are not really an industrial nation anymore. Yes, I know we use screwdrivers to 'put things together' but we don't manufacture very much ourselves do we. I presume we are trying to be a commercial nation judging by the number of business parks springing up countrywide. Mind you, there's still empty office blocks built in the seventies all over the place. Presumably it's economically viable to keep them that way. When you think about it, our wealth seems to come from the so-called invisible earnings. The number of takeovers in different industries that has gone on in the last thirty years or so is staggering. All the household names you knew as a child are vanishing. Take the motor industry for example. When I was a child, my best friend and I would make out a list of all the manufacturers we knew and stand by the curb, marking down every car that passed against its parentage. Take the number of British makes in the fifties and sixties, Austin, Morris, Wolseley, Riley, MG, Hillman, Singer, Sunbeam, Humber, Alvis, Rover, Jowett, Jensen, Standard, Triumph, Jaguar, Daimler, Rolls-Royce and Bentley. Besides the last four who have survived albeit as two companies within the luxury market we are left with Austin-Rover as the sole major manufacturing British Company. The Rootes group being swallowed up into what is now Peugeot, having dropped the Talbot range. Whereas Ford and Vauxhall have expanded their market share without takeovers in the British car scene, BMC having gradually gobbled their way through various smaller car producers and merged in the mid sixties with Rover and have continued to see their percentage of the market eroded.

I went to a Ford 'do' at Windsor Safari Park last year. It was one of their PR jobs. There's a company in London with whom I'm involved on their commercial side, supplying various vans and lorries, so I was invited by one of the dealers I use to go along for the presentation and demo rides in some of their large vehicles. Very enjoyable it was too, but at one point the narrator said something to the effect that where there was ten years ago some thirty-five truck and lorry manufacturers in Europe, there are now only sixteen and these will shrink even further. He explained how the rationalisation would benefit the customer with all the modern technological processes and advancements being made. What amazed me was that shortly before this event took place, I received an order for six transit vans. Having rang both the dealers I regularly use I was told that there weren't enough diesel engines about and we'd have to wait eight to ten weeks for delivery. The majority of the people at this 'do' appeared to be in the same boat. So much for a rationalised industry being able to give a better service. Again, do you remember all those lovely names used by commercial manufacturing companies Maudesley, Crossley, AEC, Scammell, ERF, Foden, Albion, Guy etc. They created an individuality lacking on our modern day roads.

Standing at the side of the road, our books would be full of the previously mentioned cars plus the occasional Renault Dauphine, Citroën or Borguard. I don't remember many Mercedes or BMWs. Even the names applied by the companies to model ranges were homely, something you could identify with. Take the Austin Somersets and Devons, Standard Vanguards, Humber Snipes, Hawks and the prestige Pullman. Just thought of another one – Armstrong-Siddeley Sapphires – they looked majestic. Hillman Minx, Sunbeam Rapier, Singer Gazelle. Then you had the classic British sports car – Triumph TR series, Austin Healey Sprite, Triumph Spitfire, MGB and Midget.

34

I think that's the main reason I base my model railway in 1963. They were secure, homely years when I was young. I don't think I'm looking through rose-coloured glasses, but besides the cold war, Rachmen, Suez and a few other unsavoury incidents, life for the common men was gentle. You didn't have to worry about what to eat and what not to. The impending decision by our Government on whether to allow irradiated food to be sold is going to cause a stir, but I'm sure that if the profit for those involved is big enough then it will be pushed through. Everyone wants to be No 1 these days. So much competition, pushing youngsters into careers if they're bright, with salaries way above their years and often above their mentality. Judging by the trouble ticket collectors and guards have at Fenchurch Street and Liverpool Street with yuppies of both sexes in the evening, it would appear that bright as they may be at the job pushing money from one market to another, they are nothing more than glorified louts at the end of the day – they are just dressed better.

We are having trouble with Glyn. I don't mean trouble in the criminal sense, but he's at a sixth form college at the moment with his main course being graphics. I hope I'm proved wrong, but his attitude towards everything is a 'cop-out'. He's his own worst enemy. Having dinner the other evening at some friends' house (the son of whom goes to the same college) the mother said how well her youngster was getting on and what a good report he had received. 'Report' I said 'We have not been priviledged enough to get ours!' 'Ah' She said 'I hope I haven't dropped him in it' 'No' I replied 'It's just that every time I have a chat with him, he tells me what I want to hear and then does nothing about it'. The following day at about 4.30 pm we confronted him. Bear in mind that neither of us were ecstatic when we learned that we had missed the parents' evening last October. 'I've got the report upstairs in my room' said Glyn. 'Presumably it's not good' Maureen enquired. 'No' He replied. 'You must have realised we would find out at some stage' I asked. He said nothing and went back upstairs. On his return and after seeing said report we understood why he did not want us to see it. It was terrible. What really annoys us, is that its been the same theme running through all of his reports for as long as we can remember. All the tutors and teachers regard him in the same vein as everyone else. 'Glyn is very well mannered, pleasant, polite. No trouble at all, but he doesn't work to his true potential. He gets by with the minimum of effort. Just enough to stop a phone call to you. He never asks questions and does not complete his homework'. Believe me, they've all said the same. I could write their scripts. The first day of school as a rising five saw him crying, as a lot of kids do. 'What's the matter?' asked Maureen. 'I can't read' he said. 'It doesn't matter' she replied 'That's what you're going to school for – you're not expected to know – they teach you'. It's been the same ever since. Always thinks he's expected to know. Never puts his hand up to ask. When we've offered to help him with homework it's the same reply. 'I've already done it at school'. The annoying thing is that I have always tried to impress upon him that we don't expect him to come top. If he did, fine, of course we'd be very pleased and proud, but we can be both, just knowing that he had come bottom but given his all. And that's the rub. At the end of the day he doesn't bother. If any of his teachers had been off-hand, miserable or just plain unsociable I could have said it was the school. But to be honest, I've yet to find anyone who hasn't considered Glyn to be worth trying for.

Having digested his report, I decided to ring the college and ask to see his tutors, see if we can salvage something. I mean the whole point of going to sixth form is to improve on the marks if you're in Glyn's position or take 'A' level courses if you did well enough in the GCSE.

They've got so much going for them now, haven't they? When I was at school, you took the GCE if you were good enough and the CSE if you were not. Straight exams. I always felt it would be fairer if the work, attendance, attitude etc that was displayed by the pupil during the year were to be taken into account when making the assessments. It has been said before, I know, but it is worth repeating that some children do freeze in exam conditions and fail miserably, while others that disrupt the rest of the class for long periods of the term sail through with ease. That's human nature, but I was impressed with the idea of the

GCSE when it was first mooted. The problem, however, in practice is that pupils take advantage of this facility. Apparently there is a set amount in any given subject, to hand in during the term. The teacher selects a percentage i.e. the best work and that is submitted for marking. Pupils couldn't be given a fairer – or easier – chance to attain good marks, but no, Glyn still thinks it's better to socialise and not bother.

As I said at the meeting with his year and form subject tutors, we did not push him into sixth form. He chose it himself. 'I'm glad I've got a second chance to improve my grades' he said. You see, telling us what we want to hear. I feel it's unfair on teachers. There are plenty of pupils trying hard to do well and he's just wasting their time. He works every Saturday and Sunday at a takeaway in Aldershot. A job he's held down now for about 8 months. I expect he's one of their more reliable part-time workers. He always turns up and is very seldom late, but he cannot turn the discipline of weekend work into working practice for education. Perhaps it would have been best for him to leave and go out to work at the end of the summer term. But then hindsight won wars, didn't it. The meeting, by the way, ended with Glyn promising to complete his homework and coursework, and their accepting it after the time allowed had elapsed. He doesn't know how lucky he is. Perhaps they're too soft. Perhaps if they had said during the first term that late and substandard work would not be tolerated, parents would be immediately informed if it was etc. perhaps . . . ah well.

It's funny how kids react. If Maureen and I have an argument, Glyn always takes my side whereas Deborah sides with her mother. William seems to be fairly independent and immune.

Deborah appears to have her feet firmly on the ground. She's certainly never found every subject easy, but she's always tried, and to be fair to her, it seems to be paying off. We have no doubt that next years GCSE will be successful for her. Whereas Glyn is fairly irascible and always seems negative, Deb's is level headed and reasonable most of the time. Again, she's liked at school, subjects such as English, History, Business

Studies, Science seem to be coped with very well. Maths and Geography cause a few problems but at least we get involved with her homework, and she takes hours over it.

About a year ago she advised us that she wanted to be a lawyer dealing with divorce cases. We immediately indicated that we could be her first client. But in our case it's not so much a question of fighting over custody of William, more who's lumbered with the toad. Still I feel that whatever she decides to do she will be successful. But you never know, she may become infatuated with some chap, end up pregnant and fall down the slippery slope, whereas Glyn might find a niche that suits him and do very well. You never know do you?

I wish that when I was six I had just an ounce of the confidence William displays. I mentioned earlier that he was a very active baby. Our problems started with him the moment he learned to climb out of his cot. Hours on end were spent caressing and cooing in an attempt to get him to sleep. Just when you thought it was safe to creep out of his bedroom, he'd be crying again. Honestly, no exaggeration. This went on night after night, week after week. It was an exception if we could get a good night's sleep. He was a bad sleeper even at the age of two-two and a half. He would get up during the early evening, walk through from his bedroom and crash out on the settee. We often left him there until we went to bed. I think I'm right in saying that this went on until he went to school. He just didn't want to go to sleep. When he was about four, we considered the possibility that he was hyper-active. We paid privately to see a homoeopath. He was put on a diet, tartrazine free orange drinks, goats milk etc. The end result after about three months was an increase in his ability to stay awake by about one hour per day. That was a waste of money.

Still we had our compensations. When he was about two and a half Maureen went to collect him from a neighbours where he said he was playing. No William. We searched high and low. Not in the house or the lane. We got into the car and went up to the top of the road, and searched all the local area as far as the village centre. 'It's silly both of us looking for him in the car' Maureen said. 'I'll go back home in case he turns up while you carry on.' 'OK' I agreed. As Maureen approached the house having left the car, she shouted that the phone was ringing. Both our hearts missed a beat. I leapt from the car. The voice at the other end was that of a neighbour who had seen him pedalling fiercely along the Vale Road and across two minor roads. She quickly realised that he was by himself and guided him to her friend's home from where she rang. We went round to collect him. He was a bit upset. 'Where do you think you were going?' I asked 'To the video shop, because you wouldn't buy me "Megatron's Revenge"' he replied. 'You've been told about going out of the lane before' Maureen added 'There are nasty men and women around who offer you sweets to get you into their cars and little girls and boys who do never see their mummies and daddies again' I continued. 'It's all right' he retorted 'I'd cut their heads off with Glyn's knife'. That's the way he is, always got an answer. I also made a point that he crossed roads and could have got run over. He replied that he looked both ways and anyway he didn't cross the main road, he stayed on the same side. I gave up, the pair of us just being too pleased that he had come to no harm. I must point out that 'Megatron's Revenge' is one of those transformer films that is still very much the rage. As I'm writing this I can see at least two Autobots and Grimlock. See I know them all.

We went to the Isle of Man, when he was still under three, for our holiday. We rented a cottage in Groudle Glen. We'd been to this village before and enjoyed the standard provided. The morning after a late night playing cards with the two eldest, I awoke to hear sounds coming from, I presumed, the radio. It was quite early. I looked into Glyn and Deb's bedrooms, they were fast asleep. I opened the lounge door to find William sprawled out on the floor watching TV, 'Hello Dad' he said. 'Pink Panther's on'. My eyes turned to the fireplace where a two bar electric fire was blazing away. 'Did you put that on?' I enquired, realising that he must have put in both plugs as we had taken the precaution of disconnecting all plugs from sockets the previous evening. 'Yeah, it was cold' I gave him a little lecture about the dangers of electricity, but I think the Pink Panther won.

He turned off the tanoy at Ronaldsway Airport on our return and the stewardess had to go round telling passengers individually that they could board. It was only after she'd apologised for the breakdown in technology that William pointed to a chair which he'd climbed upon to facilitate the switching off of the electrics. We all headed hurriedly for the plane.

He will make a great door to door salesman. He never accepts anyone else is right. If it looks as if I'm going to produce insurmountable evidence to back up what I'm trying to put over – he changes the subject. He asks for a cup of tea or an orange drink or a sandwich etc. Anything not to lose face.

The days when he did anything because we said so have long gone. We have one TV and video downstairs in our living room, and one TV only upstairs for the kids. The other day I was sitting comfortably watching something downstairs when he just came up, no bye your leave or anything, pushed in a video of his and sat on the floor to watch it. I toe poked him and asked what the hell he thought he was playing at. The reply was that as the only video was down here and he wanted to use it, I should go upstairs to watch what I wanted. Somewhat peeved, I added that as it was my house I could watch what I like when and where I like and that it was ill-mannered to waltz in and turn on the video without saying anything. The response was to get very upset, call me selfish and slam the door behind him.

Now if I'd done that when I was small, not that we had videos in those days, but you know what I mean, I'd have received a clip round the ear and been sent to my room. We've tried all that with William. We never had this type of trouble with the other two. They went to bed when they were told, no hystrionics if we had company. If ever they got out of order, a smart smack on the back of the legs and the lesson was learned. Perhaps we had it too easy. Getting back to when William was a baby, we'd be up and down the corridor all evening putting him back to bed. We often stayed just outside his room for hours on end because he would be up the second we'd closed the door. Whether you left the light off, dimmed or blazing, door closed, ajar or fully opened, none of these combinations produced a sleeping child. I thought that he might cry himself to sleep, but that was a false hope. All that did was to wake up Glyn and Debs, which was very unfair on them as they had school the following morning.

In May 1986 Maureen and I went away for a week's holiday in Guernsey. My Mum and Dad came down to look after the three children and the dog. William was, to quote my Mum, a little angel – no problem at all. Well they are always better for grandparents aren't they? It's still gauling to come home at the end of a very enjoyable week to be greeted by a beaming Mum who felt she had got the better of him, and a Dad who couldn't understand what all the fuss was about anyway. We got the 'he went to bed when he was told and ate everything that was put in front of him'. We were so pleased. (Enter sickly grin).

His behaviour in shops has not been wonderful. Again whereas the other two have accepted anything given them with pleasure, they have not kept on when told they can't have something, or they will have to wait because we can't afford it or it's too near their birthday, whatever. William always considered it your fault. If you're in W.H. Smith and you refuse to buy him a toy, it has been known for whole shelves to go. He's run amok in Mothercare on more than one occasion. About the most embarrassing time I can recount was when we went to a supermarket near to closing time. He had been a misery from the outset, and it got worse when he was refused whatever it was he wanted us to buy him. By the time we arrived at the checkout, having endured the endless trading back of items such as toilet rolls, bread and cereals from other people's trolleys to ours, we were already on edge. He was as quick as lightening. Another passing trolley, another exchange of goods. Anyway, he was not happy and set about kicking hell out of the wild life panda. I dashed past the checkout, but too late. He was trying to hold up the shutter as a young lad was trying to close down the entrance area. By the time I'd got to him, he made a run for it back into the fruit and veg and stood by the apples, tastefully displayed in the middle of the floor. 'William, come here' all eyes at the checkouts were on him. 'No' he replied and grasped an apple. 'Put that down'. 'No' again. This time he took a bite and threw it back in the pile. My memory is blurred after that, but I do remember smacking him hard in front of a lot of people. If only a trauma support group had heard of his plight.'

Back to our holiday in Guernsey, or rather after it. Mum and Dad have now gone home, and we are settling back down to life as we knew it. William becomes constipated, badly. Several laxatives and trips to the doctor fail to cure the problem. We put up with about a year of him going in his pants. Bearing in mind that it was embarrassing for him, it was also embarrassing for the other two when they had friends round. This was a point we put to our Doctor in the hope that it would speed along progress. We were given out-patient appointments at Frimley Park Hospitals Children Department. To be brief they were a complete waste of time. A young female doctor resembling Selina Scott kept feeling the beads around her neck and saying 'I know' 'I know'. They just wanted to feed him more laxatives. We had further meetings with a consultant at the same hospital who was a most arrogant bumptious type who considered his problem to be psychological and prescribed more laxatives.

By this time his behaviour was getting worse. He must have felt so terribly uncomfortable his irritability with the situation compounded to bring about a tension with everyone in the household. We had asked for help for the first time in our lives from social services. The local health visitor was next to useless, but the child guidance clinic produced some interesting comments, one of which was that he was probably trying to get his own back on us for going on holiday without him. A point we had not previously considered. They thought that he wanted to get our attention but it had gone wrong and there came a point where he found he was unable to go to the toilet.

An appointment was made for him to go into Frimley Park Hospital for a couple of days so that he could be 'cleared out' and they would monitor his progress. Now we foolishly and naively believed that as we were the layman, they would take care of him. I don't know where the so-called shortage of staff was in that hospital, as there were nurses a-plenty in the children ward, but parents who went home were not thought of very highly. It is such a shame that standards and expectations have dropped to such a low level. I know that nurses deserve every penny they earn and more – and I'm not unaware that ever since 'they' decided to get rid of the post of Matron, the whole cubboodle has gone down hill and a complete transformation has taken place causing low morale to spread like cancer, but it is a pity when parents have to stay all night because they cannot trust nurses to answer emergency bells at the bedside of children.

It appeared that they expected mothers to stay all day and play with, and control children. The nurses seemed to be so engrossed with paperwork. I remember one little kid whose parents were not there happily asking a nurse to look at something he'd drawn. She coldly told him she was too busy. The disappointment on his face said it all. Maureen obviously stayed as long as she could every day, but we do have the other children and the house. By saying that she was going to pick up the other two from school and she'd be back later was always received as if you were playing truant. One parent said her little girl, who was in there because she was continually sick, couldn't dare leave her as when she was sick the previous day and had called the nurse, nobody had come. If that had happened at night and she had choked would staff have been alert? I think not. A year or so of changing pants, the awkwardness of going shopping and William standing uneasily in a corner embarrassed by the situation, and you knowing that he has or is about to soil his trousers took its toll on Maureen's health. Every out patient appointment, however far into the distance the date had been, was looked forward to in the hope that the problem could be solved. The annoying thing was, that with the exception of the child guidance people, nobody seemed to care. When he came out of the hospital, he was frightened stiff of anybody in a white coat, he had a nervous twitch that took some months to go away, and we were no nearer finding a solution. Whilst he was in there, a check was to be made of the number of times he went, when he went, and how much he deposited. One day Maureen was there and found that William had diarrhoea. Even then, when she asked a nurse to help her clean him up and possibly inform someone of the situation in case it was relevant, all she got was a hand pointing towards the cupboard housing the required materials.

I tell you, I wouldn't send my worst enemy there overnight. Oh I don't know, I might send Ben Elton.

The situation unresolved, the clinic suggested a small unit in Portsmouth that dealt with physical problems in children that were psychologically linked. They wrote on our behalf and an appointment was made for William to go within a month. Time was precious, as he was starting school in September and we didn't want the problem to be still going on then. Another letter, another disappointment. This hospital sounded ideal but it could not take us after all as we lived in Surrey and Hampshire budget covered only those who lived in the County. I went loopy on the phone. When you really need help its not there. I made the comment that I was under the impression I paid into the *National* Health Scheme, that we were only five hundred yards from the hospital's border and we were actually born here, not naturalised, never claimed any benefit, but no, it wasn't to be. If only Maureen had been a black lesbian, single parent.

Back to the clinic, new idea. The Maudesley hospital in Camberwell. I remember my Mum ringing to see if any progress had been made, I told her. 'He's not mad *is* he' she said indignantly. 'No' I said 'Of course not, but they think that the people there can help and they're prepared to see us.' She wasn't very happy. To her, you only went to the Maudesley if you were round the bend. Anyway the day eventually arrived and we made the horrendous journey through some of the worst areas of London. Having parked the car we entered the hospital, having successfully managed to avoid being mugged, to be greeted by a receptionist who knew of our appointment and duly offered us a cup of tea. I kept telling myself that this was all worth it and that we were doing it for William's sake, but I could feel myself getting more and more uptight. Unfair, I know, as Maureen could see my annoyance which only made her feel uncomfortable. I'd never seen so many left-wing types in all my life. It was like I imagine the LSE. Short cropped hair, ankle socks, one girl had a ring through her nostril, sloppy jumpers covering sloppy skirts. The whole place had an air of social rejection about it. The corridors, clean as they were, held aloft posters proclaiming various trade union movements, lesbian theatre 'treats' and fund raising activities for black rights. There was also a telephone number to call if you had been the subject of Police brutality, again aimed at the black community. If there was a left wing or racial message to be put across, this was obviously the sounding board. Anyway, I digress. A consultant came to see us and we were ushered into a room. We were told that his colleagues would be watching us through a two way window (which he pointed to) and listening to our conversation through a mike hanging from the ceiling. He asked if we were happy about the arrangement. We agreed. It felt a bit big-brotherish, but I commented that we hadn't spent two hours getting up here to turn around again straight away. After about 20 minutes he went out to confer. Some short time later, he returned introducing us to the Chief registrar, a social worker, a Psychologist, the ward sister and a nurse. It only occurred to us later that as we were discussing a child's bottom, it probably crossed their minds that we could be the perpetrators of child abuse. It's a bit like walking round a shop holding a bag of sweets etc, you always feel conscious of a magic eye watching your every step willing you to go outside and get caught shoplifting. Sadly, the days of shoplifting being a rarity have gone and probably so is going to a hospital for the welfare of your children. Now, there are two ways of accessing every situation. I suppose it's a rare case of Camberwell being better than Cleveland. (Ghastly Name)

They smiled and walked out for another 'case conference'. After what seemed an interminable time, they returned and stated their belief that they could help us, but would need Maureen to go in with William, to get some rest and help in the later stages of their treatment. They were to go in at the end of the week for a fortnight. I would stay at home and kill off our other two with my cooking.

This is the stage where I eat my hat, take back everything I said about lefties, well lefty nurses anyway. They could not have been more helpful. For the first few days. Maureen hardly saw William. He was kept in an upstairs ward with a few other children, the landing of which housed a chair for the nightnurse so that any wondering child could be put back to bed without even getting near the stairs. Maureen in turn caught up on a lot of sleep, receiving undisturbed nights in a room with washing facilities and television to herself. Absolute heaven. During the day they met at mealtimes and she put him to bed at night. Aside from these few 'duties' she could relax, go shopping and take a well earned rest. I remember her saying that during the first week the social worker took her out for a meal in the evening and the staff in general had bent over backwards to make her feel as much at home as is possible in the confines of a hospital where everything has to be locked, including doorways. At night, Maureen was literally locked in. One of the problems was itinerants stealing food from the kitchen. I went up whenever I could, and at weekends and evenings took the children who had been served some appalling meals. Maureen wasn't short of visitors as my parents and hers both visited on the evenings I couldn't.

They continually disciplined William to stay on the loo until he went. They used a sin bin idea if he was bad and carrots if he was good. He used to eat so little. Milk shakes and Weetabix were about his staple diet, except when in the care of grandparents. He didn't know how far to go with them. An added dimension being that the chap assigned to 'get to know him' on a one-to-one basis and take him for treats if he was good was Mauritian. He was a super chap and William had never met anybody who wasn't white before. They got on well together, but not before William had tested the water by exclaiming a few expletives when not getting his own way and being rather upset when nobody bit. Anyway, at the start of the second week he went into Kings College Hospital where they X-rayed and tested him and came to the conclusion that his bowels were now working properly. His holding it in for so long had caused the 'normal' feeling one gets to give up the ghost, but after an intensive period of sitting on the loo every two hours or so, the discipline returned and with a gradual resumption of 'normal services' so his behaviour improved. In two weeks the change was immense, but certainly no time to slacken. Maureen and William came home in early June 1987 and he started school in September. It was hard work keeping up with the schedule the Maudesley set us, but we had a lot of help in so far as they sent us down the Chief registrar on one occasion – he came in his Porsche, flash bastard – and on several monthly visits the girl who also worked closely with him came to see us. Only after about ten months did the visits stop and we finally felt that he had managed to overcome the hang-up's of 'going to the loo'. His progress at school has not been spectacular but he enjoys it and the staff appear to like him. Quotes like 'The school nativity should be good this year, William is in it' and 'all children have a short concentration level, but William's record is about twelve seconds' seem to show he's quite well thought of, don't they?

Enough of the tow-rag, there was something I saw in a paper the other day that annoyed me, but I can't remember what it was. Better have a delve. Here we are. The booing of Kenneth Baker by a section of the audience at the BRIT awards. Regardless of politics it is crass bad manners to treat anybody this way. I'm sure though that it doesn't surprise anyone. The question is, could anyone listening have differentiated between these awards and 'Yesterday in Parliament?' If you don't set an example . . .

You almost feel as if the Salman Rushdie affair was brought about to transfer the interest from something that affects us all – like eggs and salmonella – to something that infuriates us all – foreigners telling us what to do in our own country. Once again we accept meekly the rantings of Iran. Now before anyone wants to put a death threat on me, I don't believe in any religion, so as far as I'm concerned you can be Wesleyan, Methodist, C of E, Catholic, Buddhist, Hindu, Muslim or whatever, I don't care. I only have to read about another death absolved in the name of religion to be pleased I remain unswayed despite my parents insistence on my going to Chapel as a child. Looking back you know, it really was quite bizarre. I lived just outside Clapham Junction Station in a paper shop on the corner of Falcon Road and Este Road. My Mother came from Battersea, my Father from Aberdare. He came to London before the war, they married and lived in the

47

family home. My grandmother lived with us until she died in 1964. I wouldn't have minded, but they never went to Church themselves. I was forced to go to the Welsh Chapel in Clapham Junction. I usually went with a friend whose parents were also Welsh and ran the local dairy a stones throw away. It was very cliquey and I always felt an outcast. Most of the children who went to Sunday school were Welsh speaking. I wasn't, that was the rub. We had to learn verses every week, in Welsh, and then recite them during evening service. I hated getting up in front of a motley collection of black garmented, hat covered old ladies who always appeared to me, a twelve year old, to be gossiping, they were forever looking over their shoulders for fear of the butt of their criticism catching them out. I remember asking the Sunday school teacher how, if Mary was a virgin, she had had Jesus – I hadn't gone into the details you see, and I received a clout round the ears that these days would have brought every trauma expert, social worker and television psychologist running to Clapham Junction from all directions. I also remember that outside Arding and Hobbs (a department store) in the middle of the road was a large traffic island that housed some beautiful public toilets. Of course, in the early sixties they were manned (or womaned) continually and there were only poems and expletives on the inside doors of the loos. The brass work was always highly polished. I think they had green and cream tiles, but I cannot be sure. It was, however, fairly safe to go in, on the way to chapel, if caught short.

One particular instance, I recall, I stood pointing percy at the porcelain when a man in a trilby hat came up alongside me and asked if I wanted to see some photographs. I instinctively knew something was not quite right and saying 'no thanks' ran off, doing up my flies whilst hastily jumping the stairs two at a time. Sitting in the security of the pews, I thought that it probably would have been more exciting to have had a look and risked being abducted. I mean Sunday afternoon was fairly boring.

Getting back to Rushdie, I agree it is a grey area as to where a foreigner to these shores becomes British. Personally, I've never accepted that anyone is British just because they hold one of our passports. I prefer to think of a British subject as someone who accepts our way of life, our disciplines and our freedom of speech. No, I don't want them to give up all the culture, but I feel a lot more integration into the native way of life wouldn't come amiss. No other country in the world would put up with Muslim leaders in large cities stating that someone deserves to die because of a book he or she has written. Public burning of a book is against everything our freedom stands for. The papers listen to what these people say, print it, comment on it, but nobody in Government is prepared to expel anyone who goes against our democracy. Whatever the religion, however insulted a group of people feel, no-one has the right to make threats. If they don't like it – leave. Nobody says anything these days because you mustn't rock the racial boat. In the good old days of public debates on TV and radio, immigration was often discussed. You never hear anything these days. Too near the mark, mustn't upset anyone, anyway, more of that later.

Just had a call from the architect saying all's well, and could I settle up. There is no taste in nothing so I'd better pay him. The plans look very detailed. Anyway I can now start getting some quotes and hopefully, estate agents able to sell my parents home, and if this place doesn't cost the earth to build, we can all be ensconced in our respective homes by the end of autumn.

March

Another month upon us, the year is going quickly. You remember, or possibly not, depends on whether you found it boring I suppose, that I commented on Bryant Homes wishing to build 2,500 houses in Eversley. Well the council has said that the financial offer from the company to improve roads would remove any objection they might have on highway grounds. They're getting there. Also, another council, Rushmoor, has sent volunteers to measure up a children's play area. When a local resident asks what they're doing and rings the council offices, the Chief Architect admits 'provisions have been made for housing but nothing definite has been decided'. Looks ominous doesn't it?' Why have any play areas when you can build on them? Do these people work on our behalf or not. No wonder turn-outs are so low at local elections. In Guildford Borough they've been measuring all the school playgrounds and fields. It's a pity that local councils are formed on a political basis. Used to be so many ratepayers and independents when I was young. People who represented the electorate. How times change. The common link is again profit.

Mind you, look at the number of cases of people going to court and suing another party. Everybody wants to sue these days. As soon as there is a disaster, a group of people by 9 am have contacted a solicitor and are being interviewed on TV. Be it an accident like the Clapham Junction train crash, the Townsend Thoresen Zebrugge episode or Lockerbie, everybody wants to sue. No one waits for an inquiry to apportion blame. Presumably solicitors advise so as to get their fizzoggs in before the competition to represent those affected. You often hear of a divorced couple, when looking back at the machinations of their case, state that at no time were

50

conciliation services considered as a possibility. Let's just grab as much money as we can for our client and ourselves and then 'next please'. There was a case I read about the other day where a couple who had known each other for some five years and had been on skiing holidays before have now abruptly ended their relationship because the woman is suing the man for negligence. She alleges that he did not respond to a warning signal she gave him causing her to break her leg, whilst the two of them were skiing. Obviously their relationship wasn't worth the financial enhancement a court case might provide.

It's funny, I don't know whether you feel the same, but I can read stories of famine, national disasters such as earthquakes in Mexico, volcanic eruptions etc but I'm far more upset when I read and look at pictures of cruelty to animals. Personally I would never visit Spain for a holiday. In spite of my previous comments about the type of people who go there, no country that in this day and age pits animals against people would get a visit from me, be it in a bullring or beating a donkey as it proceeds through some traditional ceremony, or the public slaughtering of a pig, again in the name of tradition. Those EEC bureaucrats can pontificate for months, years even, on the rights and wrongs of what constitutes ice cream and marmalade, but accept Spain as a full member when it allows such dreadful rituals using horses, ponies, pigs and even the poor old quail isn't exempt. They are used in live clay pigeon shoots, being catapulted into the air, only to be shot by some sick bastard. The only thing in the Spaniards favour, is that there is no covering up and no hypocrisy, they are in fact quite proud of it all, and consider these traditional days out a feast for young and old alike. I'm glad to say the natural inclination of the British public in general would not tolerate that sort of thing.

When we chase foxes, it's done in the name of sport, but with a difference. These good red coated 'gentlemen and ladies' are actually just keeping down the fox population and doing fellow farmers and gentry a favour. What a cop-out. I appreciate that foxes leave chicken sheds in a devastation, but there is not a single ounce of justification in chasing an animal for miles, often upsetting local people and other animals in the process. Are these people really any different from those other bastards who organise and profit out of dog-fighting? I think not, it's just that some have a higher IQ, are members of the right club and manage to convince (through political and business connections) those with influence that the majority of people still consider hunting to be an acceptable sport.

I am sure that if – back to referendums – there was one on hunting, there would be a large majority of people longing to see its abolition.

We are a funny nation. Whenever there is a disaster, the British seem to be the first to set up a fund, regardless of what country is involved. We also seem to produce the same feelings of abhorance when seeing an animal ill-treated. From the much publicised departure of the Spanish donkey to stoning dogs on beaches anywhere in Europe. I stand corrected but I've never read about other nationals taking home pets, spending a fortune on quarantine etc, just to give them a good home, like we do. Are we getting more like our European counterparts I wonder? The poor old RSPCA are putting down one thousand dogs a week. What kind of society are we all becoming? One that puts money before everything. I wonder for how much longer tourists, on seeing stray cats poisoned by hotel staff will be shocked by their behaviour when they visit some Tunisian hotel. Perhaps we will soon learn to take it in our stride as part and parcel of a trip abroad. I do hope not, statistics on cruelty to animals in this country continue an upward trend. Once again, penalties are not tough enough.

To me, there is no difference between tying a firework to a cat's tail and assaulting a child. Yes, I'm definitely on the side of corporal and capital punishment. The trendies have for far too long eroded discipline and respect. We breed a nation that is caring less for the fellow inhabitant, be it human or animal.

I feel we have got to get perverts, child abusers, animal torturers to understand that not only was whatever crime they committed unacceptable, but that they must pay in such a way that they will never do it again, or at least think very long and hard before committing another offence. I'm sick to death of hearing how rough a prisoner's life has been, and how once released they find there is public prejudice against them.

A prime case was recorded last month when a thirteen year old girl was thrown over a balcony as she tried to help her ten year old friend who was being attacked by three youths about sixteen years of age – and all over 10p. The girl luckily escaped death but ended up with a broken arm and collar bone. I don't know whether they have been caught or not, but I consider this type of case to be absolutely right for a flogging. It just might make them think twice.

How Britain can (again) kow-tow to the court of human rights and allow the abolition of caning and flogging I don't know. Whose bloody country is it anyway. The majority of people in the isle of Man wanted to keep it but of course they were not allowed to. We must look after the little darlings mustn't we, after all it's society fault. Balls. I was caned at school and it never did me any harm. The fact that I spend so much time visiting Madams in Earls Court asking to be tied up and whipped for two hours is neither here nor there, but I digress.

On a serious note again, I'm not convinced that the killing of grey seals is morally right either. Just because they raid fish cages, I don't think that gives anyone the right to shoot them. They are just as entitled to the sea as we are, probably more so.

I know I've gone on a bit, but I get very upset over violence to people and animals. There's no respect. Another recent case is of a thirty-two year old man being kicked to death by drunken louts in Andover. You wouldn't have had that sort of thing in a quiet country town twenty years ago. The thugs were given life. Deliberate attacks on people like that which are indisputable should be reckoned with by sentencing those concerned is the death penalty. Despite all the 'but what if's' from the do-gooders, where an act like that is beyond all doubt make the punishment fit the crime. I don't know any of those involved in this case, but it just seems typical of the pointless death of somebody through other people's lack of respect, care and concern. Kicking to death a dog, badger or any animal in my book would mean the culprit receiving the same penalty. Why is it that cruelty to an animal is considered a lesser offence than that to a human being. The pain must be the same.

Change of subject. I've looked through yellow pages and selected a number of builders, whom I am going to ask to quote me for building the house. It's amazing, that despite being labelled under the heading 'builders', when you ring they say they only build for themselves and not for the individual. Didn't think it would be so difficult. Anyway, got a couple coming this week, so we'll see how he goes.

The egg producers are going to sue Edwina for millions apparently, still don't know whether it's safe to eat eggs or not though. Being from Surrey, we will carry on regardless of course.

They can't leave anything alone can they. Apparently Popeye is too brutal and sexist, so the producers of some new Popeye cartoons are to tone-down his image and make Olive Oil a woman of today. That's obviously going to have a great affect on lager louts and muggers. I expect they will see their victim in a new light. I never thought of women as weak and feeble because I watched Popeye. Mind you I never thought all animals could speak with an American accent just because I watched Mickey Mouse and Roadrunner. It's only fun. These people are so bloody neurotic. It's strange how the media in particular want to alter things that everybody else has accepted happily for years. They must change things. Coronation Street is to get a facelift on its opening sequences. Instead of the ginger moggy sitting on the roof they are apparently to seek out a star cat – why? It's not a factual documentary about Manchester, it's a soap, it's entertainment. That roof top shot has been part of the programme for years. Probably someone waiting to put their mark on life I suppose. I can remember years ago when the ITV sports presenter Dicky Davies was called Richard Davies. More with-it? more matey? A great irritation to me in the use of the word 'strike'. 'What a beautiful strike' the commentator loudly proclaims. Cos' they are all strikers up front these days. They never shoot at goal any more, only strike. I'm not a cricketing fanatic but when it has been on the box I can't recall hearing such beautiful antiquities as 'silly mid on or off'. I've always felt guilty because I feel I *should* like cricket more with phrases like that. Of course they play 'zonal' matches as well these days. What's wrong with 'area' I wonder. A change of tack this time. Who decided that homosexuals were 'gay'? As long as I can remember they were always 'queers'. Now it has become fashionable to disclose your sexual preferences they have to take on a new name. 'Gay' to me means happy. Pity Shrewsbury Town who play football at Gay Meadow. Are there more of 'them' around now or is it just that society has changed to such an extent that it is acceptable to the masses. I saw a letter in a paper at the height of the AIDS awareness campaign and the writer commented that he likened homosexuals to the way gardeners view weeds. You accept that they're there but you don't cultivate them.

I was brought up in the belief that being 'queer' was something that happened to people who were 'unfortunate'. If homosexuals were mentioned in the conversation it was only after you had turned your head to make sure no-one else was eavesdropping and only in the smallest of whispers that they were discussed. Again, the media appear to pointedly push them forward. Frankly, I find 'Eastenders' to be the most miserable, unpleasant and gloomy programme on the air. You almost feel like committing suicide yourself after half an hour of that. The people are so unhappy. There is little laughter or fun. I accept that there are lot of people who find it entertaining – are they the same ones who go to Spain I wonder? Why did they have to show two males kissing. Besides being unnecessary, it is tawdry. Frankly I find the thought of two males having sex revolting. An awful lot of people I know feel the same – and they are from many walks of life. We all know it goes on, but why is it thrust upon us. Even on a nice family programme like Treasure Hunt there were two extremely effeminate coves taking part. I make no apologies for taking the view that it is a most unnatural act and if either of my boys grew up like that I would be bitterly disappointed. No, I'm not in favour of or sympathetic to anyone who 'queer bashes' either, just don't keep plugging it. Are these producers fighting a crusade on behalf of liberalism or are they trying to make a name for themselves with cheap publicity to keep the ratings up. I shall stick to Emmerdale Farm and the Archers, at least the cliffhanger at the end of each episode of the radio soap is likely to be the theft of two pints of milk, or someone having to pull out of a cricket match at the last moment due to a back injury.

Having managed to find an automatic car for the chap in Battersea last month, I've just come back from Sutton. The other chap my Mum put me on to has just taken delivery of the Sierra I found for him. As I said some time ago, he was the customer who was so pleased with his Cortina he's going to give it to his son as his first car. Not bad for a seventeen year old is it? Glyn still hasn't heard from Swansea about his application for a driving licence.

Apparently there has been another train crash, in Purley. Luckily no-one here knew anything about it so they weren't panicking that I was on that train. Mind you, before Monday evening's over with there will be a lot of families who will already have given instructions for legal proceedings to commence. I can see the Solicitors now, sitting watching the news in two minds. The feeling of sorrow on one hand and the prospect of a good profit in the other. I hope that's not a generalisation, but having seen these vultures on Breakfast time TV the morning after previous disasters have occurred, it makes you very cynical.

I just read that the woman who tried to sue her boyfriend over the skiing accident has lost her case. I'm extremely pleased. If she had won, the precedence would have been set for everybody. You would then have another area of concern with contracts being drawn up (giving more money to the legal profession) by both parties exempting themselves from blame should a pigeon shit on their head, or their partner's, whilst they are within a twenty mile radius of each other. Sounds far fetched doesn't it, but the skiing case itself would have been considered as such twenty odd years ago.

Getting back to violence, here's another cause for concern. The number of cases involving children is frightening. There's an instance here where two policewomen have been beaten up on the tube by two boys aged twelve and thirteen and two thirteen year old girls. Where are the parents? They

56

should be held financially responsible for any offences and made to compensate the victims until the child 'comes of age' and is legally able to take the full blast of the law by his or herself. To a large degree this behaviour stems from the liberals among us who have advocated easier divorce laws. These in turn have allowed many parents to relinquish responsibility for their children. There will always be genuine cases where the continuation of a marriage would not be in the offsprings interest, but it is too easy for parents to go their own way. A child is like a puppy. It's not just for Christmas, it's for life. How many children have ended up in sordid conditions in London's lowlife. I, like everybody else here, see programmes where the children have been interviewed and many are underage. Of course there will always be the black sheep (no that's not racist) of the family who despite any attempts to keep them on the straight and narrow will turn to a life of crime, but these are the minority. It starts at school. If 'life' was made a subject and children were taught about relationships, the responsibilities for any offspring, pets, the managing of money etc they might leave school on a firmer footing. If, as I'm sure they do, teachers consider that these subjects are covered, why do we have such a large number of unmarried parents, single parents and unwanted children. It comes back to the point that responsibility for a family environment is too easy to relinquish.

I was reading an article recently where a probation officer was commenting that out of thirty-one cases he was dealing with, only three people were over twenty-one years of age.

From those twenty-eight youngsters only *one* was living at home with *both* parents. In all the other cases a broken home was involved.

Life and marriage are not easy and they have to be worked at, but it's all part of today's economic climate. It's cheap. Even going through what I would consider the degradation and embarrassment of a court hearing, half of the offenders do not bother to show up for probation appointments. Another letter goes off to them at the taxpayers expense. If they fail to turn up after so many absences, they are brought back before the magistrate as they have broken the condition of the probation order. But they flout it arrogantly. The excuses why they have not attended are pathetic. It's only a small contribution I know, but it's all part of the general breakdown in discipline and responsibility. If they don't care whether they conform to a probation order or not at their age, what chance have we got in insuring they will not offend again; and will the threat of prison worry them, probably not.

Whenever you hear of a judge describing whatever case as 'the worst he has ever presided over' there comes a call for stiffer penalties. If it's a child that is sexually abused and murdered, parents and relatives cry 'hang him' or 'castrate the bastard'. Personally if the child is sexually abused I consider castration eminently suitable, and murder would be dealt with in the same way as any other killing where the conviction was beyond all doubt. With the DNA system able to help so much these days, the number of opponents who continually cite the Timothy Evans case will perhaps diminish and the overwhelming voice of the British Public who wish to hear a Home Secretary speak with authority and commitment for once will be placated, and their desire to see justice done will not be denied them.

Government Ministers and their 'Sir Humphries' live in a world apart from the rest of us. I was heartened recently to see that Crown Court Magistrates will now be able to increase what have been light sentences for rapists and killers, those involved in grievous assaults and robbery with violence. Prosecution will be able to appeal to the Attorney General who will have twenty-eight days after trial to ask the Appeal Court for tougher sentences. Great so far, then you get the 'buts'. Douglas Hurd said that the new powers will only be used in a small number of cases and that sexual attacks where an offender receives probation will not be affected. They haven't a bloody clue. And that's another thing. If whoever gives probation was made permanently responsible for a crime, should some pervert re-offend whilst still on that order, the judge might think twice about not locking him up.

Are our offspring born with a lower intelligence these days? I ask this because I'm continually annoyed at the 'macho' image of a vast number of people and the way it manifests itself. On the one hand, you get the ignorant yob in his Mark 2 Escort covered in fluffy danglies, obscene slogans blocking the back window and a stereo blaring from the dashboard, exhaust pipe cut off to make it sound faster and sporting a recently expired tax disc. These coves generally relax by kicking other members of the public's heads in at football matches or pubs and discos. On the other you have the well-dressed upwardly mobile yob – a close relative of the Liverpool/Fenchurch St ones – who race fellow morons in BMW320's and Porsches. Often with disastrous results where an innocent bystander, usually a child, is killed. Recently there was a case where a nineteen year old estate agent drove into a thirteen year old child. This person was found guilty of causing death through reckless driving, banned for three years and fined £2000. What a cheap life. The car he was driving being a Renault 5 GT turbo. Perhaps laws should be introduced whereby no-one under twenty-five can drive a vehicle of a certain class. To my mind, he was guilty of murder.

I know I'm in the motor trade, but cars mean nothing to me. They're a form of transport for getting from A to B. The first Company car I had was a Morris Marina 1.3. Cars have progressed in terms of comfort and performance, but how far do we go? The adverts on TV and in the press continually advocate each manufacturer's desire to get you away from the traffic lights and up to 60 mph in 6.8 seconds. Why? There's another set of lights ahead. This type of advertising is as irresponsible and unnecessary as alcohol and cigarettes. Smoking doesn't make you sexier or more masculine. It just makes your breath smell awful. Drinking pint after pint doesn't make you a big man who can take his liquor it just confirms you're a pratt.

Personally I'd put a governor on all cars making it impossible to travel over 80 mph. Why go any faster. It isn't necessary. No argument by the world of sports car manufacturers will persuade me that it is necessary to produce a vehicle capable of 160 mph when in Britain the limit is 70 mph and in America it's 50 odd.

Taking this idea one step further, I would stop the sale and production of all vehicles over 2 litres and all cars fitted with turbo. Racing car enthusiasts would be free to use larger engined and turbo powered vehicles on private circuits, but on public highways I can see no justification for any car to be fitted with a booster.

Another point. All youngsters who have just passed their test would be able to drive only vehicles with a rating of under 1100 c.c., until they have held a full licence for a year. No-one under twenty-one years of age would be able to drive a vehicle over 1600 c.c. They might learn a bit of respect this way. What do you mean 'controversial'.

Drink-driving is another aspect. It's just like the offenders lack of concern with probation orders, having been caught out 'over the top' and banned, once they get their licence back, many re-offend very promptly. Obviously a year's ban is not sufficient to deter them. I know a lad of twenty-five who has been banned twice. He's also had several other points added to his licence for speeding, due care and attention etc, he hasn't learnt. I remember last year a case where a motorist was nearly four times over the limit, having been found asleep in his car, whilst it was parked with the engine running. The 'person' in question was unemployed – nice to know that ones income tax is going to support such a worthwhile cause – and the offence happened a day after he got his licence back for a previous drink/driving ban. Magistrates at Basingstoke fined him £150 and banned him again for eighteen months when they could have imposed a three year ban. He should have been banned for life. As far as I'm concerned, anyone found guilty of drink/driving for a first offence should be banned for five years. A second offence – life. No arguments. Everyone starts off sober. Anyway I'll calm down now and have a cuppa.

You can't get away from complaints about light sentences, can you? Another pervert in Surrey who has a record of sexually abusing children since 1949 has just been jailed for five years after admitting assaulting fourteen children from five years to fifteen years of age since 1980. He is sixty-one years of age. He's been abusing kids for forty years and he gets five years imprisonment. I don't believe it. No wonder parents are angry. They must feel so bitter that justice is not seen to be done. The only way these children could have been saved from this ordeal was by locking him up for life in 1949. What will happen in five years time? Well he'll probably have been out on good behaviour for eighteen months and we'll be reading of further attacks. Still I expect the prisoners support service will help him.

A few days ago a chap who worked for Capitol Radio made the news by attempting to move his car whilst it was being winched onto a truck to be taken to a pound having been clamped for parking illegally. What makes this cove any different from the rest of us? Why shouldn't he wait the required time and pay up. People like him think that they are above the law, they presume that due to their working in the media they are exempt from parking restrictions.

Anyone who climbs into a car when it is 18" off the ground, starts the engine and tries to remove it from the winching equipment has got to be considered a pratt. The opinion is further enhanced when the car in question is a £40,000 Porsche. (If he has got so much money, why doesn't he donate a large portion to the Donkey Sanctuary in Berkshire and buy a Sierra). Now having seen the plate of the infamous vehicle, confirmation of pratthood is secured in the knowledge that he has rearranged his numberplate. The registration number is F150 OUU. He has altered this to F 1500 UU. Smart Huh! Trying to pretend it's a personal plate, some good news anyway.

If ever I were rich I would avoid such embarrassments. OK so personalised number plates are worth money. But if you're collecting them for profit, fine, but don't lower yourself by actually having one on your car. I can think of very few things more pretentious than that. This chap's going to be charged with causing £310 worth of damage to the lifting gear.

Education chiefs never learn either do they. I see that because of new reforms, hundreds of small schools are likely to close. You get what you pay for in life. The larger the town the less the heart, the less the heart the less the respect. The less the respect the more the louts and thugs will thrive. Small schools obviously cost more, but is it not worth it for the social behaviour that comes from a community where everybody is known. The 'Ivory Tower' view by Ministers is confirmed when you realise that no announcement will be made on small school closures until after the May council elections as all parties know it's a vote-loser. If they know that, why oh why do they all do their best to close down what the majority of people want to see retained, and realise the value small schools have over giant pre-fabricated portacabin look-alikes that breed the yobs that spend their time spreading graffiti over every public building or installation they can lay their aerosol spray upon. With a Prime Minister like we have, surrounded by 'Yes Men' we haven't a chance of heading off another cut back. Is there anybody out there in Government with the guts to stand up and say enough is enough. We need to build *more* village schools, *more* local schools for large towns and cities with the obvious lower number of pupils that that would bring. Get rid of all Governors, Head Teachers and any other Administrator who so much as sympathise with the view that the Police should not be invited to speak on the school premises about any range of subjects. They are here to protect us, and the I'm sick and tired of the abuse showered on them from every left-wing corner. Without Police we have anarchy. We need children to respect the law from a very early age and to know that they are also their friends to whom they can go if in trouble. I'm not naive in believing there are no rotten apples, but you will get this in all walks of life. I sell cars but am not endowed with tattoos and I don't wear a gold chain either.

The racial problem in this country is not going to go away, but I foresee every cultural and religious faction jumping on the bandwagon and wanting separate lessons for their own kind instead of joining in Christian assemblies etc. But we'll deal with that later.

Every walk of life has its neurotics, but they seem to be an ever-increasing breed, especially in race and education. In London recently, some well-heeled parents decided to raise money for a new art block by holding a fashion show. This didn't fit the requirement of the teachers. They commented that pictures taken by a top photographer of nine of the school girls were 'exploitive and sexist'. Their leader adds that, and now we get to the nub of their annoyance, the girls did not represent the school as at least a third are black. So biased in favour of a minority are these teachers that they were prepared to ignore the show completely if the 'offending' poster was used. Frankly I find these left wing downbeats insulting in their attitude. They should be thankful some parents are interested in the school. But what can you expect when you have a 'chair' of a committee. What's wrong with Chairman or Chairwoman. Mark my words it will get worse. What these people fail to see is that the views of the moderate man in the street, who is prepared to tolerate and accept a multi-racial society, even if he was never asked if he wanted it, will be tinged with bitterness and anger if he is pushed into a corner due to the pressure of these political animals who cry 'racist' every time something goes against their narrow ideals. This is not the first instance of white teachers spoiling tactics being used when black parents have also agreed with a particular idea or scheme. Half the time it's not the black community that complains, but the white stirrers who purport to represent their cause. They are the same people who 'approve' reading material for their ratepayers. Who the hell are they to tell parents that in their opinion Beano and Dandy are acceptable, but Beezer, Roy of the Rovers and Whizzer, are, for whatever obscure reason 'racist'. I have yet to find out, but even Girl Monthly is regarded as offensive. I suppose it's full of white, middle class girls who speak properly and go to school in uniform with teachers seen to wear respectable clothing. No other country in the world would put up with the crap that we do. As I said earlier, I do not believe in any religion, but I am not against religious lessons being taught. This is a Christian country, whatever that means, and many points made in the Bible regarding treatment of other citizens, greed, tolerance etc are acceptable to followers and non-believers alike. I think that all these factors, minor as they may appear, when taken alongside the type of education taught, the standard of teachers, the size of schools etc combine to make a pretty dismal view of the type of future worker we are bringing into the market place. The House of Lords were surprised last year to hear of witchcraft and Marxism being taught in religious lesson time. Why should they be. Where better for the left to infiltrate and twist the minds of impressionable youngsters.

Remember, these are the same people who refuse to accept the Police in their schools. How dare they. Only last year the publisher André Deutsch was dismissed as irresponsible for publishing a game book called 'The Fear Factor – Terrorism in the City'. This book is aimed at the school libraries and talks about the overthrow of the Government and terrorism being an extension of the will of the people.

A large number of children in this area speak badly. Now I'm not perfect by any means, but it was drilled into me, and I mean drilled, that you pronounce 'th' and not 'f' ie the fink and fank brigade. H's and T's were not dropped. What can you do however when companies with a large presence on TV like Weetabix continue to show adverts where the word 'eight' is pronounced 'eigh' and even their brandname is pronounced by dropping the 't' to 'Wee'abix'. Terrific influence eh, I rang their head office and spoke to the Marketing Manager. Very pleasant chap he was too. Said I was the first one to complain and that this particular campaign was drawing to a close. I pressed him to give me an assurance that in future adverts correct grammar would be used. He concluded by saying that he would 'take my point on board'. We shall see.

I've just written my letter of resignation from the Conservative Party. I rang the Chairman (in this case a woman) and gave my reasons. She asked if she could pass my letter to Cranleigh Onslow, our MP. I agreed, of course. Whether 'her upstairs' would ever know my feelings only time will tell. It's strange but it's only when you write down your views that you actually realise your sympathies spread from one end of the political scale to the other. When will I find a party that represents the majority of my views, it's so frustrating. When it comes to tough measures against union actions that have crippled the Country for long periods, secondary picketing and block votes, I'm Tory to the man. It's the same with the retention of nuclear missiles, how could anybody sympathise with the woolly liberals or the vote-losing labourites and their unilateralism. When it comes to immigration, at least the Tories have reduced the numbers, although we still take on board far too many for the space available. No, that is not a racist comment either, it's called practicalities. A large percentage of the public elected this government on a law and order ticket. They will be feeling particularly let down. It's a sad day when we have to rely on American style Guardian Angels to monitor peace on our underground system. We have 350 London Transport police while New York has 4000 for a much smaller railway. But then, the police are just another mouth in the underfunded nest competing with hospitals, schools and everybody else. Where does all our wealth go? Without going over already well-trodden ground again, the continual debate on hanging will never reach the required majority when it comes to a vote, so the people of this country will continue to feel that their voice is not being heard. Education and Health are probably the two main aspects that will lose this government the next election. It will be suicide if they do. They have so much to gain by actually allowing the sound basics advocated by parents who just want the three R's taught properly, good old-fashioned discipline and smaller queues on the waiting list for surgery. To lose what was the best National Health Service in the world because of their obsession with profit is to lay the foundation for the return to stagnant socialism. An even more frightening prospect to look forward to when one considers the standard of Councillors and MP's representing some of our boroughs and constituencies. The other suicide act is the privatisation of the utilities. We all owned them. Water privatisation does not have to be the only answer to an improvement of standards and services. If we had invested continually over the last few years the present problems would not have arisen. I wonder if these financial restrictions imposed on various industries were made just to privatise. Well, they're not winning the public over on that one. I'm really pleased that our local water company is now owned by the French. In this respect the Labour Party scores. If there was true competition I could understand it, but I still get gas from the same Gas Co, electricity from the same electricity company and water from the same pipes owned by a profit making water company, and I use a phone, the line of which is rented from BT. You cannot go anywhere else. *All* these utilities should be state owned, of this there is no doubt.

Ah well. I met a chap earlier today, who used to be a milkman at the same time as me in the late seventies. I left the recruiting bureau I worked for in Weybridge and decided that what I really wanted to do was try some manual work for once in my life. No major decision making, no driving through London and the Home Counties to see clients, no meetings, no living by the watch. It was September 1975 that I joined Unigate in Sand Hill, Farnborough. Milk was 5p a pint then, although it was going up $^1/2$p at the end of the week.

I spent a couple of months learning the ropes. Getting up at 4.30 am wasn't a problem once I got into the swing of things, but lifting five full crates of milk from ground to float proved just how unfit I was. In these opening weeks I managed to build up the muscles without damaging my back in the process. I told myself that this was to be a paid holiday and that I would do this until Christmas. Shortly before the Festive Season was upon us I took over 'round 4'. This number started half way up West Heath Road and took in the estate of the same name plus Minley and Fleet roads with the obvious offshoots as well. Some 420 houses in all as I remember. Besides one young mother who whenever possible came to the door dressed in a revealing nightgown and insisted on bending down and picking up the milk whilst passing the time of day, I never had the sniff of an amorous housewife. Couldn't have been me, could it? Anyway the winter came and went, May reared its pretty head and the Summer of '76 unfolded. Having endured some pretty cold and wet mornings during the previous six months I decided to enjoy the peace and tranquillity of a milk round that I had organised to a point that by being at the first drop by 5 am meant that I was back in the depot by 9 am. Having unloaded and ridden home on my newly acquired moped I would arrive at about 9.30 am. This was the case for Monday through to Wednesday, Thursday was my main collecting day which would finish at about 2 pm. Friday I also collected and finished at about 12 midday and Saturday I was home at about 10.30 am. Sunday was a doddle. Home by 8.30 at the outside. At weekends I had a lad to help me. When I left in March 1978, yes I did stay longer than anticipated, but I did enjoy it – and boy was I fit – I had gone through a few weekend helpers. There was one who was helping when I left having seen about eighteen months service with me. It was one day as we unloaded on our return to the depot that I was challenged to a dual. Bets had been placed that a colleague of mine could load up his float first and be at the exit before me. Others had commented that in such a competition, I would win. Being the sporting fellow that I am, an agreement to 'run the gauntlet' was made for the following day. The ground rule being that we would unplug the battery chargers at the count of three and then load up the days milk plus the provisions and the remainder of yesterday's milk from the walk-in fridge, reverse into the main area and head for the door. Whichever float reached the main road first would be adjudged the winner. This being achieved by turning sharp left out of the door and driving up the slope to Sand Hill – the main road. The contest underway and it was neck and neck, both of us being urged on by our mates in quite a loud manner. I was marginally ahead when reversing, I moved into forward gear and made a mad dash at 10 mph to the door – Exciting isn't it – I took the inside position, the doorway being just wide enough to facilitate two floats leaving side by side. Around the left hand corner and up the slope. This was when disaster struck. Just as I turned the corner still slightly ahead, surrounded by baying milkmen, I struck the curb with my nearside wheel. The float tipped slightly and five metal crates of sterilised milk tumbled off the back and onto the concrete road. My colleague grinned and waved goodbye – Bastard. It wasn't the losing that annoyed me but the time it was going to take to clear up the glass, which now prevented any other float from leaving. Phrases like, pratt and plonker reverberated around the depot while I scooped up mess and flushed away the milk. If I remember rightly, it was put down as a handling accident by the foreman, but it took quite a while for the ribbing to end.

The lad who worked for me had a brother who helped another milkman. The two of them obviously used to swop notes on the attractions and the irritations of their respective jobs. We were always back before the other lads round. On one occasion my helper said that his brother was happy today because from now on they'd be back earlier on a Saturday. I asked naively if this was because some of the homes were being swapped to another round. 'Oh no' he said 'He's been having if off with a woman on a mobile home site and while he's inside giving it one, Jack (the brother) does the milk for the whole site, then sits in the float and waits. Sometimes he's waited half an hour.' 'So' I said. 'So one of them's chucked the other haven't they' he beamed. Later that morning I saw the newly deprived milky. 'Hello' I said, 'Got someone else now have you' 'Well I'll have to find someone' he replied looking a bit upset. 'The times been shorter and shorter like recently and today I knew that was it. She was lying on her bed. I was giving it a good seeing to, like, and just as we're going at it Hammer and Tongs she says 'By the way have you got $1/2$ pint of cream and a tin of peaches!' Well you know it's over then don't you, like?' I agreed it was a grave situation, and hiding my amusement carried on about my business.

I learnt quite a bit about people during these two and a half years. There was a customer who put out a note saying one extra pint or No Milk. I ignored the requests and on pay day she asked if I'd read the notes. 'Oh yes' I said 'but if you don't add please you can't expect any response can you?' I added that just because I was doing a manual job, it did not mean I had be a moron. One customer used to write things like 'I know Aldershot lost last night, but another pint would be appreciated' Now these sort of people I'd do anything for. There were a number of elderly people living in Minley and Fleet Roads who always watched out for me so they could have the kettle on when I reached their house.

Happy days but by the beginning of 1978 I was itching to get a suit on again and that's when I applied for and successfully acquired a salesman's position in the motor trade.

It's Wednesday 22nd, I've just finished dinner, it's 11.15 pm and I'm knackered. It's been a most odd day. The post arrived this morning. There was a letter from one of the builders, it completely threw us. This chap came down about a fortnight ago. He had the same spec. as the others and said it would take about a week for him to give an estimate. A week later I'd heard nothing. I rang him 'Nearly finished' he said 'I've got the plumber with me now and we're working out how many rads and the size of the boiler – I'll send you the estimate in the next couple of days' He ended the conversation by saying that he was at about £90,000 and did I realise how much it was going to cost. I expressed surprise at the amount and he said he would have a look at the final figure and try to cut it down. The next 'couple of days' would have taken us to last weekend. I only ring people once, so I wasn't expecting to hear anything. Imagine my surprise when I opened the letter to find his quote including a basic kitchen of £78,000. Maureen and I sat down. Here we were about to go to the bank with three estimates. One for £84,000, one for £85,000 and another from a large building company who gave us quite the worst service at £98,000. Now this last builder also stated that he would have the estimate ready in a week to ten days. What service, I rang after a fortnight to be told by his secretary that he was away that afternoon, but he would be in the following morning. No 'Can I get him to phone you' was uttered by the secretary. Anyway, I phoned the following day 'Ah yes, I'm going on holiday tomorrow, but my manager will be completing the estimate' 'I need it now' I replied 'have it for you tomorrow, can you ring then' They obviously save quite a lot on phone bills. I rang again because I needed the three estimates for the arranged meeting at the bank today. Eventually got through and received the figure of £98,000 with some relief. I did not want them to give a low figure as I would have had to consider using them. My back was put up originally when the builder came round. Nothing more ostentatious than an expensive sporty coupe with personalised plates. I cannot stand flashy people. 'I go for a workout at the gym before I go to appointments' he offered as an opener when we first met. I'm not against wealth, and I'm certainly not jealous of it, but I can't stand it being flaunted. If he had enough money for an ego trip like personalised plates, why didn't he give it to a Seal Centre.

Anyway this newly received figure of £78,000 as I said included a promise for kitchen fittings, whereas the others did not. We had been recommended to a builder, the one who quoted £85,000. We had been able to see his work, nine houses in fact. A friend of mine in the motor trade – Henry – rang one night and said he had been having a chat with a friend of his and he would get me to ring him. Apparently he's generally a spec builder, but occasionally builds for other people. I rang him on the Friday night and he arranged to come over the following morning. He was here at 8.15 am. Now that's what I call service. Showed him the drawings and stated the personal requirements such as a brick built interior wall in the sitting room and the dining rooms. Beams in both rooms plus kitchen. Thick skirting boards with scrolls as opposed to the 2½" ones, leaded lights all round, reclaimed bricks etc. 'Get in the car' he said 'and I take you up to Albert Road'. Now that's only a stones throw away in Farnborough. Actually it's now called the 'Farnborough Park' area so you add another £25,000 to the price of a house. We then went to see his home in Church Crookham and finished up in the desirable Cranmore Lane area of Aldershot to see a further seven houses he had built – Yes there is a desirable area in Aldershot – just the one. This builder obviously had the same ideas as us regarding the aesthetic appearance of new houses.

I rang the builder whose quote we had received and he confirmed that £78,000 covered all the specifications I required. I asked if we could see any of his work. 'We built a bungalow about 2 years ago in Fleet' he said 'But the last house we built a couple of months ago was in Kent'. Maureen and I decided to see the house in Fleet and then continue on to Aldershot for our meeting at 11 am. Things have to change don't they? For the eight years that I've been self-employed I've dealt with just two assistant manager's. During that time there have been two managers with whom I have never had the pleasure of dealing. That's all changed. With the retirement of our last manager, and the promotion of the assistant manager late last year to Chichester, I've just had to start all over again. All my letters start off 'Dear Mr' as opposed to the use of my christian name. I rang the new man who appears to be wearing both managerial hats as due to rationalisation more loan work is to be done in an area office. Anyway, this was last week and he said Wednesday 22nd would be OK as the 'loans' man is at the Aldershot branch all day Wednesday and he'll be able to give authority for the loan.

We saw the bungalow in Fleet, red brick, pantile roof very boring, and made our way to the Great Metropolis that is Aldershot. We were introduced to the Woking Office 'Loans man', who apologised profusely for being ten minutes late – roadworks in Worplesdon – One up to us I thought. Now you may have gathered that I can talk a lot. Well combine this with the fact that the 'Loans Man' stuttered and you can guess that the conversation was very one-sided. He did throw us a bit however. I had shown him the plans, the builders estimates and the estate agents valuation on our house and he asked which builder we had chosen. I expressed my preference as we had seen his work and that he appeared sympathetic to the cosmetics we wanted but also put forward the case for the builder who had quoted £7,000 lower and provision for kitchen. He concurred that it was better to pay the higher amount and know what you are getting than enter the world of the unknown. We had told the builder we wanted that it would only be a formality and I'd ring him to confirm that evening.

How much money are you putting into this project your-selves?' He asked. Maureen and I looked at each other. 'Pardon' I exclaimed 'You own us, lock, stock and barrel. Our children have the words Midland Bank tattooed on their foreheads from an early age' 'We're brassic lint' I added. 'Oh' He replied quietly 'You see it's usual for the person building to put up the money for construction up to ground level, then we loan them the rest' He continued. 'I'm not in a position to loan you all the money, I'll have to check with Head Office and give you a call just after Easter' 'That's too late really, they want to get cracking on Tuesday' I replied. 'OK I'll ring you tomorrow' he suggested.

The time was now 1 pm. He had wound up the meeting by raising the matter of costs. £85,000 at 1 per cent fee is £850 he had told me. 'Is it negotiable' I asked 'No' was the answer 'In that case I won't bother to ask for a reduction then' 3 per cent over base was agreed on the amount to be loaned and he suggested we tried to sell our house as soon as possible and move into rented accommodation so as to minimise the costs. To be honest I'd never thought of that.

Maureen dropped me at Aldershot station and I caught a train to Wimbledon so that I could change for the Sutton line and alight at Morden Road. A company I deal with rang me yesterday about a Peugeot Estate needing a little attention to the engine. Having arrived and seen the car a deal was struck and I took the car away – that is as far as the Hook underpass on the A3. Just before going under the tunnel a con-rod pushed a hole in the engine. There was quite a bang. I managed to pull it off the road and came to a halt at the top of a service road out of harms way and outside a telephone box. Not a proper one of course, but one of those bland, open, cold types where the wind really bites. I suppose I should be thankful that it worked. I tried to get through to an Uncle who lives in Tolworth - no reply. I tried Dad, who willingly offered to be over in half an hour. Now my original plan was to go straight to my parents from Morden Road and tell them of our decision to have a more expensive house built, as that would be the best way of ensuring a more sound financial future, but it would mean they could not afford to buy ours. I was not looking forward to this conversation. When it became apparent that the car was not 100% I decided to go straight home and go back up to Wallington and tell them tomorrow (Thursday). In the event I locked up the Peugeot, suffering in the process, several passers-by telling me that there was 'something black' running out of the car, and waited for my Dad to arrive.

It was a bitterly cold day and I really appreciated the warmth of my 'chauffeurs' transport as we glided through the tranquil havens of Merton, St Helier and Mitcham. On the way back we had to pick up a friend of my parents' and take him home so the amount of time left for a long discussion was rapidly diminishing. Despite my Mother's attempts to force feed me I compromised with tea and biscuits. Dad had told me that he was going to his Masonic Lodge that evening and would be leaving at 6.30 pm. It was 6 o'clock now.

To be fair to my Mother, when I eventually plucked up the courage to tell her what we had decided to do and why, she said 'You have to put Maureen and the children first' I could

72

see she was upset but she held up well. For once I wanted to open up and explain all the financial pressures we've been under for the past two years, but time was against us. I decided on telling them everything except the 'Spanish episode'. 6.30 came and Dad dropped me at Hackbridge Station. I gave him a brief synopsis of the aforementioned saga and promised to tell all the next time we met, when we would hopefully have more time. I had previously rung my cousin Simon who lives in Epsom so that he could pick me up at the station, have a quick chat at his place and then go to play squash in Guildford.

Having been at his house for about ten minutes, the phone rang. It was Maureen. Said 'loan chappie' rang at 7 pm saying he had checked out our builders, had a word at Head Office and everything was fine, we start the Tuesday after Easter. Maureen apparently thanked him and he asked if he could 'go home now'. One bit of good news huh! Anyway the evening ended in the 'bar' if that's the right word for the Guildford Sports Centre, where having thrashed my opponent out of sight we retired for a few 'bevvies'. Maureen picking me up and driving me home. Funny day.

Here we are, Easter Monday, and we're just about to go up to Putney to see Maureen's parents for dinner, so not much time. Last Thursday went without incident. The Peugeot Estate which had been sitting overnight distributing oil had not been vandalised and I had it picked up by a breakdown truck and taken back to the mechanics I use in Aldershot. Thursday produced the last evening in the garage with which to play with the model railway before demolition over the weekend. Nice chaps from the Railway Enthusiasts Club in Farnborough came round, some bearing gifts of beer and lager – I like them. It had taken me about four years to bring the layout up to the standard I was happy with. And now it all has gone in two days. We have an unusual shed which is another story, in our garden across the road next to where the new house is being built and has provided shelter for most of what I rescued from the model railway. The next layout will be even better.

Well that was painless, had an enjoyable afternoon and evening at the out-laws, it's 9.15 am on a bright and sunny morning and I'm just about to contact the most objectionable occupation in all the polls – the Estate Agent. After last week's 'chat' with the bank it will be interesting to see if the buying public agree with the valuation we have received.

Man of the months award goes to Tim Midgley (no I'd never heard of him before either) who has apparently bought a rain forest in Zaire and turned down a fortune offered to him by the Chinese in order to save the wildlife and the trees. These are the sort of people to hand out medals to instead of bureaucrats in Whitehall who have spent their lives coniving ideas and snivelling around MP's in the hope of appearing on a TV chat show.

April

The start of another month. It's Monday 3rd. I haven't been in contact with my colleague in Bracknell, so I don't know if we've sold any cars or not this weekend, we certainly need to put two away at least. Last weekend, Easter, was a complete waste of time. Bank Holidays are like that, you either sell nothing or do really well. I'm looking across at the building site. We had four brickies here by 8 am – lots of activity, sand and cement being mixed, blocks being carried to strategic points. It's quite exciting when it's your own house.

Some friends of ours came round on Saturday night for dinner and we were discussing song titles. It got a bit silly and we focused on renaming well known songs for Surrey purchasers. 'He ain't heavy he's my brother' became 'He's quite light really, he's a relative of mine'. 'You ain't seen nothing yet' became 'I've been looking for quite some period of time, but as yet I haven't observed anything of interest'. You're right, they're not so funny in the cold light of day. I shall make a cup of tea.

It's mid-morning. That bloody cat belonging to a couple who live nearby is becoming insufferable. To be fair to it, as Barbara Woodhouse used to say, 'It's not the animals it's the owners who are at fault'. We had been friendly for six years with Janet and Kevin, but we hadn't spoken since we went in there for drinks at Christmas. The husband's nice enough, but he is very quiet and soft. Janet is the bustling one who actually has a great sense of humour, makes the best of herself and is fun in Company. She organises the mortgage, housekeeping and insurance etc, he plays cricket during the summer and watches local football club during the Winter. Odd relationship really. She told my wife that she never keeps spare tins of food in the house. 'Kevin got liver and bacon tonight' she once said 'What's wrong with that' asked Maureen. 'He doesn't like it' She replied 'but it's all we've got' They're not poor, she's just tight. They have one son. I'm sure she only had him for the Family Allowance, then realised he cost her more than she was getting and decided not to proceed in enlarging the family. You'll never believe this but she had a cold that just wouldn't go away. No going to the Doctors for her. Janet works at a vets so she asked for some tablets. According to her, what you get from the chemists on prescription is the same as they give to an animal. Anyway, after a week or so she still had the cold and asked the vet for something stronger. Having been given some new tablets she commented that they didn't taste very nice 'Well they are flavoured to suit dogs' came the reply. Still she managed to save on the prescription fee.

On her Mother's birthday last year they took her to a local Berni Inn or similar. But instead of making an evening of it, they booked for 5.30 pm as you get one meal free. Must have made her mum feel really wanted. Still, I think that's where she gets her funny ideas from. Her mum is forever burning rubbish. In fact she's caused half the hole in the ozone layer. Her father doesn't drive. The reason apparently being, that as he was, before retirement, a teacher, he would not have made a very good pupil. No I don't understand that either. So he continues to cycle around Ash Vale. Still you save on petrol don't you!

She's a terribly sad person, we refer to her as VFM – Value for Money. At the start of last Autumn's term, Janet, Maureen and Pam, another friend, started going to Keep Fit. Maureen would come home and say that Janet had really put herself into it, going very red in the face in the process. When commented on one night, Janet explained that by sweating like a pig and feeling dreadful she felt she was getting value for money. For one reason or another she had to drive two weeks running – it's only five miles at the outside – there and back – so they couldn't stop for a drink afterwards as she'd have gone over her budget! She gave up at Christmas and started going with some friends from work to another class. I use the word friends loosely. She probably doesn't have to drive so much and it's possibly 20p cheaper. She apparently fell out with her neighbours at her last home. She's always falling out with teachers and getting herself very worked up. I think her meanness is causing her to be her own worst enemy. I'm sure she only got the cat as it was free. It's a lovely animal, but like everything else, it's not allowed indoors. By 7.45 am it's outside. To be fair the catflap is unlocked, but I expect the poor animal's instincts tell it not to go 'home'. Instead, it shits all day in our garden. The other night was 'fun'. Just got off to sleep when there was a shriek from upstairs. I dashed to the bottom of the stairs to find Glyn standing at the top holding the cat. It obviously wanted a bit of love and affection – the cat not Glyn – and had climbed through the velux windows and leapt onto his bed. I pulled on my trousers and carried the cat back to its home, knocked on the door and handed over the animal to a very sleepy Janet, asking her if she could keep it in during the night at least. We've spoken only once since and that was a couple of days later when an apology for the cat's uninvited entry turned into a slanging match, but I'll refrain from boring you with the details. Suffice to say that their cat's still semi-resident in our garden, a venue it prefers to its own kitchen. Ah well, they could be foreigners.

How much of a soft touch has this country become? Muslim leaders here are using the threat of not voting Labour unless their respective MP's back their stand against the sale of the Satanic Verses. Personally I couldn't give a stuff what's written about any religion, and I stand by the old adage that whilst I may disagree totally with somebody's views I will fight for their right to express them. When you witness situations in this country where effigies are burned in towns and mass demonstrations are being held by adults who take along very young children the effect on our race relationships becomes extremely strained and does not auger well for the future generations. I don't remember these goings on when the 'Life of Brian' was shown. It shows the two cultures in their true light. One totally committed and unable to accept any other view point and us, just bloody soft and taken for an international ride week in week out.

77

I watched with anger as the couple who are being sued, by a girl they fostered some twenty odd years ago, were interviewed on the TV. The implications of her winning the case are enormous. Now I don't for one minute doubt that this girl has suffered, but it was an accident. You're talking about a couple who volunteered to help. They didn't have to do it. I've yet to see the young lady being interviewed, and I would like to know who suggested it to her. I can only surmise that whoever it was either did not think of the possible repercussions of the action or they were motivated by financial gain. It's like everything else. In the end, people will stop coming forward to adopt and foster. Even if you lose one couple because of this case, one child in the future will be confined to a home instead of the chance of integrating with a new family, and all because of this lady. A friend of mine's wife works in the Osteopaths ward of a hospital in Bucks. She has been told officially, that if she comes across an accident, she must not interfere, because if she does and anything goes wrong and she is held responsible she could be sued. What a state! Fortunately, she is one of the 'old school' and would always stop and help.

I see that teachers are blaming lager adverts for the large number of school children who turn up for the afternoon lessons in a state of inebriation. Surely if school uniforms were in use nationwide, off-licences would not be able to get away with their off hand phrase that the pupil 'looked eighteen'. Anyway, let's be honest, if they can smell profit, they're ability to 'look' properly is lost to monetary gain anyway. Personally I'd make it like drink and drive laws. No second chance. If you sell to under eighteens you lose your licence. Plain and simple.

Well, I'm over Eddie Edwards. The problem is, just as I thought it was safe to read the papers again, even though there's some kerfuffle over his selection for the England team, the new bore of the quarter has reared her pretty head. Yes Pamela Bordes. Why every paper assumes her bed life to be of interest I can't imagine. So she's been screwed by the world and his wife. Does anyone give a toss? I have honestly yet to meet a single soul who has brought up her name as a conversation piece, or who has been remotely interested in her 'story'! Who cares. Mind you, it is a sign of the times that twenty-eight years ago this sort of thing was a major embarrassment to a government regardless of political colours. Now it's only the newspapers who consider it important or just sensational. That's another thing. The news on the TV does pig you off when you see so much foreign news? Whether it's a trip to Moscow or some minor African state or Oliver North's trial, it is still of very little interest to the British viewing public, but it takes up a large percentage of the allocated time. Is it yet another secret government directive to distract the viewer away from our problems? Surely something of interest has happened in Britain during the day. Talking of news, another item that seems to have been lost, I hope not for ever, is the early evening magazine. I don't mean the dirge they serve up in the form of ITV's 'Thames Report' or the BBC's regional news programmes etc but the old fashioned Nationwide when Michael Barratt and co would report a family's mundane, but interesting daily events. Nowadays it's usually some story involving corruption, race discrimination, sex discrimination and road building through built-up areas etc. Have these items later in the evening when you've wound down, but early on, all I want to see is light entertainment, nothing heavy with bitter and twisted oiks pointing fingers at the interviewer in menacing terms while verbally attempting to put over their grievances.

I see that a report to be studied by Kenneth Baker, actually asked parents and pupils their views. It seems, surprise, surprise, that many parents felt that the amount of homework set was insufficient and that schools did not get the pupils to work hard enough. Pupils also felt that more discipline was required. Will the government ever learn to heed this warning? Get rid of these card carrying anarchists and install 'Rhodes Boysen' who commands respect. The report also comments on the number of subject teachers who are not available and when this happens, children are given free periods to revise. I know this happens as we had it when Glyn was in the fourth year and science was not taught for several weeks. Probably the worst comment was the low expectation teachers have of a child's achievements. Why do we tolerate the dreadful standard in the teaching 'profession'.

It had to come. Roy Hattersley is defending the right of free speech whilst trying to defend his seat at the next election. I don't believe this man. In his article in the Mail on Sunday, he asks why is it that elderly Australians arriving on these shores are considered visitors but Asians, here to visit children are immigrants who will be deported unless they hold an entry visa. He also states that Catholics and Jews educate their children at voluntary-aided schools within the state system and obtain religious instruction of their choice, whereas Muslims are not allowed the same chance. Does he honestly not know the problem. He is an intelligent fellow and not that naive. This is a clear case of sitting on the fence and a reasonable majority. This is not a racial comment but an honest and fair appraisal of the way white Britons feel, I hope you see it like that anyway. Elderly Australians are perceived to be 'from this country'. They are white. They are unlikely to stay after the holiday is over. I can't remember seeing investigative TV programmes seeking sixty year old Australian grannies who were 'holed up' in deepest Accrington. I can however think of many instances where the immigration authorities have been let down by visitors from Asia 'disappearing' into the back cloth of Tower Hamlets and Ealing. They could be red skinned, polka dot or silver. The colour doesn't matter it's just the way the problem has evolved. Catholics and Jews have been here for centuries. Yes of course they have come under fire from their peers about their religion, culture, clothes etc. But it is the growing black community who have necessitated the taxpayer to underwrite the race relation commission, the various local authority committees and education officers. It was not necessary with the Chinese, Greek, Italian communities, but special powers have to be introduced for Black and Asian immigrants. that is what irritates the man (and woman) in the street, they feel threatened. It is because we are such a tolerant race that we put up with it. The laughing stock, the soft touch. I can't think of another country that would put up with what we do. If for no other reason than Mr Hattersley's pronouncements or appeasements, nobody should vote labour in the next election and expect a fair hearing for the native population. Mark my words, the day labour return to power the lefties will infiltrate at all levels and the next generation could be totally anarchic, unable to discuss controversial topics, unwilling to listen to anyone else's point of view and forcing their own narrow opinions on the general populus through aggression. Our children are the product of an age when teachers with skills are declining day by day and formal education and discipline are becoming dirty words.

I've just read Mr Hattersley's article again. Another question he asks is that if Muslims tolerate what they see as libellous rantings, why shouldn't we tolerate the serving up of school meals acceptable to Islamic law? How far do we go. Do the Chinese, Italian and Greek communities want traditional fare in schools as well. If you are going to be fair and provide living equality for all, then Welsh school children should be served with leeks on a regular basis. But no, the examples I have given are white (or nearly white). Perfectably acceptable for European immigrants and their kin to accept this country's hospitality and it's way of life, but not if your skin is black. As I said earlier, half the time, it's not the black or Asian people who complain but subversive animals who stir up a situation and then leave to fester into a political and cultural storm, gaining them Kudos and easy access to a media platform they would have trouble standing on in any other sphere.

At the end of the day it's all to do with numbers. If only some of the black and white activists would step back and see the situation through untinted glasses they just might understand how the 'silent majority' feel. We don't have race wars with the Chinese, Italians or Greeks or anyone else. Sorry to harp on these examples, but there are fair few of them and they don't appear to have created many (if any) problems over the years. Everyone concerned seems afraid to comment on whether an offender being described on Crime-Stoppers is black or white. They describe him (usually him anyway) by height, clothing, age etc but never mention that he was black. If he's white, he's described as white. That's OK then. Apparently this is another case of racial equality only going one way. It's definitely them and us. A year ago Scotland Yard tried to infiltrate black mafia style groups but couldn't penetrate the close knit West Indian communities. Children automatically see the police as an enemy. If a group of immigrants be they first or second generation want to be taken seriously in their quest to be treated as equal they will have to try harder to integrate and become 'British'. Other nationals have succeeded. You only have to look at the Jewish population and the amazingly large numbers who have made it to the top. They accepted this country as their home. They found their niche and built on it. And don't tell me it's because they're not black. You can be black and succeed in this country, but the chip must come off the shoulder and a far less arrogant, aggressive stand must be taken. Bearing in mind the fact that you only get out of life what you put in, I feel a lot of Black and Asian people would gain a lot of respect in this country if they weren't so eaten up with jealousy. If I went to Saudi Arabia, I wouldn't expect to drink and not be punished because I can consume alcohol legally in this country. When in Rome etc.

If proof were needed that we're becoming a neurotic nation then think of the owner of a pedigree dog who shot his neighbour's dog up the rear end because, quote 'his dog was being raped'. Did it matter so much to the killer from Norfolk. I've never personally had a lot of time for pedigree dog owners. They are akin to those who drive fast and flashy cars. They think that they are above all others. Frankly I consider them to be somewhat lacking. I suppose it is like having an adult security blanket. The old mongrel is far less prone to illness, usually much nicer natured and you have the knowledge that a good home has been given to an animal that might otherwise have ended up an RSPCA statistic. We have some friends round the corner who have a boxer. It's a pedigree. One evening when in their house for drinks, the conversation turned to dogs, I remember commenting on their dogs lack of a tail. The husband said they were docked as pups. I countered that I'd been listening to a programme where a vet concluded categorically that it was not only totally unnecessary for this 'tradition', to continue but the owner was depriving his pet of a needed organ. 'If it had a tail, it wouldn't have all its papers' he replied 'You'd rather have papers that a complete dog, would you?' I asked. I don't remember his reply exactly but it was one of those muted apologies where you know *he* knows he's in the wrong but will go along with 'because'.

Getting back to the 'bastard' who shot the dog. Having been fined fairly severely, he appeals and not only gets let off but is awarded costs. It's a crazy world. He should have felt grateful to have got off with a fine. I would have liked to have seen an appeal court agree that his sentence was wrong and impose the death penalty. This 'person' has no right to own a dog himself and in my humble opinion the flood gates are open for anyone to take the law into their own hands should they feel their precious pedigree is in the least way being pestered by an immoral and upsetting mongrel. Our neighbours had two pedigree red setters. They paid quite a lot of money for them. Only one survived and suffers fits. The other died or had to be put down when still very young. It was basically a question of inbreeding being taken to excess for the financial rewards the breeders receive. We're not talking about conservationists wishing to preserve a breed, a cause which would be commendable, but in most cases we're dealing with 'traders' whose only interest is profit. I much prefer the 'Scruffs' Show to Crufts, but then I always supported the underdog – boom – boom!

The pratts at the equal opportunity commissions slay me. A new report commissioned by them (who else) says the compulsory wearing of skirts in schools should be outlawed as girls are subjected to rude comments and indecent assaults. This is the cream though. Apparently skirts remind the teachers and male pupils that the wearer is female. Her waistline, legs, make up, hairstyle and possible bust count for nothing in this analysis. I'm so pleased my tax is going towards such a worthy cause.

I don't know whether it alters your view or not, but although I'm not a Coronation St afficionado I always admired Roy Barraclough when he co-starred in the Les Dawson sketches of the two fat ladies. Always appreciated the diatribe, and felt he was the ideal foil for Bet Lynch with the ability to deliver some good lines. Now I see he's confessed to being a berty woofter. I know, I know. His ability to act has not altered one iota because of this declaration, but I cannot honestly say I'll be able to watch him in the same light and with the same affection as before. Sorry Mr B, mind you, you're not the only one, I felt exactly the same when I read about Russell Harty, but I didn't feel sadness following Gordon Kaye's revelation, I never did find him funny.

When it comes to public relations, that Kenneth Clarke gets full marks, I see he told the Royal College of Nurses that the NHS reforms will go ahead regardless of how many people oppose the plan. Could there not just (and I mean just) be the possibility that the doctors, surgeons, consultants, nurses, admin officers etc could be right. No I don't suppose so either. After all, this is a government that listens to what we want isn't it? Well it must be, Mrs Thatcher has told us so many times that she knows what we want. Funny nobody's ever asked me. Still I'm sure Mr C knows best.

Still no conclusion to the great egg debate, there's just less about it.

The 'close relationship' between the government and the agricultural industry grows stronger and more obscene daily. Scottish farmers are to be allowed, under licence, to shoot the Greenland White Fronted Goose if they damage crops. Apparently the goose is extremely rare in Britain and this move goes against all the good work being done to try to build up stocks.

Pool old John Nettles is still having problems with trying to become a Jersey citizen. From what I've read, he has the support of a vast majority of Jersey people. ie. Those who should really count, but not the few who actually make the decision, democratic that. Mind you, what a lovely position to be in whereby this State can allow in, or reject who they like and no-one accuses them of sex or race discrimination.

Old people are so afraid of gangs and vandals, that they are staying indoors at night, rather than chance an attack. No this is not about inner-cities, but here in Ash Vale, Surrey for Christ's sake. The populations gone up by a quarter and we have the same contingency of police as we had a decade ago. Mindless morons have recently spent the evening slashing tyres of some 100 cars. Now don't tell me that the little darlings are bored and have nothing to do. They seem to be the only ones with money these days, especially since the interest and mortgage rates have increased so much.

You remember last month I mentioned that the council workmen were seen measuring up a play area, and the councils comment when asked, was that it had been earmarked for possible housing development. Well a group has been formed to protect the said play area and they've had a petition signed by some 1300 people and a deputation has met Rushmoor Councillors to discuss the situation. Still, what's a play area when you can build up to another fifteen houses on the land. I hope I'm wrong, we'll have to wait and see.

We've had our home on the market with the local estate agents for a fortnight now and not a sound. The builders are cracking on with the site across the road and all the outside and inner support walls have been built. Once the slab is on its surprising how quickly it goes up. Some of the window frames have arrived. They don't look up to much at the moment, but when fixed and the leaded glass is added I think the effect will complement the yellow bricks very nicely. It's still disappointing about the number of punters. You expect to get tourists I know, but we haven't been greedy and have put it up for sale at less than the valuation price. Still it's early days. The problem is that our financial situation is like walking across a very fine line. If we sell our house for nearly the asking price we can afford to pay off the bank overdraft and purchase a better kitchen for the new home etc. If we have to wait a while and eventually drop the price below a certain figure, we might have to sell the new house and pay capital gains tax etc and still be in the financial mire. It would also break Maureen's heart to see something we planned and built sold off to pay debts, before we'd even had the chance to move in. Anyway, why despair – we have a little time yet.

If proof were needed about racial neurosis then read on. Paul Daniels, not exactly known for being controversial, was lambasted last week by ninety viewers for making jibes about Asian words ie, is a vindaloo an outside toilet. Not funny in itself but probably mildly amusing when placed in the context of Every Second Counts. As he said, he makes fun of all the home countries including England and no-one complains. Still, if ninety offended viewers rang or wrote in to complain out of an audience of some ten million I suppose you have to take notice – provided those offended aren't white.

We had an evening of totally opposed emotions last night. Whereas Deborah will help around the house, Glyn has the ability to disappear into thin air just prior to being summoned for housework, only to re-appear about 10 pm. Anyway, after an ear-wigging from me about his 'never offering' his 'surly attitude', his 'untidy room' etc the row escalated down well worn paths concerning his never telling us where he is going and who he is with etc. This all welled up into a nose-to-nose confrontation. The decibel level rose and Glyn stormed out before I'd finished shouting at him, declaring his intention to leave this house in no uncertain terms. 'Come back here at once' I ordered, having absolutely no effect. The door slammed and Glyn left to walk out of the garden and along the lane. 'Go after him' Maureen pleaded. 'You want him back, you go' I retorted angrily. Of course, I didn't mean it but it was the heat of the moment. I opened the door to get my final four pennyworth in and slammed the door shut despite Maureen's sobbing request. Deborah was comforting Maureen and William stood looking up at all the 'grown-ups'. 'Isn't Glyn coming home again' He asked. 'No' I snapped 'I wouldn't think so'. There was a lull, I could see William's brain beginning to work. 'Can I have his bedroom as a playroom then?' He beamed. Mercenary little sod isn't he. It was just the ice-breaker we needed. I couldn't help it but laugh. Some while later William was pushed off to bed and at about 11 pm Glyn walked in, muttered goodnight and went up to bed. I said nothing. I awoke at about 2.30 am to find William lying between Maureen and I with his eyes wide open. This is unusual as he rarely comes down in the night. 'You okay' I enquired. He ignored my question and asked 'Is Glyn home yet'. 'Yes' I replied 'he's been home ages'. Before I'd finished, he'd closed his eyes and his mind was at peace, happy that his big brother, who he idolises, was back in the fold.

Surely the understatement of the year belongs to the judge who cut the bail from £600,000 to £15,000 for the skipper of the Exxon owned ship that has caused so much death and destruction off Alaska. He concluded that the original figure was not commensurate with the seriousness of the crime. If mass extermination and ecological disorder is not severe enough, I don't know what he considers a major problem.

I see the number of tourists to these shores will be plummeting unless we do something about litter and dirt. Whatever happened to Richard Branson's brigade? Less tourists means less money. God knows we need it right now. I suppose the problem with cleaning streets is that we don't have the money to finance it properly, it's the cuts you know!

Paul Channon's still hanging on in there, as they say. I would have put good money on him being ousted in view of his lamentable performances during and after the various disasters we've had over the last couple of years.

I am sad to see that so much money has been placed on the Grand National. Frankly having seen the number of instances where horses have had to be put down on this course I think the race should be discontinued. It comes to something when bookies are taking bets on how many horses will finish, but why put animal welfare above profit and spoil a fine record of greed and suffering.

Can anyone tell me why, in a country like ours that depends so much on tourism, we allow our beaches to get into such a state. It comes to a pretty pass when only thirty-eight out of 364 bathing beaches are clean enough to be entered for prizes. Apparently a large number cannot be considered because the pollution problem is so bad. But then if you're going to privatise the water and sewage industry you must run down investment to make it look so efficient when the City buys the shares and hopefully repairs the years of neglect, but at what cost?

When we were at the outlaws a couple of weeks ago, my sister-in-law said that she dreamed about a railway accident the night before the Purley crash, and in it she was standing holding a rabbit, looking up an embankment when two trains collided. She also remembered that in her dream a station was visible, but in the distance. We asked her if this was an isolated incident, but she said it had happened once before but not so accurately. Apparently about two weeks before the Hungerford Massacre she dreamt she was walking along the embankment at Putney when there was considerable confusion and a man in army fatigues was firing indiscriminately and a policeman was killed. This particular dream she relayed to the sister who lives in Southfields about a week before the fateful event. Strange isn't it?

My father-in-law is the original salt of the earth. He is very mechanically minded and would have loved a son. Instead he was 'blessed' with three daughters, Maureen being the eldest. We get on very well as he has a love of railways in particular, although he likes all forms of transport. We were talking recently about our earliest recollections and I still remember the trams rumbling around the bend in Falcon Road, Battersea, as if it were yesterday. I think they finished in 1951, so I would only have been four years of age, but the memory of those beautiful, graceful machines, coupled with the shunting all night on the railway and the 'whoop', 'whoop', 'whoop' of the tugs in the fog will live with me forever. You remember a couple of months ago I sold the automatic Maestro to the chap in Battersea, well, when I took it up there the memories came flooding back you know. I travel quite a lot up and down York Road when I visit F.J. Keens, a Rover dealership who have been situated at Queens Circus, under the arches for years. I used to deal with them when I worked for Heath and Wiltshire, and I'm glad to say the relationship continued when I went self-employed.

When I was young, at the junction of Battersea High Street, Battersea Park Road and York Road, there was a pub called the Princes Head. I can remember when there were no traffic lights there, just a policeman on point duty and Battersea High Street wasn't one way. The public house disappeared during modernisation in the sixties.

I recall my father telling me that we might have to move as we lived on a bend and the Council were going to knock down all the houses on our side and straighten out Falcon Road. Today 'our side' is one of the few remaining areas left unaffected by redevelopment and the road is, I'm glad to say, still unstraightened.

I spent half my life at Clapham Junction. I could 'trainspot' from my bedroom window. Our newsagents, inherited from my Grandmother, was the local centre for gossip. As a child growing up surrounded by sweets and ice-cream I probably had less chocolate bars and products from the freezer than paying customers because it was always available. Probably accounts for the reason I don't smoke. Thinking about the latter again though, I do remember bunking school with a mate and sitting on Ealing Broadway Station at the age of fourteen trying to perfect the art of inhaling. We bought five Senior Service untipped ciggies between us and after the second I was promptly sick. Perhaps *that's* why I don't smoke. Anyway as a young child my world was full of terraced houses in Este Road, Lavender Terrace, Falcon Terrace etc. I suppose it was the late fifties that saw these houses demolished. One or two houses survived in the truncated remains of Lavender and Falcon Terraces but Este Road kept the 'beautiful' array of terraced and detached houses and Frownes Street became a modern road with pedestrianised walkways comprising two story houses, an elderly persons flat complex (immediately behind our shop) and three blocks of flats called Eden, Ridley and Temple House. As I write people and faces come back to me. There was a woman we called 'Ilfracombe' – as she came from that town, well it wouldn't have been relevant to call her 'Melton Mowbray' would it? – who retained a strong Devon accent despite having spent most of her life in London. Her weekly paper bill, paid in full and on time was always preceeded with my asking her (deliberately) for her address. 'Twenty-two Garden of Eden' she would reply, every time; year in year out; She always laughed as she said it, indicating an unused line. She also used to say to my Mum. 'You're boy must be twelve in the October as my so and so's twelve in the August'. The line was the same, it was just the age that altered yearly, but her heart was in the right place. I used to witness customers asking furtively if they could see my father. Often they held back until the shop was empty. After my dad and the customer had finished discussing the letter or papers that appeared to be the talking point, the face on the soul would indicate whether the news was good or

89

bad. It amazed me just how many people couldn't read or write. The corner shop was where you went for cheques to be changed, legal advice or just human gossip. We were surrounded by three pubs and an off-licence. Opposite us was the Lord Auckland on the corner of Lavender Road, looking to its left was, and still is, the Meyrick Arms and to the right on the corner of Ingrave Street – again still standing – The Queen Victoria. The off licence has long ceased to be a going concern. The wholesalers William Pull & Co was opposite us, across a zebra crossing. In those days, if we didn't have the customers requirement in stock I would dash across the road to see if they had one. Often, if we knew the customer and no-one else was in the house, Mum or Dad would leave the customer while they went across instead. You could leave people you knew by themselves without the thought that they might steal anything ever entering your head. During the final year of my Grandmother's ownership the shop went downhill somewhat. After my parents took over, Mum looked after it while my Dad went out to work at a hosiery company as a rep. We had only ever hired a car for holidays and we knew a vehicle went with the new job. I spent all afternoon standing on the shop steps looking for him returning from Leicester with his newly acquired charge. When he came round the bend it was beyond all expectations. They'd given him a Ford Consul. One of the very first, and definitely something to be driven about in. This was followed by two Wolseley 1500's. A change of employers saw Dad driving a Ford Cortina – PYT 69 F. The only other registration number I remember was that very first Consul NJF 460. Before the acquisition of any car a summer's evening was spent on my father's cross bar as he push-biked me along Falcon Road down the High Street and up Gwynne Road to Lombard Street where the dry dock was situated. We would look at the barges in for repair in between observing the tugs and general traffic on the Thames. It was the High Street that provided us with our Ice Cream. Not for many years did we succomb to the 'delights' of Walls prepacked identikit products. It was my job to take the empty aluminium tub to Notorianis and replace it with a full one. One day I returned with a new tub and the change, less ten shillings

– a fortune when I was young. After remonstrating that they hadn't given me enough, as opposed to my parents theory that I had mislaid it, I retraced my steps to find a ten shilling note lying in the gutter. That wouldn't happen nowadays. Falcon Road as I remember was cluttered with people, on both sides of the road on Saturdays. Next to Pulls, opposite us, was the grocers. Not necessarily in this order, as the mind plays tricks, but there was Arthurs the Outfitters – two shop fronts they had – The Chemists – where the poodle was the spitting image of the owner's wife – Max's radio shop, a very dirty café and as the road curved to the left a rag and bone merchants and a timber yard next to it. If you carried on across the road from our place, up Lavender Road and turned first left you entered Grant Road, where there was a café used by trolley bus drivers as this was the end of their routes. No 625 was one of them. The tradition of turning round at this point was carried on after the routemaster buses took over. If ever a bus has carried its spurs and earned a place in history it's the routemaster, but I'm not here to spout about buses – sod it, it's my book, I'll write about what I like.

Andoe Road branched off towards the station from Grant Road. It was one of these two roads that possessed three shops that remained unused and windowless for the whole of my youth until demolished in the redevelopment that swept away all the shops and terraces. Many of these roads had fine trees which all perished in the mass eclipse of fine houses. I remember even as a child telling my parents that flats looked awful. I couldn't put my feelings into words but I knew those being rehoused would live to regret it. The thought of an inside toilet, no damp and straight walls appealed to many a resident, but the lack of garden, four flats to a landing and the eerie silence interrupted by the lift, when working, sadly led the appeal to diminish rapidly. A classic case, carried out in the name of modernity and improvement, where a whole community was destroyed. When you hear so much news about Afghanistan these days it still seems strange to hear the capital pronounced Kar – Bull. We in Battersea were surrounded by Middle Eastern and Indian names, apparently, according to my Mother this was due to the visit early this

91

century by an Indian Maharajah. We had Candahar, yes with a 'C', Afghan, Khyber, Kambala, Musjid, Mantua and Cabul (pronounced Cerbull, spelt with a 'C') Roads. There were also Heaver and Kerrison – whether they had any relationship with the former I don't know.

As you walked down Este Road, you passed our side door and then the back yard, used for the storage of our car and housing our outside toilet, and then the entrance to the Fownes Street development. On the other side were terraced houses with their 'airys' or areas, basements these days, until one reached the fire station. Battersea being one of the last utilising the services of an open fire engine. Perhaps you remember the early matchbox specimens with full length ladders, the type used in Norman Wisdom's films. After the fire station used by the youth of the area for all their football matches you had George's house. He was quite a character, unable to remember anyone's name. He would come in our shop with his alsatian and relate a long and funny experience and hardly ever refer to anyone by name, preferring to call them 'thingy' or 'whatsisname' or 'you know' whilst gesticulating with his fingers and fag, otherwise perched in the corner of his mouth. A couple of houses down you passed the Canty's and the Hodgetts. Mrs Hodgett was a little lady with three sons, two of whom lived at home with her. She died some few years ago but was well into her eighties having smoked Woodbines daily from the age of thirteen. Then a green and white painted shop, the proprietor of which was Ronnie Ansell, the cobbler, the smell of leather permeating the surrounding area. I remember a family, the wife of whom was German. They had a daughter called Astrid. There was also a Ruby in the street and locally we had one of the first 'Dawns' a 'Storm' and a 'Rocky.' There was a family called the Pannells whose kids had a mongrel called Oddsod due to its Heinz 57 varieties. If my Mother wanted to go to the loo and she was the only one in the house, a customer would be asked to 'keep covey' whilst Mum disappeared to the yard. We had a hot peanut dispensing machine on our counter by the fridge, which unfortunately never served anything other than cold peanuts on account of the fact that a plug was never affixed to the cable! Domestic freezers were not within everyone's financial grasp in the early sixties and we made do with the one in the shop. Often a customer would dive in for an orange lolly and come up with a bag of frozen peas or a chicken. We used to have a telephone kiosk just inside the double doors that fronted the shop. These doors by the way were open from about 5.30 am to 8 pm at night. Boards were placed, by way of hooks at the top of them, to the doors and they displayed the various paperbacks and periodicals including the girlie mags such as 'QT' and 'Spick and Span' which as a child I would leaf through when left in charge – well you had to have some perks didn't you? Anyway, one night we shut up shop and were digesting our meal when there was a knock on the door leading from the shop to what we called the 'shop parlour' (storeroom). A woman had been chattering away on the 'phone and been completely unaware that the shop had been closed, doors locked, lights turned out and that the staff had retired for the evening. It caused quite a laugh and some embarrassment to the lady in question.

Living in a newsagents you obviously had to have a paper round, and mine took in the newly developed area behind us, Este Road, Shillington and Stainforth Streets before returning back up Wayford Street, along Kerrison Road and into Falcon Road, down to the 'grove' and back up Este Road on the other side. Home in time for a fry up before school. On the corner of Wayford Street and Este Road was Schoolings, a super bakers, everything fresh. The smell in the early morning was gorgeous and a sticky bun was had on most days, often free if I remember. Ernie and his brother whose name escapes me ran it. All gone now.

As I said earlier, the memory plays tricks, so I've got a map in front of me – well actually it's by my side with a reading lamp illuminating the area – so I can check that places are where I thought they were. Like all maps, you get side tracked into looking at other attractions. All the railway lines that run through this 1930's map are still there with the exception of Nine Elms shed and goods depot. Between the lines that crossed London from Clapham to Willesden there was one road, always run-down as I remember, Latchmore

Grove. This was demolished while I was young and turned over to a small park which is still used by joggers and dog walkers alike. I often see it from the train as I travel towards Waterloo. Along the railway line runs Sheepcote Lane. Still there in name, but home to early council brick built blocks and later built concrete monstrosities that no end of privatising and painting will redeem. Sheepcote runs into Longhedge Street, early home of railway works and one of the last sites in Battersea where farm buildings could be seen as late as 1956. What tales these places could tell eh?

A friend of mine, now a very successful business man and resident in Northamptonshire used to live in Dagnell Street, very close to the wonderfully named Freedom and Reform Streets. Near his old house is Culvert Road, where his grandmother once told us of an open waterway, where in her youth she and her friends would fish. How things change, and rarely for the better.

If you turned right out of our shop and carried along Falcon Road passed the off licence there was an Italian hairdressers, the owner of which had a gorgeous daughter who I used to go out with. The only problem being that I'm a nose man. If he nose isn't right that's it, and nice as she was the nose just wasn't right for me. To me the perfect nose is that 'carried' by Melandra Burroughs, Kathy, in Emmerdale Farm. A programme worth watching for her alone. Off the rails again. Past the hairdresser's and a red and white painted row of shops that were always a bit run down, can't remember what they sold, and then on to Kitty Asts. The nameboard for this ladies fashion shop is still in evidence today. The apex of the bend produced Halls the tobacconists – wonderful smell from that shop – and next door Lewis' the Dairy, home of our best friends when I was young. Mrs Lewis, still going strong, and still a Battersea resident, Mr Lewis, alas no longer with us, and their two sons, Glyn now living with his family in North Wales and Mel, my oldest friend, a successful General Manager for a company publishing puzzle books and living in rural Kent. Milk was delivered from their dairy by battery float. Not one you sat in though, but one you pulled along. They eventually sold up the rounds to one of the monopolies.

They had chickens which produced a large number of double yolked eggs – another rarity nowadays. Mel was never in the best of health and his success is all the more remarkable bearing in mind he spent a large percentage of his life either in hospital or indoors. When he was ill, I was nominated to feed the chickens. This was OK, the problem was getting past Tina the labrador who positively hated me and took every opportunity to nip me. Bloody animal.

Carrying on past the dairy were some fine houses, I believe still in situ. The last definitely is, lying on the corner of Falcon Road and Falcon Grove it's now a mosque! Falcon Grove was a beautiful tree lined road with well stocked gardens fronting semi-detached family homes. I took several slides of this beautiful backwater before it was swept away. Now the grove is truncated and leads to unattractive flats. The whole area is dirty, graffiti ridden and the air is heavy with the smell of curry instead of fresh bread from Schoolings. Carrying on along Falcon Road was an array of small shops, one of which was the Carpet shop – Yes the Maestro man again. I remember being attracted to his window as a youngster because he had a Dinky Bedford van with his Company name printed on its side. When I delivered the car, I asked him about it and he said he still had it somewhere, being somewhat surprised I had remembered its existence. The next block after Kerrison Road was 'David Thomas' a fine store with several departments. My Dad used to work there full time before I was born but helped out on Saturdays when he was a rep. On a Saturday evening when I delivered the classified papers, I would call in at about 5.15 pm to tell him the good news if Cardiff, Newport Co. or Swansea had won. Wrexham never counted as they were a North Wales Team, which to a South Walian was as far away as Timbuktu. Towards the Princes Head on the same side was Walters, a clothes shop, various small shops again and finally the Co-op. Most of these buildings are still there, but the quality of the business will never be seen again. The whole area is tatty and dirty. The opposite side of the road developed beyond recognition into a sprawling mass of high rise flats with few concessions to shopping. The pavements are bereft of the human life that trod its knowing way, locals battling for space between displays of goods lining the shop fronts, or hanging from the blinds which protected both shopper and passer-by alike, and the pavements edge. Well it's all gone now, just another urban damnation.

Still no bloody punters on the house. Here we are a fortnight after the Hillsborough tragedy and the writs are starting to fly. I've had all the 'I don't think I'll ever play again' 'I can't play for England' 'My hearts not in it' I ever need to suffer. Liverpools 'We will have to decide whether to continue in the cup or not' takes the biscuit. Of course it's tragic, of course there's grief, but you don't just give up. What about the Second World War when German planes raised whole areas and destroyed not just one family but streets of families in minutes, and they didn't have council leaders asking for everybody who was there to ring in like they are doing over Hillsborough or support groups and trauma experts. They had their grief, of course they did. No more and no less than anyone who lost someone close to them in the recent spate of disasters that has befallen Britain, but they carried on. Not for them Solicitors able to sue the Luftwaffe. Not for them a fund raising millions, and Gerry Marsden leading the singing. It might seem cynical, but I can't help but feel there is an unreal spectre reigning over these tragedies, a sort of synthetic veil. Will some of those who cried publically on TV not put the boot in when the opposition scores and they take it personally. How long will that be? I keep hearing sports commentators express the hollow belief that this latest football disaster could be the turning point where the barriers are taken down and fans can be brought together to enjoy football as it rightfully should be. I can't see it happening myself, still let's wait and see.

A pat on the back for Tescos, I see they're not prepared to sell aerosols that contain CFC's any longer – well done.

Whilst I think of it, a public plea to Cross and Blackwell. Please don't ever change the formula used to make 'Branston' pickle. I've never looked on the jar, but if you do use additives etc I'm prepared to forego my usual stand against such chemical intrusions. Mind you I'm not keen on the sandwich pickle – the bits are too small. Just thought I'd let you know.

The price of free speech eh – Over £1000 per day to protect Salman Rushdie from the threats against his life. You can always rely on the British taxpayer to fund such worthy causes.

What a terrible reflection on our society and a sad day for morality. The London School of Economics, Students Union have elected Winston Silcott, who is service life imprisonment for murdering PC Blakelock in 1985 during the riots in Tottenham at the infamous Broadwater Farm Estate, as honorary president. Obviously mass condemnation has been made by MP's on both sides of the house, the police and other notable personalities. You always get one loony but how do so many anarchists, because make no mistake that's the kind of people we're talking about, breed in such number at one educational institution. The power they have got to get a motion like this carried is small fry to the power they will wield in subversive and intimidating practices when let out into the streets and social work departments of nuclear free Brent or Hackney.

Well, this month saw another crack in the once solid masonry of the health service. The incentive to obtain private treatment for optical problems were dealt a blow by the sight test fee not including checks for cataracts, glaucoma etc. Apparently out of a million examinations a year over 40% are found to need some treatment, but of course, how can you sort out a problem during the early stages when the patient can't afford the checks in the first place. Talk about a false economy, but then this government wants blood.

Near to my heart now. The Government have refused to set up a national register so that car mileages could be recorded. Good idea I say. Frankly I get pigged off when I have visited a Company, bid on a vehicle, and lost it by a couple of hundred pounds. When the car in question has done say 90,000 miles and my price was fair it usually means the car will turn up in an auction with 40,000 miles showing.

You read of it all the time, some trader is taken to court and is fined £1000 and has his wrists slapped. He's made up his fine within two cars and spends his life 'clocking'. I've bought just over 2,100 vehicles since I went self-employed and have never clocked one, I don't need the aggravation. You throw your hands up in dismay though when you have the Trading Standards people suggesting that the DVLC at Swansea should take this operation on board as cars are re-registered and you have Mr Bottomly sitting on the fence asking for more information and proof of the problem. It isn't just confined to traders either, which is why I'd welcome any record system. The press can always use phrases like 'cowboys' and 'sharks' to describe the motor trade, but I've sold cars to three private people, you know S/.Det, 2.2 kids with Fiesta and Dire Straits cassette who have asked me to do a part exchange with the car I sold them say two years ago. When I look at the car it's done less mileage now than when they bought it from me, but because I'm in the 'trade' it's supposed to be OK. Turn it round the other way, they would be most upset if I sold them a car that turned out to be clocked. The motoring public are definitely not whiter than white, but it doesn't make good reading does it, spoiling the illusion of the poor hard done by motorist being ripped off by unscrupulous trader.

That little tow-rag of ours is definitely getting above himself. He loves Faulty Towers and has developed a way of expressing his reaction in a very adult way. The other day I told him to go upstairs and stay there until he could behave himself. I can't remember exactly what sin he had committed, but going to his room is one of those things that seems to calm him down. He knows he's lost by virtue of the fact that he has to open a door and physically go upstairs when he wanted to watch TV, so to make a 'last defiant stand', he shouts or sings loudly so that you can't enjoy the box, slamming the door and stamping all the way uttering comments, calling me 'selfish' or 'nasty and horrible'. I admire the spirit, but you can't say one thing and then give in. He has to go. It acts as a 'time-out', because when he comes back, all aggression has gone. It's as if he's saying 'Right, new sketch, we'll start again'. Now, however, we're into this new tack. Having sent him packing he retorted. 'Thanks Dad, I've always wanted to go upstairs, now I can go on my own, thanks a lot' Sarky little sod. He's picked up one of my phrases which is 'I really don't need all this'; and to be fair he uses it correctly. We were over the ranges and Deborah told him to stick to the path and not veer off onto the muddy areas with his bike. His aggressive response was 'It's a free country, isn't it'. I put him right on that one later. Another favourite of his is 'Well give us a break'. This one is applied when asked to pick up toys that are lying around the place. He can't do anything without making some comment.

Last summer, when he was five and a half, I was outside one sunny morning at about 7.30 am weeding – impressive isn't it – when he joined me. 'Hello daddy' he said brightly, 'Hello William' I replied. A voice from the house which backs onto us said something and William started up a conversation. It was one of the children from the family and while I carried on weeding I was aware of the voices getting louder. 'Was', 'Wasn't', 'Was', 'Wasn't', 'Was', 'Wasn't', 'Fucking Was!' I stopped weeding. No it must have been something else that I heard. It was William's voice all right. 'William,' I said 'Will you come over here'. He came, and not sheepishly either. 'What did you say just then?' I enquired. 'When'. 'Just then' 'I don't know, why?' 'I'm sure you said a word that's very naughty, now I'm not going to tell you off, if you didn't know it was rude, but I need to know what you said, so that I can tell you not to say it' I felt confused, and William definitely was. 'I don't know' he repeated. His wide eyes appeared to be hiding nothing. 'I don't know' he insisted again. Just as I was going to drop the subject he spluttered out 'Oh I know what I said – bother' 'William', I said with renewed vigour 'What happens on Thursdays' 'It's video day' (Thursday is video day, because they're half price – cheapskate) 'That's right, it's video day, but it won't be today or any other day unless you tell me the truth!' 'All right, I said "fucking was"' 'Thank you' I gasped 'If *ever* I catch you saying that word again I'll make sure your backside is so sore, you won't sit down for days, do you understand?' 'Yes' He replied quietly, 'But I can say bother, can't I?' 'Yes you can, now go in for breakfast' I followed him in, he was remarkably bright considering. Then I realised that his devious little mind had found a situation on which to capitalise. 'Glyn' he shouted 'Debby, Dad said I mustn't say "fuck" but I can say bother! Mum, Dad says it's all right to say bother, but "fuck's" rude, so I mustn't say "fuck" must I. 'Go on, get it over with' I said 'tell the world.

About a fortnight later and having had no recurring incidences, we were sitting at the dinner table one Sunday when William was humming and singing the 'yellow polka dot bikini' song which was being used for an advert at the time. Well he hummed his way through the boring bit and then he sung 'it was an itsy, witsy, teeny-weeny fuck . . .' silence. We all looked at him. He put both hands across his mouth and then brought them into the position outstretched ala Manual in Faulty Towers and said 'I didn't know I was going to say it, it just came out'. Talk about butter not melting. We hid our mirth well, but fell about later that afternoon.

It must have been some three or four weeks later when he approached Maureen and I and said 'You know that word I mustn't say?' 'Yes' I said, looking serious 'Well I've forgotten it. It's just gone!' 'Good' We said, waiting to see what the following would be.

His face was a picture of innocence. 'I don't say that word now do I Daddy' 'No' I said trying to dismiss this comment. He started to walk slowly away and said 'But it's all right to say huck off isn't it' 'No' I said with mock severity 'it sounds very similar', but he'd already gone.

A good example of William's ability to compromise to his advantage happened on Bonfire Night just as the adults were about to go inside to start eating after witnessing a super evening's fireworks. This was at the home of some very good friends of ours, and the teenagers were setting off the last of the rockets. 'I want my firework lit now' said William to a seventeen year old. By firework he meant sparkler, but the lad in question replied that he was going to light his rocket first. Back to the 'Will', 'Won't' I believe. Anyway William got annoyed, as is usual if you don't jump to his demands immediately, and exclaimed 'Fuck it'. Unbeknown to him, Glyn was behind him as he pronounced his annoyance at having to wait and said 'I heard what you said and I'm going 'o tell Mummy and Daddy. You've been told before about it and they'll probably take you home' He looked worried 'Don't tell them Glyn' he asked 'I'm going to' he said, and moved towards

100

the door. 'Glyn' he pleaded 'If you're going to tell them, say that I said "shit" instead!' Glyn didn't tell us until the following morning but it kept him on his best behaviour for the rest of the evening.

May

Did you see that a Surrey Motor Company are to launch a new Jaguar supercar with the ability to reach 200 mph. It will cost £120,000. I began to read the technical data, but I'm afraid I got lost and bored after the first few digits. Perhaps the picture I saw was unflattering, but I couldn't help but think that it looked as if someone had taken an XJS and added plastic 'bits' to it. Given it the widest and most classless wheels they could find and offered this rare beast as the latest 'ultimate driving machine'. It only needed a nodding dog to complete the impression, that whoever buys it has the unfortunate imbalance of class, quality and money. I stand corrected but I haven't read that the speed limit has been raised. Mind you, if the government felt they could move more traffic on motorways and save yet again on public transport they probably would.

Apparently there is a National Motivation Week looming near the end of this month, will I be 'motivated' by it I wonder?

There's still a lot of debate over Sunday Shopping Laws. Personally for once I agree with the church, but not for the same reasons. I can see no justification in large stores opening on Sundays. Garden centres, yes, because the very nature of their business reflects the leisure time available. Petrol Stations and Paper Shops too. Small grocery shops are a very grey area. Do you prosecute someone who sells a tin of baked beans and a pint of milk? I feel that small shops should be allowed to sell food and be given the advantage over large chainstores for that one day in the week. Definitely no clothes shops, banks, building societies, large department stores etc. Keep Sunday different. It's a bit like the BBC, you'll only appreciate it when it's gone. Here's another couple of 'nos' – Estate Agents and DIY stores. I'd close the lot. The latter are open from 8.30 am to 8 pm in most cases six days a week. If those working shift work can't find time to get what they want during this period, they're either extremely lazy or they're earning so much money that they could afford to pay someone to go for them – anyway why not send the wife. She's only sitting down knitting something no-one will ever wear, or watching Neighbours!

This Animal Rights Militia aren't doing favours to those trying to alter the way 'Joe Public' thinks by playing soldiers at McDonalds. It only needs one child to be injured and years of work building up public sympathy goes by the board.

I never thought the day would dawn when I agree with an idea mooted by the French. Here was I, under the impression that the only thing we had in common were birthdays once a year, when I see that the French Government are looking at plans that would make cars that can travel in excess of 100 mph – illegal. Naturally car bosses are enraged and put forward their extremely weak and financially biased argument. It won't happen yet, but perhaps the seeds are sown. I'll stick to my argument of an 80 mph limit by dint of a governor.

Well Liverpool have announced the decision we all knew would eventually come. They are going to play in the FA cup. Why it should ever have been in doubt I do not know. You don't stop flying aeroplanes because of Lockerbie. You don't stop travelling by train because of Clapham Junction and Purley, and you don't stop playing in any competition at football. Life has to go on. I still hope Forest win however, if only to take away the dominance that the City of Liverpool has had in British football. Another derby between these two is all we need.

There is a picture of a fire engine in our local paper this week, accompanying some article about narrow roads on a new estate. Put safety before profit? There's a novel idea. What annoys me is that the fire engine has the word FIRE painted twice, either side of the Bedford badge on the cab front, but spelt, as is usually the case nowadays, backwards. It's insulting isn't it? If I'm driving along and see a big red thing with ladders on it, red lights flashing, siren going, men in blue with yellow helmets sitting in the cab and travelling at high speed, I feel pretty sure I'd know what it was coming up behind me. The same goes for ambulances. Is the education system so bad that newly qualified drivers would not be able to rearrange the letters into a well known phrase or saying.

What makes a lad of twenty-two turn from an apparently normal run-of-the-mill life into a killer. That poor British Telecom chap who happened to be in the classical wrong place at the wrong time and died, and the thirteen people shot and injured add yet more weight to the cause for concern over gun laws. I know it's hard on those who enjoy shooting at clay pigeons and targets, but I feel it's time they took up cricket or something potentially less harmful. No guns of any kind should be licenced to members of the public for leisure purposes. We will wait to see whether a 'voice' told him to do it. Stiff penalties like long prison sentences for possession of firearms and floggings for using machettes, cleavers, axes etc would not be acceptable to the soft left but certainly acceptable to the majority of law abiding middle of the road citizens. If you don't possess these items, you've got nothing to fear have you? It's a bit like identification cards. I'm all in favour of every person in this country having one. The only people, apart from those politically motivated, who let's face it, are usually sympathetic to anarchy in varying degrees, that would not want to carry a card are those with something to hide. A National Identity card would help stop football hooligans gaining passports and visas allowing them to continue their trail of havoc across Europe and would also help the Police immensely in the pursuance of criminals and illegal immigrants, but then that's why the left are against the idea, isn't it?

When you hear that Mrs Thatcher has been described as a 'worse menace to Britain that Hitler' it gives you a good idea of the kind of member that is prepared to pay subs to the 'National Union of Public Employees'. Now I know that there is always going to be, regardless of party, those who defend their leader by using the staged phrases like, 'disgusted', 'obnoxious', 'totally unjustifiable' etc, but to be fair, I think for once their response is reasonable I don't like the woman, but I cannot for the life of me see any reason for this analogy, yes it is insulting.

Why does this government have to continue its relentless pursuance of water privatisation. Everybody is against the idea of it being in the hands of companies with a mandate for profit. No-one wants the risk of even larger areas of land being developed, even for housing purposes. But no, regardless of the fact that this will be one of the main 'contributory factor' to the end of the 'Thatcher Years', they go blindly on, despite all the warnings. With someone as dislikeable as Mr Ridley in charge, what hope have we got?

An attempt to reverse the decision to elect the Silcott fellow as Honorary President has failed, I see, but the students have sent a bunch of flowers and a note of apology to Mrs Blakelock. How nice of them, their consideration is touching.

It slays me you know, there are lists of phone numbers in the papers these days at the usual fee of 38p peak and 25p off peak so that you find the answers to such questions as – 'Am I queer?', 'Impotence in Man', 'Masturbation' 'Oral Sex Explained'. It's all so easy these days – dial a number. It took a lot of sitting at school and public toilets to fathom out some of the drawings when I was young, but I got the hang of it. Mind you, I took a lot of convincing that you couldn't catch syphilis from toilet seats. One joke on a wall will always stick out (if that's the right phrase). A VD germ was crossing the road right in front of a bus 'Oh Oh' he said. 'I'm a gonner 'ere'. Next.

A side of this government's economic strategy that many rail travellers are unaware of is the continuous slashing of support grants to BR. Every year the subsidy reduces. Now Ministers will hold up file after file and quote you figures substantiating their claim that investment in the railways has never been higher. Part of the 'we've never had it so good' syndrome. Certainly an extension of it is in their eyes, anyway. Every coach is pushed into use. The continual annoyance to passengers when they are about to board a shorter than usual train, or the newly re-opened lines that have two car diesel sets instead of three outlines the problems facing BR. I read recently about a company in the North who have for years chartered a train to take their staff for a days outing. This year they had to hire coaches because BR could not manage to put together a spare train. Now I'm not suggesting we return to the ludicrously inefficient fifties where coaches would lie in sidings for what amounted to two weeks use a year, but the imbalance has to be reversed. You speak to railwaymen, you know, those who actually work day in, day out on BR and ask their opinion. Don't talk to the Area Manager. Obviously there are the odd one or two who genuinely enjoy their subject, but unfortunately too many are accountants. The higher up the ladder, the less the railway (and Passenger) has to do with them. For years I've advocated the privatisation of the system. When the Southern Railway was independent, for instance, it ran services to remote areas such as Torrington, Seaton, Lyme Regis, Sidmouth, Bude, Padstow, Bodmin etc. Now a lot of these places had good high season passenger levels but were financially unviable throughout the rest of the year, but they didn't close them. The SR maintained that branch lines were 'feeder routes', that it was 'part of the service'. The country suffered the short sighted and in many cases short term closures of stations and lines, but if BR were to be privatised now, we're talking about a new philosophy, a different breed of business man. No give and take when BR is sold off. Remember a few years ago there was a suggestion of the Victoria-Gatwick and London-Southend lines being privatised, well that's the problem. Piecemeal sales of the most profitable lines only. What happens then. You have a country where only profitable lines survive or where a still nationalised BR picks up the pieces with private enterprise licking the cream. My idea of privatisation is a return to the old system where companies competed for business. Say Paddington – Exeter and Waterloo – Exeter. A classic case the latter. With all the machination of political intrigue the Western Region took over the Southern's Exeter route in the sixties and immediately down-graded the route by cutting out feeder services, local services, and the ultimate sin – singling the track. Now I use this route a lot and the number of times I and fellow passengers have to wait in a loop at Gillingham or Tisbury because of the late running of the opposing train is endless. This isn't efficiency. It's cost cutting for the sake of it. There is now talk of electrifying the line as far as Salisbury and possibly Exeter. This could have been done years ago. It's like the privatisation of all the other services, it's no good unless there is competition. With only one main route up the main west coast, one up the east, the Great Western main line to Birkenhead, lost twenty odd years ago etc, there is no competition. Therefore BR must be kept in the nation's hands and not in a few greedy shareholders whose interest in BR will wane as soon as Baked Beans look a better bet for a quicker return.

I can't help feeling that the after effects of the Hillesborough tragedy has gone too far. Mind you, sportswriters headings don't help. Liverpool have just played their first game since the ill-fated match and there has quite rightly been a minute's silence before the start of their game with Everton, but then you read in Today – 'Brave reds are back'. 'Brave? Brave? Why Brave? They're playing a game of football not returning to the Falklands for the recommencement of war against Argentina. It still feels very synthetic, this 'everybody being nice at football grounds' bit. People don't change overnight. Liverpool and Everton supporters are some of the best behaved, but then they've had a feast of success for years. Not for one minute should that excuse Cardiff, Millwall, Portsmouth or any other club's supporters who are often in the limelight for the wrong reasons, but it might help 'mellow' some of their more aggressive tendencies. If I became aggressive every time that Aldershot lost, I'd be forever behind bars, whereas, if I become mellow in front of a bar every time they won I'd still be sober!

There's definitely something wrong with that child. I wouldn't have dreamt of saying 'no' when told to go to my room. Smacking has absolutely no effect. You literally have to push him up. The favourite sayings at the moment are 'I hate you' or 'You want me to suffocate'. Now we don't know where he has got the last one from, but it's yet another in the long list of his 'I'll make you feel guilty' rantings. We heard him in his room the other day having been sent up there once again, talking to himself. He was saying 'Why is it always me, they always pick on me, never Deborah or Glyn. Oh no, Only me, always me!' All this was said in a mocking, sarcastic tone while throwing Lego on the floor. The reason why William was sent upstairs in the first place was because it took three attempts to get him to do a simple task like take a plate, after tea, from the sitting room into the kitchen. He screamed abuse all the way, asking why I never took anything out. It didn't help when he dropped the knife and had to pick it up. Much screaming from the kitchen, led to him returning somewhat quieter to announce that the plate was broken. 'How did that happen?' enquired Maureen sharply. 'Just because I took it out, doesn't mean I broke it, does it? It just broke' 'I expect you threw it in the sink in anger' I added. Deborah smiled, William glared at her and collapsed on the floor in his normal bout of hysterics exclaiming 'You're selfish, you're all selfish!' He was promptly toe-poked upstairs.

The other day he asked for something which Maureen did not understand. Her query was responded to by him asking 'Are you thick or something?' This was promptly followed by a demand that he went upstairs until he could behave himself and not be so rude. 'Great, great, I love it upstairs, oh thank you Mummy, thank you so much' What *do* you do with him.

Until she moved there was a little girl who lived next door to us. Sweet little thing she was, very gentle. She'd knock on the door. William knew it was her 'Come in' he'd shout, no opening the door for her, he'd just sit there, eyes glued to the TV. She'd sit down with him 'Go and make us a drink!' he'd order her. She would get up and go to the kitchen and quietly ask Maureen if they could have a drink. Drinks would be served and five minutes later he would tell her to turn over the channel. 'I'm not allowed to touch other people's TVs' she would say. 'It's all right, I've told you to' he would add, eyes still not giving her the courtesy of a glance. She used to run around after him like a wife. He misses her, well he misses her not getting up to do something and having to do it himself anyway.

One evening we were going out. The two older children, were I believe, on holiday so it was down to Maureen's Mum and Dad to babysit. We returned to find the home still intact and the outlaws still in one piece. Having asked if everything had gone OK, Mum said that he had asked for something which was not immediately forthcoming. William apparently ran to the front door and ran out. Now they're not infirm, but being in their late sixties early seventies he did have a slight edge on them. They looked high and low, up the lane, into the side road. After some forty-five minutes of searching he was found laying prostrate on one of the two benches in the kitchen, under the table. They'd had all the cupboards open and continually called his name, but to no avail. 'Why didn't you answer?' exclaimed a relieved Grandad. 'Because you didn't find me' he replied. 'We thought you'd gone out into the road' continued Dad. 'I shut the door and came back in' he beamed, pleased as punch that his ruse had fooled them. On our return he was obviously fast asleep in bed. Mum and Dad went home, and our first meeting with him when he crawled into bed with us sucking his 'silky bit' (security blanket), at about 7 am. 'Nanny was crying last night' he said openly. We looked at each other, they hadn't told us that, well they wouldn't would they. 'They were worried they'd lost you' one of us said, 'you shouldn't hide like that' 'Well they said I'd have to wait and I didn't want to, can I have breakfast now please, I did say please' Big beam, end of discussion, start of breakfast.

I very rarely tape anything, but am I glad we have the award winning Victoria Wood show to play. She is absolutely superb. Without a doubt the best female comedienne this country has and probably has ever had.

Off to Yeovil to deliver a car the day after tomorrow, so if you like I'll tell you about the station buffet then. Can't wait can you?

I got a letter back from the DVLC this morning. I sent back a tax disc from a car I've purchased and claimed a refund. The letter states that as whoever taxed it issued a cheque that bounced I cannot have a refund. Now that's fair enough, but isn't it a bit incompetent to allow the driver to drive around unhindered. The tax had been purchased three months earlier, so he'd had that amount of time free. You'd have thought something would have been done wouldn't you?

It's Wednesday evening 10th May at 8.30 pm and I'm sitting in the bar at Guildford Sports Centre. You have to ring up and book a squash court a fortnight in advance, but two weeks ago I asked Maureen to drop me off at a garage to pick up a car, on her way to work. I returned home at just gone 8.40 am, rang and found all four courts had been taken. You literally have to ring within ten minutes of the place opening at 8.15 am to be sure of a court. A friend of ours came last week. Maureen goes swimming while I play squash, so it's company for her, and this week Tony her husband came as well. A great couple, these two. They're the ones we went to Yorkshire with for a weekend last year. Going away for a few days is a great test of one's friendship. I've heard of many a relationship breaking down on holiday. Anyway we survived four days together so we're going for a week to Southern Ireland with them in late September. We're looking forward to that as it looks like being the only break we're going to get this year, one in which, as I said earlier, we are walking along a 'very thin financial tight rope'. We've had a couple of people round to look at the house, but nothing that gives you hope of a quick sale. One couple said it was just what they wanted but they'd had their home on the market since January and were still trying to sell it. The other couple finished looking round by saying 'Sorry to have disturbed you' So you know they're not going to buy.

When we came here last week there was a sign by the door proclaiming a change of ownership. Pity is, the change of ownership has not corresponded with a change of service. There are usually two girls who serve while an older woman spends her life taking money out of the till and putting more back in again. I have yet to work out whether it's the same money or not, but she never leaves the till alone. We've been in here when they've been out of all snacks, nuts, crisps etc. This week there's no crisps, bloody useless isn't it. Because I couldn't get booked in I'm spectating, well sipping beer and writing this. I can't stand swimming. Can never see the point of getting wet unnecessarily. The older woman behind the bar is serving this week, she's been joined by another about the

110

same age, they're both as slow as tortoises. In total, as I sit here, there's five women 'working' behind the bar, the queue's still as long. The other side of the bar is given over to a Cafeteria. The tables are always in need of a good clean, and there's usually crumbs or crisp remains on the floor. Let's see if any change will occur under the new management. Have to close now, I'm about to be joined by the swimmers.

It makes my blood boil you know, there's a severely disabled man in Aldershot who is also epileptic. His wife has to wait on him twenty-four hours a day. They applied to the DHSS for a 'higher rate' of allowance in 1986. Since then various letters have passed back and forth but the board concerned are unable to commit themselves to a decision. With the backing of the local MP for Aldershot the case is still being looked into and a decision is likely to be made in October. It's bloody disgusting. No-one wants to put their name to a decision these days. The best committees are those with two members, one of whom never turns up. The main problem this couple face is that they do not have the back-up of an ethnic support group able to slam the DHSS for racial injustice. Being white means you are at the back of the queue.

One bit of good news is that a very fine church in Grosvenor Road, Aldershot is not to be demolished after several years of closure, but will be turned into offices keeping all the external stonework intact.

It's early evening on 12th May, we've got friends coming tonight so not a lot of time to spare once I get back. Maureen's making a Mexican supper which I'm looking forward to washing down with some earthy red wine. I'm sitting in the penultimate coach of the stopping train from Exeter to Waterloo having started mÿ journey at Yeovil. This departed at 5.21 pm and I'll get to Basingstoke at about 10 past 7 to 'connect' with the 7.25 to Farnborough where Maureen will be waiting to pick me up.

Started the day by travelling from North Camp to Reading and changing for the Swansea train. I was met at Bristol Parkway by a very friendly chap whose car I was taking away to sell on behalf of the company he worked for. We drove back to his house between Yate and Chipping Sodbury, an area like so many today that only a few years ago boasted small town centres with character, surrounded by open fields. Absolute devastation. The place looks like an urban sprawl. No local material used here. You could be in Harlow or any other planners blight. Estate after estate of boring red brick houses converging onto new feeder roads for 'easy' access into Bristol or Bath. Roundabouts everywhere and the obligatory out of town superstore.

They built a Sainsburys in Merrow near Guildford on a site close to the A3 a few years ago. 'A green site' they call it. What a joke. Whenever they build a new supermarket or DIY structure in a previously undeveloped area you know it's going to be followed by housing or office complexes and be completely boxed in within a couple of years. I don't know who they are trying to fool, and it's just the same in Merrow, every square inch is being built on right up to the 'sound barrier' they're constructing alongside the A3. Anyway, nice chap that he was, he drew me a map of how to get out of the rats maze and find my way around many roundabouts and several estates to Keynsham, where I could pick up the main road which would lead me to the delightfully named Farrington Gurney where I would see the sign to Yeovil. Although you don't go through all of them, you pass signs for quaintly named places such as Pucklechurch, Mangotsfield, Norton Malreward, Norton Hawkfield, Compton Dando, Midsomer Norton, Chewton Mendip, Shepton Mallet, Evercreech, Keinton Mandeville and Charlton Mackrell. There are plenty more but I can see you're nodding off. The chap who met me off the train must have been about my age. As he was drawing his map for me and he mentioned the name Keynsham, we both blurted out K-E-Y-N-S-H-A-M, Keynsham near Bristol. The name Horace Batchelor lives on.

These twinnings really pig me off. I don't want to look forward to driving through the same pretty village only for the ambience to be spoilt on my arrival with a sign proclaiming 'Pucklechurch' twinned with – and then some foreign town whose name you can't pronounce and have probably never heard of anyway facing you as if it's something everybody's proud of. I want to travel through unspoilt villages and hamlets where the character of the place enhances their lovely names, and I definitely do not need to see twinning proclamations bold as brass, as if to tell you that they've arrived in the big time. Looks cheap and nasty to me and profits only those concerned and is of no use to the ordinary man in the street who pays the rates but has no say.

Seen it all now mind. Just as I was being dropped off at the station, a taxi drew up at the rank to allow its passenger to alight. It was a FSO. Can you imagine using one of these as a taxi: Wonder if he was driving it for a bet, he couldn't have bought it with his own money, surely?

I'm glad to say that I had a bit of time to soak up the delight that is the buffet on Yeovil Junction Station. You can sit there and transport yourself back twenty-five years to when steam reigned supreme on the West of England services of the Southern Region.

Most buffets in steam days contributed a certain atmosphere to the proceedings. In the mid-sixties you could still find plenty of buffet rooms last decorated many years before, often faded grandeur, but always quality. Tea urns polished regularly, hand pump beer dispensers of brass, mounted on wooden plinths, the orange and lemon glass bowls – we've just arrived at Templecombe – solid wooden seats of varying designs, smoke discoloured ceilings and walls, but then it changed. As steam turned to diesel, wood turned to plastic. BR swept away as many examples of Victorian and Edwardian architecture as it could get away with, taking at the same time priceless artifacts that had not been 'discovered' by the masses, but relegated under the all embracing tag of railway fanatic souvenirs.

BR introduced the 'modular' station building (open fronted porta-cabin) with 'modular' seating. Plastic was now one of the major components used by the railways from carriage interior to drinking vessels. Gone were the china cups and saucers, silverware, hallmarked cutlery etc. Instead the plastic cup and 'see through' ruler to stir your tea and coffee with. But at Yeovil Junction on the one remaining platform left to receive passenger trains, the green and white plain tiles, the time-stained mirror and the marble top, mounted on solid carved wooden supports and facia gives one the feeling that everything is right with the world. A sense of security I suppose. A brief return to a world inhabited by people with time to care, when the only Policeman to have been murdered was Jack Warner in the 'Blue Lamp' where all the police cars were black Wolesleys and steam engines with immortal names like 'Hal O' The Wind' galloped up the East Coast, 'King George V' flew to Bristol, 'Coronation' sped to Glasgow and here at Yeovil you could spot to your hearts content the likes of 'General Steam Navigation', 'Peninsula and Oriental Line', '66 Squadron' and many more. Locos named after famous shipping lines, West Country resorts and towns, famous World War Two airfields and squadrons who protected these shores in times of crisis. A far cry from today's diesels sporting cheap aluminium nameplates offering such pathetic titles as 'Top of the Pops', 'London School of Economics', 'The Royal Bank of Scotland', 'Fina Energy'. A sop to big business. Chairmen of the pre-grouping railways would be turning in their graves if they knew the devaluation and cheapness that surrounds the current railway scene.

Back at the buffet, however, the picture continues as you can sit in wooden chairs of different designs. In the winter a coal fire burns warmly beneath a traditional mantelpiece. The books and magazines on sale take you back. 'Reg Harris has just won the so and so race' proclaims the headlines on a cycling periodical. A lot of these mags for sale dating from the 1950s and 60s– we've stopped at Gillingham. I've purchased several back numbers of railway journals from the buffet over the last few years.

I remember pointing out the buffet to my wife when we watched a TV drama some time ago with Hywel Bennet. I don't mean we watched it with him, I mean he was in it. Oh really. He was driving up the station approach road in the programme. He then ran across the bridge, down onto the platform and disappeared into the buffet. 'That's it' I exclaimed 'That's Yeovil Junction buffet and that's the lady I always have a chat with' 'Probably an actress' replied Maureen, annoyed that I had interrupted her viewing. Anyway, a couple of weeks later, I was able to confirm my observations having had a chat

114

with the said good lady (Hazel) on a subsequent soirée. Here we are at Tisbury.

Clean station, Yeovil Junction, no graffiti yet, flowers, BR are going mad on them, not that I'm complaining. They certainly brighten stations up. Beautiful scenery we're passing through, rolling hills with stone cottages and farmhouses, some tempting you like a petticoat, peeking out from behind trees and bushes. Sheep, cattle and more green hills, but very few people – glorious.

I can't remember the last time the clock was working properly at 'Y.J.' as we refer to it in the great metropolis that is Ash Vale. Ironical isn't it. Station clocks always worked. You set your watch by them, not any more. They have a particularly fine specimen at Yeovil – one of those double sided, forming a point type. Pity it works so infrequently. I wonder what past station masters – that's another title to conjure with - would have made of clocks not working under their charge. Well they wouldn't have – would they. I expect a committee needs to commence before expenditure for repairs to be carried out can be considered. Part of today's general lowering of standards I suppose. A bit like the schoolgirl across the way who has put her feet up on the seat opposite. At least she's dressed smartly in the black school blazer, striped tie and clean white blouse. There's about eight of them in all, pleated skirts and socks to match. Luggage on the racks, I expect they're going on a school trip somewhere. They don't appreciate the travel opportunities that they're given these days, my kids certainly don't.

We're just leaving Salisbury. Ah no! The girl sitting next to the one with her feet on the seat has decided to tell the carriage the contents of her bottomless bag she has in front of her on the table, beside the coke, Mars bar and sarnies she has just devoured. Another girl has just exclaimed 'gross' on hearing her endless list. What a dreadful word 'gross' is. It's the sort of word you expect a loud Jewess to shout in 'Rhoda' and receive a dubbed howl from the audience while giving a sideways glance (as only American's can) to whoever fed her the previous line.

115

These trains usually have a mini buffet on them. I invariably had the pleasure of hearing a gentleman (Eastern European I suspect from his accent) informing passengers (sorry customers) 'light refreshment please, coffee teas in the bar please'. He must have walked up and down that train five or six times each journey advertising his wares. An ambassador for the catering corps, I'd say, but I haven't seen him for a couple of months. Business is still very patchy, the continual high interest rates are killing used car sales. Ah well, it can't last, can it? We've just closed in on the Ludgershall branch and we're approaching Andover fast. Nearly all the sidings have been lifted to the West of the station and a very fine wooden goods shed was demolished during the last few years to provide more parking space.

Another sign of the times this. Under the name 'Andover' – which never looks to command authority painted in the lower casing used by BR – is a second board in light grey proclaiming the legend TSB. Very laudable to fund (I don't know whether completely or jointly with BR) the repairing and repainting of the station, but doesn't it smack of commercial interests cashing in and being involved in what should be routine BR maintenance work. Light blue canopy stanchion do not seem very appropriate for the station but they are the banks house colours. Southern Region green and cream would be much warmer. Can't have that, it reeks of quality.

At last, she's moved her feet off the opposite seat. They've got signs about that now, on BR and the underground. The obligatory symbols now so prevalent that written English seems to take a back seat. A bovver boot above and a stiletto below – surely sex equality should be used here so that both shoes are level with the red line running through them and not giving rise for complaints by feminists. Ah! I've got it. There must be two versions of the ad and I've probably missed one where the shoe positions have been reversed. I can see the order at the printers now. So many ads of each version. Can you imagine what would happen if there were too many 'male' shoes on top? There would probably be a support group formed to protect feminists interests. The problem with the feminists is that the majority

116

of them are not feminine. Is that why they're hard faced and bitter I wonder?

Where does it end? I can see Breakfast Time now with Mike Morris interviewing some sloppily-clad, spiky haired unemployed oik/social worker (some thing?) who will give her reasons for forming a major offensive against advertising agencies who create ads where the male is perceived as being on top even in an innocuous ad like the 'feet on seats'. Mr Morris doing his early morning best to inject sensibility and reality into the subject and her, pouting, finger pointing, never listening, never wavering from her 'cause' and being paid money which will probably be used to support some ugly confrontation ending with yet more police being beaten senseless in the name of free speech (ie the 'right' to stop workers passing a picket line through intimidation,, or the secondary picketing in support of Union 'brothers'). We're passing Whitchurch.

Of course if they use two shoes on the level, should they be facing each other? This could indicate sex taking place standing up, or should both shoes be facing the same way, indicating they're still having sex but being a bit more imaginative. Oh, the endless permutations.

Basingstoke. Another ruined town. Full of roundabouts, mini or otherwise, estates of box houses, office blocks in concrete and glass. Another 'growth area'. No soul, no heart, no atmosphere. Just Urban sprawl, what a bloody hole! They've recently repainted the station, tiled the subway and generally repaired and 'tarted up' the area. It looks a vast improvement. The problem is one which surrounds a lot of 'restored' buildings. Having spent a fortune on refurbishment, they never see a cleaner. Clapham Junction had a full scale repaint a few years ago and then no cleaning was done up until it came up on the schedule for more painting. They put up flowers and assume that it covers all ills – it doesn't. The frustration is that to the passenger (sorry, customer) it all seems so obvious. Gates, fencing, window sills etc. We're not talking about looking for dirt. I expect its the cutbacks, can't afford the staff. BR have spent a small fortune on the restoration of North Camp station. Even won a prize, but

117

a few months on, and a visit will show you the paintwork peeling off the plastered walls because proper sealing has not taken place. The door to the platform slams due to the lack of vacuum equipment to stop this happening. Now wait for the dust to appear. No finish, no care, no interest.

Ah well, I'll have a quick cup of tea while I wait for my train to Farnborough, talk to you later.

Well we had a super evening last Friday. The Mexican fare turned out very well. The rest of the weekend was spent making sure the house looked as near as possible to the proverbial ideal home, so as to tempt the many prospective housebuyers who never materialised.

Justice has a very funny way of rearing its financial head. A woman gets her bottom pinched, tells the police and has the offender prosecuted for indecent assault. The chap concerned is fined £80 plus £17 costs by the magistrates. Now if he had stolen a handbag, mugged an old lady, or vandalised a public building the sentence would have been considerably less. Being white probably wouldn't have helped him either. How can some women be so hard faced as to involve the police and the courts, many women of thirty-nine would have been pleased to have attracted such attention.

I've always found Rowan Atkinson extremely funny, it's a pity he's moving to ITV. Perhaps I'll be able to purchase Black Adder tapes eventually to remember his wit by. From Hancock through Mike Yarwood and on to Morecombe and Wise, no comic who made the switch from the Beeb has ever enhanced his career in my eyes. The scripts are never as funny and the commercial companies always seem to flog a horse that died a couple of series previously. I hope I'm wrong, time will tell.

One's faith in the judiciary is blown apart again when a High Court Judge is let off with a fine instead of a driving ban, and all due to a technicality known probably better to Judges than members of the public. Drink-Drive is a serious business and the effect should be the same for all. It adds insult to injury when you also discover that his fiancée was also over the limit. Don't tell me he didn't know.

The good news. That poor couple sued by the foster child for damages against them over the scalding incident in 1966, have been rightly cleared of any blame. The bad news is that they have got to find £27,000 to cover the costs. It beats me. How anyone defending, and winning a case can be lumbered with the expense is beyond my comprehension. I'm sure that it can be satisfactorily explained away legally, but I think the whole thing stinks. Kingston Council who were very happy to have the couple look after the girl have been very 'active' in moral support but somewhat lacking in practical areas. Phrases like 'I decided to press on so that people realise that kids in care have rights' doesn't ring true. The pressure that the case has inflicted on the couple concerned is immense, they didn't deserve all this. Of course I feel sorry for the girl, but you can't morally blame people who were trying to help, trying to give a home, albeit temporarily, to a child – especially as it was twenty-three years ago. Despite the fact that the foster parents will look very closely at their insurance small print, anxiety as to whether it is worth it or not is bound to cloud some decisions, and if you loose one foster family, it's one too many.

There's some more of these numbers being advertised to help you worry over diseases you didn't know you had, or discover you're a transvestite. Perhaps it's to tell you how to become one. Well at least I now know who to contact about premature ejaculation. Oh how I miss those sheep! When will I discover the delights of the male menopause, perhaps one of these contact lines will help me out. Christ, there's a line for everything. Surprised there isn't a service for throwing pills and money down the phone at you – it will come.

Pamela Bordes is still bloody boring, she's just prettier than Eddie Edwards but then . . .

I'm sick to death of these 'Family Credit' adverts extolling the virtues of taxpayers money being foisted on families. What amuses me is that the powers-that-be have obviously hedged their bets by incorporating as many regional accents as they can find, plus the obligatory black family who would automatically qualify, as rejection would result in chants of 'racist' if not given and probably retrospectively as well. I look at the ads and ask myself 'If they can't afford to live on their own earnings, why have such large families in the first

119

place?' Ironically, the only family you wouldn't mind living near you are the black family who are dressed the smartest and the nicest. The rest portray a typical council house family with pet alsatian (that's never bitten anyone) called Duke, a Cortina with dice, no tax disc (Why spend 'Family Credit' on legalities when you can smoke and drink for free) a week or two in Spain paid for by another social handout while the council re-decorates your tip on the rates, and the obligatory bottle of dye so that the oversized matriarch can stay forever twenty-five despite the increasing constraints of the dress or skirt that's two sizes too small and six inches too short.

Two would-be purchasers have been to see the house. One didn't like the size of the two upstairs rooms, the other pair, an older couple fell in love with the place, but still have their own house on the market with apparently little interest being shown. We'll press on regardless. Across the road the upstairs windows are now in and the panelling is complete around the dormers. The chippie is completing the large boards and we've been asked what colour stain we want on the wooden surfaces. The scaffolding will apparently be in situ for another four weeks until the tiling and guttering has been completed. Once all the scaffolding has gone one can get a better idea of the scale and proportion of the building. We've been looking at kitchens, but until we sell our home, we're unable to make any decision as we don't know how much we will be able to spend.

I was reminded of a comment made by someone recently when I read that a lawyer had received a refund after he complained to BR that the First Class seats in the new Class 321 trains were too small to be comfortable on long distance journeys.

In March I attended a preview of the Model Railway Exhibition which is the premier modelling show held in Westminster every year. The Chairman of the organising club was talking about a recent venue when vintage Southern Railway electric trains were used and how people could have been forgiven for thinking that the carriages were BR's new design in comfort. It's true you know. We've had railways in this country for over 150 years, and the standards of seating both

120

in standard (Second class to you and me) and 1st class pale into insignificance when compared to the sumptuous finish of pre-war stock. Even the coaches known as Mk1 and two built from 1951 until the late sixties/early seventies has seats matching windows. But numbers is the name of the game. The accountant's pen rules. One coach body and cram in the standard class seats with half the paying public peering at large laminated pillars. The windows also get higher with of course no manual ventilation control. Progress definitely doesn't mean improvement in many cases, does it.

I see that the BSB have put back their opening date, and Sky doesn't seem to be doing too well either, judging by the slow take up of receivers. I do hope they loose a packet and are forced to close. I've had a look at the type of houses that have had these dishes installed, and whilst there are some on the 'middle of the road' houses, a vast number seem to appear at each end of the financial scale. The large expensive house where they probably don't watch it but consider it necessary and the cream painted council houses where the TV set rules anyway. Pity they don't screen twenty-four hours a day elocution lessons.

You know my annoyance with people who 'sue' for what I consider to be the wrong reasons, well this takes the biscuit – until the next time. A girl who was stood up on a date is suing the chap concerned to cover the cost of her shoes, hairdo and flowers she had paid for especially. It's rather amusing, but can you imagine the implication if she wins. At least it happened in America, so it should take another couple of years before we see a similar case brought before British Courts.

It was never going to be long before another group of downtrodden foreigners found the good life, it was just a question of who. Well it's the turn of the Kurds this time. Despite severe doubts as to what harm, if any, might befall these people if they stay in their own country, there is already a support group, with clerical links as usual, operating in London to house these people here. Now every Country's got its problems, and so have we, the main one being that we are an island with limited space for our own people. Why do we continue to be the 'soft touch'. We appear embarrassed or guilty about a problem many countries continue to sort out to the satisfaction of its own Nationals, unlike Britain, who regardless of political party, continues to allow immigration to take place. It will be interesting to see what happens in 1997 with regard to the Hong Kong British passport holders. Let's just hope we don't have a socialist government again or the flood gates would really be open.

Besides my own personal reasons for cynicism of the Spanish legal system, and the much publicised case of Ronnie Knight and the others wanted back here on extradition orders, which appears to be continually thwarted by the authorities, the case of a young girl who suffered terrible burns in a gas blast five years ago and is still awaiting compensation really drives home the farce that surrounds European harmonisation. When you think that it can take up to ten years to get a case like this through the courts it reinforces my hope that the turnout in the forthcoming Euro election will be as low as possible. Still as long as those elected can further enhance their Euro prospects and their bank balances it's got to be worth it to stand.

Well, the lessons of Hillsborough didn't last long, did they. Out of every disaster some ray of hope for the future should appear. The hope was that by taking down the barriers not only would scenes such as those witnessed on that sad day be impossible, but that normality and sensibility might return where fans from opposing sides would watch the match together. Here we are four weeks on and there's a pitch invasion at Crystal Palace by morons amongst the Birmingham City fans and at Portsmouth nearly sixty Chelsea supporters are arrested while at Bristol City's ground 'fans' were fighting with the Police. I just can't understand the mentality.

I'm off to Aberdare with my Dad for the weekend. We're going early tomorrow (Friday) and Mum will be staying here for the weekend with Maureen and the kids while we take a journey back to my holiday childhood and my Father's birth place. Because he looks so fit still and he and Mum spend a vast amount of time out with friends, attending functions and travelling around with choirs and rugby clubs I tend to forget

122

that he's seventy-five years of age. Anyway, having planned this some time ago I'm looking forward to him showing me the places I remember as a child but haven't seen for twenty-five years at least. Must have an early night, don't want to get too excited.

Man of the month, regardless of the fact that we still have thirteen days to go, is Lennie Lawrence for managing to keep Charlton Athletic in the First Division. I've always admired his quiet modesty, but to continually strive against all odds and no hope, year in year out is surely a testimony to the guts and determination this man has. I've always had a soft spot for Charlton. Living in Battersea meant that my friends and I usually walked over the Bridge and watched Chelsea, but I never felt at 'home' there. Probably something to do with Charlton being 'underdogs' I suppose. The vast escarpment and wasteland that lay behind the gates always brought a feeling of warmth and pleasure. I've stood in a crowd of three thousand watching a Third Division match on a Saturday afternoon when sheep were grazing on the terraces opposite the stand. Looking back it seems amazing now, but I'm not exaggerating. Funnily enough I was with a friend of mine recently who used to come with me and we were discussing these days in the early sixties and the subject of the sheep came up then. Still they should be back at the Valley next season hopefully – no not the sheep.

Looking forward to reading about the annual disasters at airports. Usually makes good reading, seeing the yawning, bored children and parents who have paid £3.80 all in for two weeks in Sol-de-Somewhere. It's like everything in life, you get what you pay for.

Poor Mr Kinnock, he just can't get rid of all the shackles and chains that embrace him. It will be interesting to read the result of next month's by-election in Vauxhall, London. Even his party's black MP's and other activists are having a go. It's a bit like Henry Ford's Model T. You can have any colour, as long as it's black. It's the first time I've had the misfortune to see Bernie Grant's name mentioned for some time. Perhaps I'll have better luck next month. By the way, whatever happened to that other black male MP. Can't remember his name.

123

Speaks very well, but is usually heard blaming the police for something or the other.

Definitely not the flavour of the month with the cat owners. I went to see them, but they're not prepared to do anything about keeping the bloody cat from messing on our lawn, so we will not be resuming the relationship that's been soured over pets. Mind you, at the end of the day it's probably better not to get involved with someone who considers keeping a tin of baked beans in the cupboard as uneconomic but would have to participate in an ego trip by wearing a *real* Rolex watch and be able to impress workmates and 'friends' – I use the word loosely. Perhaps I could build a house out of Lego, that would certainly improve my social standing – tourists could come and see her watch and my modelling.

Well here we are, nearly at the end of another month. Business is extremely bad. I'm not even selling the bread and butter cars like Metros and Sierras. There's a general lack of calls, one or two pockets of resistance, but generally everybody I know is feeling the pinch.

It makes you wonder sometimes if perhaps a comment or opinion has actually served its purpose after all. Weetabix are to stop their current advertising campaign because the standard characters are too aggressive. Well that was one of my concerns when I rang them a couple of months ago. Unfortunately, my other concern about the voice over using the word 'Wee'abix' and leaving out 't' is still being perpetrated. It makes you laugh when you read that the company are looking for a more sophisticated image. Obviously doesn't include good diction.

I'm not the greatest fan of John Prescott, but he and virtually everybody else echoed the view that if you build wider and longer motorways you just carry more cars faster to the next traffic jam. Now why can't Mr Channon see it. Are these people so far removed from common sense. You can build an eighteen lane motorway and the result will be the same. For Christ's sake, see the light and get the freight off the British roads and onto the rails again.

I see it's beginning to emerge that although the police at Hillsborough were not conscious of, or ignored the calls and cries for help over a short but critical period, the view that all the fans were whiter than white is becoming a little tarnished. When one local resident states that up to twenty yobs were urinating in her garden, it says a lot for the kind of mentality we are supporting. You can see how the police must feel, week in, week out dealing with the morons, but then when it goes wrong, their reaction is tainted by mixed feelings and disaster occurs.

That wonderful Mr Channon's latest idea to allow construction of private toll roads built alongside existing motorways enlivens the imagination taking it only a few years further when they will be sponsored, and advertising will be placed every few yards in true L.T. (Sorry L.R.T.) escalator fashion offering you the latest range in playtex bras, films, cornflakes, Renault cars (think of a number) and of course the opportunity to partake in a game to win the last remaining satellite dish available – besides the other ten million which only Mr Murdoch and the suppliers know about, having officially been sold years previously – and last but not least the ads for lager. Now *I* know you shouldn't drink and drive, but if the government can sell our soul publicly, it can have no qualms over its own, besides you can make a fortune out of brewers through advertising.

It would have been nice to have signed off the month with some good news, but with the rain forests disappearing by the minute, seals, dolphins, elephants and god knows what else being slaughtered indiscriminately and those 'nice' Japanese people trying to overturn, (or if unsuccessful) flout the laws governing whaling and shark fishing, it seems to be all bad news. Even the chance of a Wembley cup final of which the papers publicly stated a preference for Liverpool winning 'for the people', a golden opportunity for progress was lost when 'fans' ran onto the pitch and the traditional lap of honour was lost in a sea of bodies. God knows, I'd love to cheer on Aldershot in a Cup Final, and if they won I'd clap and hoot, but I wouldn't need to run onto the field or fight, having drunk myself senseless beforehand, but then that's the difference between living in Liverpool and Surrey I suppose.

June

Well, this month sees two by-elections and the blandly titled Euro-elections. My hope, as you know, is that no one votes. I believe the turnout was about a third last time. It amazes me that the figure was so high, how can anyone have any affinity with the names of the constituencies. It will be interesting to see how the 'Green' party fares. If I were to vote it would be for them, but in protest form only. Outside of the major issues that any political party worth their salt should be tackling such as the state of our water, pollution, acid rain, the relationship between radiation from B.N.F.L. plants and children with leukaemia etc. I find I have little in common with them. They want to throw out nuclear missiles, I'd keep them, they tend to support Amnesty International, and I'm not convinced of some of their motives. They are against Capital punishment. They should do well, however, and it will be interesting to see their performances against the SDP and SLD.

I see that Lenny Henry is quitting comedy to help in Africa. Good news this, I never found him funny, and before you say it I never liked Bernard Manning, Frank Carson, Jimmy Cricket or Little and Large and they're white.

I'm sure he's as nice as he is painted, but I'm getting fed up with pictures of Dustin Hoffman in his Shakespearian guise. It is his job after all. Then there's the picture at the Rose Theatre and promoting Ark products. Still it could have been Eddie Edwards.

There's a telling comment with wider implications that I've read about today. A British travel firm has scrapped skiing holidays in France because the place is being taken over by package holiday makers who do not go there for the enjoyment of embracing the quietness and 'frenchness' that

126

the up-market punter expects. More and more take-aways and pubs are opening which invites you to tell the difference between their Alpine towns and Harlow – except for the snow of course. I mean the litter will be the same, cheap concrete and glass monstrosities harbouring under the name of leisure centres will spring up, and mugging and rape will replace peace and enjoyment. Isn't this instance of a local holiday problem the same as we have with our villages? Thousands of people from Inner Cities directed to Council estates and creating all the problems that go hand in hand with the mass infusion of 'Townies', the end result looking like Yate and Chipping Sodbury.

Now this isn't confined to C.H. tenants, but I do get aggrieved when I see that someone has won half a million on the 'Pools' and then declares that he, or she, is going to continue to work. In the meantime of course, they are going to take a cruise, buy a Rolls Royce and have a party in Poplar for the whole family, plus of course friends they never knew they had. A lot of business failures later and they publicly state that it was the money that altered their lives (although they said at the time it wouldn't) causing their marriage of 30,000 years to break down and friends to shy away, declaring how lonely they are, and how they wish they'd never done the 'Pools'. I think there should be an intelligence test before anyone enters a competition where the winnings are above, say £10,000. Those with mentalities of morons would thus be eliminated from taking part.

The good news is that a man who worked for the British Medical Association involved in child health care and child abuse has had his claim for unfair dismissal turned down. What I find annoying is that someone in that position convicted of taking indecent photographs of children considers it reasonable to continue in the post, he must spend more time on fullers earth than this one.

I wish Mr Baker, the Education secretary, well in his bid to raise the spelling and grammatical standards in schools. A move made all the more helpful by teachers actually encouraging him this time.

For years we felt as if we were banging our heads against a brick wall when confronting a teacher, of any subject about the bad spelling or the grammatical errors that have appeared in set pieces by our offspring. All we got was 'We mark or point out factual errors in the piece that has been written, but we leave out anything that isn't relevant to the subject'. Now we thought that English was encompassed by all subjects. How wrong we were. We had one teacher tell us that if she underlined all the mistakes made, it would undermine the child's confidence. I told her in no uncertain terms what I thought. She was not a happy teacher.

There's more to it than just a spate of dog attacks, isn't there? Doesn't matter what the age of the victim. A child will probably fear most animals for the rest of his or her life, while an older person, in some cases out walking their own pet which is then attacked, killed and ignored, will feel sick and bitter, and think very carefully about going for a walk in a park again and possibly not get another dog for fear of the same thing happening. I don't blame a breed of dog, it's the breed of people. I know I'm categorising, but the owners are generally the 'macho' type who like to appear authoritative and need to be taken notice of. A big fierce dog implies power, aggression, and to its irresponsible owner – one-upmanship. The dogs are very often kept in box houses or flats, taken for walks at the end of leather studded leads, and paraded for all to see to watch in awe and fright. But then, that's half the turn on. Again, there should be an intelligence test before ownership could commence. Mind you, I'd do that with drivers as well, any public sighting of hanging dice, pathetic stickers and extra lights would automatically disqualify anyone from ownership of anything other than a car up to 1100 cc. No car tax would lead you to a five year ban. I'd get the bastards. You'd kill two birds with one stone as they usually own alsatians as well.

So it's goodbye to Barry McGuigan. They're never the same second time around.

It comes to a pretty pass when a local authority – there to represent the people I may add – cannot stop a developer from building on what apparently is a lovely woodland and meadow area. When a Council, in this case Bolton, decides they can no longer continue to fight the development and leaves the public to go it alone, the whole sham of greedy builders and our rights as residents of an area are clearly put into perspective. I'm not usually a violent person, but I can see the day coming when large armies of laymen will rise up and stop the developers from building, either by the courts, hopefully, or by guerilla tactics, ie the sabotage of machinery etc. Threats of taking individuals or groups to Court will hopefully be difficult due to the numbers involved. Yes it is anarchistic, but the option is the complete destruction of our countryside by companies whose only aim is greed. In the Bolton case it's those nice Barratts people who are involved. Let's hope the foxes and badgers win. If not I hope something befalls those responsible for this latest example of legalised destruction and they look back and think 'if only'! Bastards.

While I'm incensed, there's a chap here, you may remember, who was told by a judge to go back up North as it was more suitable to alcoholics than here in the South. Well he's been done again. What gets me is the bit about him having just cashed his dole cheque before getting caught. He hasn't worked for twelve years, a fact he appears very pleased about, adding that he gets by without working. Can anyone give me a good reason – Any reason, why he should get a penny from you and me. No work, no money. Why *do* we have to support the likes of him. Beware, with a Labour government, there'd be a lot more.

Bearing in mind my comments about the 'type' of owner we're dealing with over the dog attacks one chap I see here whose rotweilers (three) savaged a five year old boy has given them away to avoid them being put down. The heading in the article I read was 'Attacker dogs face Execution'. For a moment I was elated. I thought it was relating to the owner until I re-read it. Wishful thinking I suppose, but what sort of person can renounce responsibility in that way.

I know I can go on a bit about drink and drive but there's another chap here who turns around on the M5 and starts driving into the traffic coming the same way. He's got three previous convictions for D & D and here he is again. This time he's put on probation for two years and banned for three years.

129

Now I suppose no-one was injured or killed in this instance or it would have been mentioned. If the other three offences were injury and death free as well, the man is extremely lucky, but wouldn't you think he'd have learnt by now. Obviously not. He should never be given his licence back again. The chances of him remaining free from future convictions seems fairly remote, and if any further incidences end in loss of, or injury to, life then the magistrates who imposed this latest sentence are as guilty as our 'friend'.

Not much news these days about Salmonella and eggs, and not much from Mrs Currie either.

We were with friends over the weekend and we discussed who we would have in charge of various government ministries. As the wine flowed we, well I, became more thoughtful, everyone else became bored. People could be hypothetically deported in a drive to rid this country of those I felt were unnecessary in the vision I perceived of a Britain returning to being a 'nice' place to live in. Now don't read anything into this, no-one has been gassed, only deported. Mind you, my decision was final with no Appeal Courts.

First of all the 'Government':-

Prime Minister – David Owen

Minister for the Environment (with power to compulsory purchase all architectural eyesores, demolish and replace with parks and woodlands) – Prince Charles and Jonathon Porritt

Minister for Health – Miriam Stoppard

Minister for Education – John Harvey Jones

Junior Minister for Education – Rhodes-Boyson

Junior Minister for Education (special responsibility for Elocution and Grammar) – Dianna Moran

Minister for Agriculture – Anyone not connected with farming

Minister for Defence – Cyril Smith

Minister for Overseas Development – Axed – Whole Department

Chancellor of the Exchequer – Richard Branson

Treasury Minister – Alan Sugar

Home Secretary – Teddy Taylor (Con. Southend)

Foreign Secretary – Willie Rushton

Minister of Common Sense – Cyril Smith (again – well he's big enough for two ministries isn't he!)

Junior Minister for Common Sense – Joe Ashton

Everything else to be decided by Rosie Barnes

Those Expelled –

Lord Longford, I've long detested his view on Myra Hindley and Ian Brady. Those two of course plus all inmates who have murdered, raped and attacked innocent people. I know this is a sweeping statement but you know what I mean, and anyway it's only a rough draft, isn't it?

Ben Elton, who I've never found funny, only loud.

Mary Whitehouse, for continually telling me what I should be watching, when I want to tell the country what it should be watching.

Eric Heffer, Dennis Skinner, Tony Benn and Arthur Scargill for obvious reasons.

Tam Dalyll, for continually whingeing on over the Belgrano. I mean for an Argentinian he has a very good Scots accent.

Salman Rushdie, because he knew the furore he'd cause.

Nicholas Ridley, for being here.

Eddie Edwards and Pamela Bordes, for being boring.

A few from Overseas:–

Dustin Hoffman, for over exposure in his Shakespearian guise.

McEnroe/Lendl for being allowed to land. I'd allow Pat Cash providing he doesn't climb over seats to hug father again.

Back home:–

Douglas Hurd, for being soft.

John Aldridge, for bad sportmanship.

Nina Myskow, for being a pain.

General:–

All religious leaders who do not accept women priests. All male councillors who do not wear a tie when attending Council Meetings. All those on Council Twinning Committees. I know you'd have to go through them individually in case there was someone worth saving, but virtually all, Brent, Camden, Lewisham, Islington, Tower Hamlet staff, be they health, housing or education, would have to go.

Owners of dangerous dogs. A large number of architects, the ticket collector who was rude to me at Waterloo Station in July 1983. All Company Chairmen, and Yes Men who weald the power that damages our countryside. All muslims who cannot respect freedom of speech in their adopted home. All drink/drivers and those convicted of drink related offences. Football hooligans and vandals of all classifications. Drivers of cars who, when overtaking, or parking do not indicate. Those named Kelly, Kylie, Dawn, Roxeanne, Crystal, Darren, and Jason. All the Clints, Waynes, Duañes, Dirks . . . and any others you can think of in like vein. Residents of houses/boxes named Costalot, Dunroamin, Thistledome . . . again plus all the naff names you know locally. Others to go would be inmates of houses called 'Somewhere', 'Brialey' – Brian and Shirley, 'Colinda Cottage' – Colin and Linda – the cottage bit makes it original – doesn't it? residents of semis and terraced dwellings who call their abode 'Something house or lodge' – talk about pretentious. Those with personalised car number plates. Anyone who says 'Darling' patronisingly, those who practise vivisection (for whatever supposed medical reasons). Scottish Salmon farmers, Tattooed persons (except young women with a butterfly on the inner thigh, because it turns me on. Actually the tattoo I *really* like is the snake that winds its way around the belly and curvaciously disappears up a pretty girl's arse. Now that's erotic – time for a shower). Those Scottish Nationals who precede a statement with eeers all the time – see how generous I am to the rest of the Scottish people – allowing them to stay. All businessmen who have 'designate' or 'executive' on their card.

Reliant Robin, Skoda and Lada owners/drivers. Monsignor Bruce Kent for being naive to the point of absurdity. All car owners still 'sporting' red noses (which look suspiciously like miniature safety helmets anyway). The Leeds City Council employee, Mr Stephen Kitten, who decided that all council staff should work to a metric clock.

This could only happen in Britain. A teacher who left his previous job in Somerset because of unseemly goings-on with children, gets employment as a teacher again in Lowestoft. To be fair he tells the Governors at his interview and they (amazingly) employ him but add the proviso that he must live outside town. Isn't that a hoot? He of course continues his fun and games with youngsters and he's just been sentenced to one year imprisonment, so with remission for 'good behaviour' (well there are no under elevens in prison to jeopardise his chances, are there?) he should be out by the end of this month.

I don't know whether it's true or not, but a Somerset County Council spokesman, remarking about their problem with badgers burrowing under a by-pass at Montacute and de-stabilising it said 'We won't hurt the badgers, they were here before us!' If that is a factual comment then more power to his elbow. There's a ministry that needs him.

I see that students at Wadham College, Oxford have voted 43–41 in favour of a re-trial for the LSE students glorious leader, one W. Silcott. Where on earth did these 43 come from. So nice to know I'm contributing towards their education, well England beat Poland at football anyway.

I sincerely hope the court do not let the fact that because there is a well known face, in the shape of Ken Dodd, sitting before them, sympathy, and fond memories of the hours of pleasure he has given people, will cloud their judgement over his ability to stand trial. If someone has been defrauding the tax authorities he should face it, irregular heartbeats or not.

I see that the Environment Minister, Mr Howard, having stated that swallowing sea water off our beaches produces no risks or ill effect, has declined to taste it himself, an offer put to him by the newspaper 'Today'. Now if it's not good enough for him – fine, but what about us. If he'd said it was OK for the residents of Labour controlled boroughs, and new towns like Bracknell and Basingstoke I could understand it, but how can he include the good residents of Surrey.

It's beginning to look more and more as if the thought-less supporters who arrived from Liverpool without tickets contributed greatly to the decision to open the gates at Hillsborough. The Police, trying to avoid confrontation and the ensuing trouble, tread softly and the advantage is taken, culminating in the tragedy. At the end of the day, the Police are in a no win situation.

133

Well it's now two weeks since I went to Aberdare for the weekend, time to reflect, time to analyse.

Firstly, and very importantly, I think my Dad enjoyed it. For me it was great hearing him describe activities, walks, train services over areas now vastly different from what he grew up with sixty odd years ago. The Friday we drove up there was roadworks free and with a peerless sky. That is until we turned off the M4 and headed up Aberdare Valley. As we approached Abercwmboi the blue faded into a dull grey haze and the sky looked heavy and laden. Naively I commented that it was our luck that the weather should change just as we were arriving. Dad answered by saying that once we got past the phurnicite plant the clouds would go. Apparently the joke up there is that this large local employer produces the cleanest coal available, but everybody living in the vicinity suffers in the process. Talking to people later on that evening, I was told that although a lot has been done to purify and reduce the effects from the plant, the sky is always like that.

We stayed at the New Market Tavern in a street now pedestrianised. Nice job they've made of it. Pity nobody wants to keep it clean. Despite several bins placed conveniently near the seats, you could be in Soho for all the muck and rubbish there is left around. A very enjoyable meal at our Hotel was followed by a trip to Aberdare Low Level Station, from where we used to depart back to Cardiff to connect with the main line to Paddington all those years ago. Now the site houses a bus depot. The crumbling remains of walls and the platform edge stand defiantly. A large portion of the track bed has been given over, to a new by-pass. The goods shed and BR staff clubrooms remain. They look semi-derelict with dirty windows and vandalised doors. A dusty unmade car park now sits where wagons were once shunted and in the corner by the rusting remains of the yard gates, still attached to the stone retaining walls, I found a length of wood displaying chocolate and cream paint. An upright from a shed? A lamppost? A post proclaiming some instruction or order with dire consequences if not obeyed? I was going to bring it home, to do what with I do not know but I felt it should stay. A testimony to the days when working for the railways earned respect, a far cry from today.

Next we visited Aberdare High Level Station, now re-opened but the usual 'shadow of its former self' phrase appears here again unfortunately. We spoke to the linesman on duty who kindly showed us over the main building situated on a platform that was not included in the plans for re-opening. The beautiful goods shed and associated offices and sheds disappeared some years ago but the derelict track lies abandoned, the buffer stops looking towards Hirwaun, vainly awaiting the arrival of a coal train headed by a pannier tank about to busy itself shunting. But in 1989 all the linesman can tell us about is how vandals set fire to the station and watched it burn. Luckily fireman (as opposed to fire fighters or fire persons) were promptly on the scene and despite all efforts by the yobs to destroy it, the building lives to see another day and possible listed building status. Parking the car at Gadlys, an area near Abernant, we walked alongside a stream where I last walked some thirty-five years ago. I always remembered my Aunty – now unfortunately passed away – and my Father talking about a tramway running alongside the stream. My memory was hazy, but the pictures in my mind were rewarded as we made our way over the stone steps still in situ, their purpose given away by the spike holes, where crude rails were laid all those years ago. We later drove as far as we could up the old road from Abernant to near the remains of the 'Halfway House' pub, where Dad spent, or misspent, much of his youth, before retracing our steps and continuing to the other side of Aberdare and up the 'grieg', a mountain road connecting Aberdare with Maerdy stopping at the site of the Black Lion halt where my Father relayed childhood memories of steam motor services to Cwmbach. We walked briefly along the trackbed now used by the locals as a path affording quite dramatic view over Aberdare. The grieg was, as I remembered it but oh! the filth. A large area of roadway has been cordoned off from the surrounding moorland by fencing. The effect has been for the fencing to trap litter for hundreds of yards at a time. Is there nobody available from the Local Council to clear this mess?

A fish and chip supper was followed by a walk to the Conservative Club to meet my Uncle, with whom we quaffed a few ales. Later we continued our foot journey up the hill to Trecynon. This entailed what I thought would be a walk over the old railway bridge by the 'Little Theatre'. The building is still there, an old railway structure given over to the arts many years ago, but the trackbed is now a new road, and the bridge area has been transformed into a roundabout. I remember sheep being here in previous visits – but not now. A pleasant evening was spent in the company of my Father's friends and what did surprise me was how little the pubs have changed. Dominoes, cards, cribbage, and darts all form a part of the social network. Not for these pubs the age division of young and old. One of my Father's friends, Glyn, is seventy-nine but there were fellow drinkers nearer twenty who passed the time of day or nodded across the bar, acknowledging the existence of people who were friends regardless of age.

My Father commented that he couldn't get over the number of taxis travelling backwards and forwards from the pub to the surrounding terraces and estates. A far cry from when he walked home from pubs in Trecynon as a youngster, being passed by very few motor vehicles. As we got closer to the town centre around midnight the place was alive with youngsters. Night clubs have sprung up and I remembered the words of Ken and Christine at the last hostelry. 'Aberdare is the drink and drugs centre of South Wales.' Young girls in very short dresses and skirts were acting promiscuously with boys on or around the seats in the square, Police vans stood stationary in side streets, and bouncers in evening dress stood talking to tattooed youths outside clubs and pubs. During the day the town is bustling and enjoyable with its surrounding escarpments closing in on both sides, but at night the image is one of a certain fear for personal safety. Youths, somewhat the worse for wear urinating in the shadows of a derelict cinema, the voices of people arguing in another street. Back in our Hotel we went to bed almost immediately, but although I heard Dad snoring I was constantly woken by the thoughtless, unsociable antics of the lager louts spilling from the nightclubs at about 2–2.30 am, shouting and singing

136

as they wended their way. The clipping of stiletto heels on the bricks made a hell of a din, but I eventually succumbed to tiredness despite the noise. The following day we awoke to another fine morning of sun. After an early breakfast we worked out a route and headed up the valley to Hirwaun. Spectacular views can be had as you travel on the A4061 over the mountain towards Treherbert, and there are very few tourists, well actually we didn't come across any, all in Spain buying straw donkeys with a bit of luck. Anyway a brief detour led us up a long cul-de-sac on the side of a mountain in the Rhondda. The side roads became smaller and smaller until terraces of only two or three houses disappeared to our left as we climbed. A pick-up van dispensing milk and groceries passed us with two very young out-riders carrying goods to houses and returning to jump on while the van carried on down hill. I pointed out the name 'Ocean Terrace' to Dad who commented that it referred to the Ocean Mining Co who were large employers at one time. What close communities these are. Having left the narrow ledge that is Cwm Parc we returned to Treochy and carried on over the mountain through Abergwynfi and Caerou, a village no trip to the area should exclude, and on to Tondu, a once great railway junction with engine sheds, today exemplifying all that is great in railway nostalgia. I could have stayed all day and never been happier. We drove along to Pontypridd to take in the once beautiful station building. Still there, but the proverbial shadow. What a dirty place it is. I haven't seen so much litter in one town centre in all my life. The place was bustling, throngs of people, cafés full and shops taking money, but oh the rubbish in the streets. One thing that struck me about the roads was that anyone signalling when overtaking was about as rare as a flying pig.

On our return to Aberdare we went through Llwyn Pia. Travelling North, if you look up to your right the hillside is lush, and just as you take in the beauty of the escarpment, a council estate appears on its peak as if some schoolboy has built a scenic model and then been silly. Three good memories now.

1: I didn't find any towns that were twinned.

2: Virtually all of these towns and villages have small shops only. No multinationals or conglomerates. Don't think I saw a McDonalds anywhere.

3: The sheer delight in being able to drive through rugged, inhospitable countryside with no traffic, only sheep.

The evening was rounded off at the Red Lion, Penydarren – well worth a visit and the Conservative Club again. We left on Sunday taking in villages down the Merthyr Vale to Caerphilly and travelling home late in the afternoon. Probably never have another weekend away with my Dad like that. Fond memories though, fond memories.

We went out with friends for a drink last night and on our return a local resident was walking up the lane looking at our friend's car. 'We've had some trouble tonight' he said 'and I thought you might be the Police coming'. Explanation unfolded to reveal that after he went out and his wife had gone to bed (complete with ear plugs) yobs had walked along the railway line, climbed over our fence into the lane, opened their side gate and thrown a brick through a window. The same oiks had been thought responsible for a similar incident two streets away earlier in the evening. 'Why pick on yours?' I asked 'Well, we didn't have the outside lights on' Came the reply.

The following day a friend of ours told us that the wife doesn't leave the outside light on now to save electricity. Can you believe it. She always gets it wrong. She told us some time ago that she'd been 'horrified' at the quote given to repair her car when it failed the MOT. Not one to throw pennies around, she took the car away and saved about £2 on the cost of repair, took the car back and was asked for the full fee for a re-test. End result she's down £10.

She went to book a holiday which if booked by the weekend meant your taking a child free of charge. She went home to think about it, I mean two weeks for 3/8d is dear so a major decision with sub-committee had to take place. She went back on the Monday to book up, only to be told that the offer had closed. Anyone else would have snapped up a bargain there and then, not her. Even when she did book her holidays, she haggled over the deposit. It must be us I think. We had a neighbour like that at our last home. She

138

borrowed a lot though, tea, sugar, milk. Never whole packets that could be replaced, but cupfuls. She once came rushing in asking for some toilet paper as their little girl was on the loo and they'd run out. Maureen and her took the kids to the Safari Park. This neighbour insisted on the children all going together on the rides to save money. You know those rocking horses or spaceships that have a slot to take a coin? Well they were 4p a go. Her idea of pleasure was that if you put three children on at once you saved money. The fact that the metal creature bucked back and forth because of the weight instead of giving a smooth ride was neither here nor there. The interesting thing is that they have so much in common. In both cases the wives come from 'funny families', it is they who organise things, are quite ebullient, neurotic, innocent flirts and bloody tight, while the husbands are quiet, easy going sorts, with few hobbies and interests, but genuine people all the same. Funny that!

I went a couple of weeks ago to visit Ford's Truck Factory at Langley and I've spent the last two days in Stuttgart at the invitation of a local Ford dealer from whom I occasionally obtain vehicles. Now the two factories are virtually identical in their assembly line layout and vehicle construction, but what struck me was that at Langley a large percentage of the workforce was either coloured or Asian whereas in Germany it was young Germans. I expected to see a lot of Turks or Eastern Europeans. At Langley, yellow safety lines are everywhere and the walls full of frames with safety pictures of do's and don'ts. At the Ulm factory the frames are full of pictures of completed vehicles. I don't know whether one reads anything into this or not, and if so what conclusions are to be drawn. Another thing is that workers in Germany are allowed to drink alcohol on the premises. One overriding impression was that all the workers, from top to bottom in Germany seemed to be working for the same company with the same goals in life. Here, it seemed the 'Them and Us' situation that continues to dog British industry was prevalent. I may be wrong and would certainly stand corrected but that was the impression I got. One frightening statistic that I did take note of was that 95,000 new lorries will be on the road in Britain this year against 65,000 in West Germany. Is this anything to do with the fact that they rely, like the French, on moving a lot of goods by rail. There are private sidings and marshalling yards at central locations in both Countries, here we offer the land to Barratts. On that note, standing in the centre of Stuttgart you can look either side of you and both hillsides coming virtually down into the town itself still possess vineyards. Can you imagine the same being true in a British town of comparative size. Here in the South, Charles Church, would be building a new development called 'Vineyards' as a sop to the past and a trendy name for their latest expansion. Another chap, who like me, had never been to Germany before commented on how clean it was and the fact that at night, cafés could leave tables and chairs outside, retailers could leave cake stalls and the like, fairly safe from vandalism and graffiti. Never saw any of it. Here the chairs and tables would be fair game for our beloved lager louts. 'Probably have to go to Ethiopa to find somewhere dirtier than Britain' was one of his more succinct comments – where is Richard Branson and his band of street cleaners?

Getting back to the brick through the window, it was obviously a big event in their lives. The husband was out looking around the following morning. A Police van came up the road and he was out like a shot. The glass had been replaced extremely early, puttied and painted, the area cleared. The plain clothes Policeman walked across the road and onto our property to dust the fence for fingerprints. He never said hello or anything to us, no 'Is it OK if I go across the road and look over the area' No bye your leave, no bugger all. Crass bad manners. Police cars had been down all night. Another neighbour had been there until late to comfort the victims of the 'brutal attack'. I've never seen so much fuss over nothing in all my life. All this Police time expended on a brick. I lose £25,000 being defrauded and they can't get the bastard back from Spain. Doesn't make sense.

Well, we're becoming extremely depressed about the house selling game. The one or two people who have been interested are still unable to sell their own properties. I placed an ad in both local papers, the only response so far being from a woman who looked at the wrong column – it's been under 'homes to let' for three insertions, but they've got it right now – and a chap who rang and made an appointment, then rang back at the time he was due to say he had, quote, 'Mislaid his wife and could he ring later to make another appointment' If he doesn't want to come why doesn't he just say so. The financial situation is getting progressively worse, and unless we can sell our house soon we'll be in the unenviable position of 'owning' two houses and not being able to pay for either. We've reduced the price, all the estate agents tell us it's the type of property that's selling as opposed to estate houses, but still no definite interest. Coupled with the fact that car sales are still very patchy, it's not a good time, and Maureen is particularly worried at the moment. She keeps getting up in the night to make some tea and read a book, falling asleep in the chair and coming back to bed as dawn's breaking. It's such a fine line we tread, and getting thinner by the interest rate increase.

I can foresee the situation arising, where, in a couple of years time the men from the Ministry of Agriculture will be stating that at the time of the go-ahead there was no scientific reason to suggest that irradiated food could cause 'whatever' disease or contribute towards some fairly terminal illness. After reading all the bumph on this subject I have yet to see the advantage of this sinister sounding treatment. I understand what they are saying about killing off more bacteria, but the suspicions remain that more harm than good will come by its adoption, and anyway, I've not heard anyone I know saying that they're going to buy irradiated food – listen to the public – that's novel.

In the People today 11 June 1989 the Voice of the People commented that one should vote Labour in the Euro-Elections, as a vote for Mrs Thatcher would be against public interest as she is quote 'Blind to the need for better drinking water, blind to a better deal for workers and pensioners, blind to the benefits of the E.M.S. and by being anti Europe she is being anti Britain'. How is this so. The comments made by the paper are really no different from opposition statements and other media observations and I cannot see it. Why do we need to be in Europe to expect a continuation of the

141

high standard of water purification we have been used to for yonks. Why does being in Europe mean pensioners should get a better deal. I'm not in a position to comment of the E.M.S. but why do the media consider her stand to be 'Anti British?' Now that the elections are over and the SDP and SLP vote has been transferred to the Green Party, the obvious comments are being made that the Tories lost seats due to Mrs Thatcher's attitude to Europe, as I've just mentioned. It isn't the case at all. It's not that deep. The majority of people couldn't give a toss about Europe. They voted Labour because of the mortgage and interest rate rises, dissatisfaction with the water situation and the general cutbacks. Labour's cheers should be tinged with caution. The public at large have short memories. A cut in income tax and low interest rates along with stiffer union bills will bring about another Tory victory. How many Tories during the 'Falklands Factor' election thought about the increase in VAT from eight percent to fifteen percent made in 1979 when she first got into power. It is an iniquitous tax as it is. Another instruction from Europe. It would appear that the percentage of votes is up in comparison with the previous Euro-election. A friend of mine voted to stay in Europe because he thought that wine would be cheaper. Sums it up, doesn't it.

Someone reminded me that it isn't long before Wimbledon is once again upon us. I remember as a kid enjoying the likes of Laver, Newcombe and Roche etc, the later years of Borg, but like most things now money is king to the point of exclusion of everything else. Winning is all. I just hope McEnroe is dismissed early, that if Lendl wins – he smiles, and that people are pleasantly surprised with the low price of strawberries. Personally I wouldn't allow that loud mouthed oik to land on these shores. His behaviour is definitely not needed when trying to teach self discipline and manners. His continual brushes with authority are tiresome, but then, when such huge sums are being paid out what can you expect.

You know, all this wailing by the Hong Kong citizens about coming to British soil should the Chinese Government be of the same political ilk in 1997 leaves me bewildered. We don't have the room. It's as plain and simple as that. I'm not interested in the arguments that Britain has gained so much from

Hong Kong and they are passport holders. Hong Kong has done very well out of Britain over the years, allowing them a Western and prosperous lifestyle in complete contrast to their fellow Chinese. I'm continually told that the world is changing and I must get used to change. Well that's what they have to accept as well. If however the roles were reversed and it was (heaven forbid) Britain that was in a state of anarchy, would these loyal coves be so intent on coming here and helping us. No. They'd be cosily dealing with their own problems like the rest of the world. We're doing it again. We're bogged down in diplomacy instead of telling a colony the facts of life. We've been thrown out of many a former Commonwealth State when the inmates have considered that our usefulness has expired and we accept it meekly. Now I'm waiting for the general hints to be dropped telling us how necessary it is for a 'slightly larger' number than was first considered to be given sanctuary here and for us to receive brickbats from other countries informing us of our duties and obligations. I know it is a long time still and anything can happen, but if the present situation continues any number allowed over 'none' is one too many and unacceptable. We will of course accept, because we are a nation of 'acceptors'. It is not our nature for the middle of the road layman to demonstrate in squares and town centres. I'm sure the various left wing organisations will eagerly be mounting campaigns, and the church will get involved offering Christian views on Utopia. What if we have to build new towns in Hampshire and Bucks for these people. I expect the development would have been on the cards anyway. It is just a question of that esteemed Minister of the Environment rubber stamping what our greedy builders want and several thousand residents don't.

This erosion of our way of life is continuous isn't it? For those of us who use 'troy' for measurement, a concession has been made for it to remain in use, but for millions who use one fifth or one sixth of a gill at the optics, life will never be the same again, we are to be served our drinks in millilitres and centilitres like everyone else, in the quest for harmonisation. We are definitely a nation in a quandary when it comes to measurements. Some authorities use yards while others use metric for their signs. Public footpath signs offering miles and some proffering their distance in yards. It wouldn't be so bad if the standard of mathematics was any better but it isn't. I recall an argument being put forward in the sixties that one hundred pence to the pound would help youngsters. I was probably witnessing the start of the educational decline during that period. If anything the standards are worse now than when we had LSD to contend with. God knows what todays 'unlearned and unteachables' would make of a system that had twelve of one thing and twenty of an other. We coped, but then we had teachers who taught, not slapdash, political animals who consider knowing the names of Winnie Mandela's football team to be preferential to the Country towns of England. Anyway, it's nice to know I'll still be able to ask for a pint of bitter. Actually I still ask for 0.86 of an imperial pint of paint. I refuse to recognise litres.

I had to get a passport before my trip to Stuttgart. Said youngster behind the screens in the Post Office asked me for my post-code. 'Don't use it' I replied narked. He bored the pants off me telling me how it would speed up my mail. It's a system only convenient to the GPO, certainly not to me. I received two letters the other day, both from my bank. One posted First Class with code, the other posted Second without and one day later. They both arrived together three days after posting. It's an absolute farce. I asked said youth if anyone at Stuttgart Airport would be interested in my code 'No' he replied 'but I have to fill it in'. What a waste of time, and I also didn't know I was 1.73 whatever tall, as far as I'm concerned I'm 5 ft 8½". Never forget the half.

Another example of our guilt feelings towards former territories coming to the fore was exemplified by the announcement by Mr Hurd, The Home Secretary, that DNA testing is to be used to confirm relationships between immigrants here and their kin wishing to join them. Whilst the government does not want the taxpayer to pay for this service, it wishes to minimise the cost to the applicant. Why? We native citizens have been paying through the nose for inefficient transport services and other nationalised industries, dental and medical care for years. Why not get these people used to a system they will have to partake in eventually, despite all the help they'll receive. Still the good news for them is that as the costs would be horrendous for large families, poor loves, an all- in fee is likely to be announced. Start where we mean to carry on. I see. What I expect to hear is the predictable comment coming out against such a move. Yes they're all there. That unceasing bureaucratic machine the Racial Equality Commission, The Immigrants Advisory Service, The Joint Council for the Rights of Immigrants, and of course Mr Hattersley who called the moves 'racist'. Well he would, wouldn't he. God save us from another labour government.

We're not the only short sighted nation though, far from it in fact. There is a move in the USA by the local Bureau to sell areas of forest for logging. That's OK I suppose in small doses, after all we need wood. The problem arises when chopping down trees means the destruction of the habitat of animals and birds in large numbers. In this case it's the Northern spotted owl. If anyone had any sympathy for the loggers in the first place, one's sentiment certainly goes out of the window when one knows they have a slogan 'Save a logger, kill an Owl', pity it wasn't the other way round. To finish off one's indignation, I find that the majority of this wood is going to be sold to the Japs. They really are a most obnoxious race aren't they? Now the likes of Mr Hattersley and Kaufmen will be unable to consider this as a racist comment because we are talking of a colour other than black so that's acceptable criticism, however unpalatable it may be to them personally.

I know it won't do any good but we've stopped buying tuna fish in the forlorn hope, I expect, that if a lot of people act likewise the poor old dolphin will not be massacred to the extent it is at present. When you think that 100,000 die each year it brings home the problem. It's always those Japs who end up the main culprits in these stories. They now claim this slaughter is part of their religion. It's the cop out for anything, the catch-all phrase. I'm surprised I haven't read that the Japanese Minister responsible receives messages or hears voices telling him to do these things, a la British rapists when asked why they committed their brutalities. Which brings us back to the Japs. Leopards never change their spots and the slit eyed race of the sun only change their barbarities from humans to animals when the power of the yen is greater than the power of conquest. With the number of Jap owned companies and golf courses in this country it probably amounts to the same thing.

Now as I said previously, I'd be quite happy, for someone to blow that potential death trap, the channel tunnel, to smithereens. I read that the French in the event of war will not allow British troops to cross into Europe via the tunnel. Something to do with their being somewhat less than equal partners in NATO I believe. Anyway, it's apparently going to be down to us to ferry our troops across. I suppose that means using Townsend Thoresen. Sorry P & O. What a bloody cheek the French have. It wouldn't be so bad, but they will have capitulated anyway by the time we get there, you know, two hours after the non nuclear battle begins, still as long as they have a free area in the south they should be quite happy.

Who do we have more kinship with, Europe or America. Debatable as some people find it, when it comes to language, America wins hands down. Yes I know they're rather common, but it's similar isn't it? The plans to limit the amount of non-European television broadcasts does take the biscuit. Who the hell wants subtitled or dubbed Euro crap. It won't mean more people ending up watching French or German soaps and game shows, but more people having videos. We have had American and more recently Australian programmes on both channels and happily accepted that whether you like them or not the nub is that you can understand them. Why should we in Britain be sentenced to a diet of sixty per cent European programmes. Another case of a free trade dream entering a world it was never designed to and abusing the privilege in the process.

I watch little enough ITV these days with their extended advertising periods, finding it better to watch recorded programmes and slip through the dross, not looking at Maureen Lipman or the water privatisation propaganda. If they proceed with the idea of sponsored weather forecasts I will switch permanently to the Beeb. It appears, and not at the viewers request, that we are supposed to accept this intrusion by big business into our TV life with open arms. This is not America, and I wish it as much luck as the Channel Tunnel.

At the end of the day it's another change of life we are indebted to Mrs Thatcher for. Thirty-three years of reasonable standards of advertising will go to the wall. I honestly looked at the date of the newspaper I was reading to see if it was April 1. I don't suppose many people wish to see sponsored DIY, gardening, cooking and sports programmes but then in football you have the Vauxhall Opel League, the Beazer and the HFS Leagues. Notwithstanding the Nene Group, Stopshops, Danair, Key Consultants, Green King, etc. Gone the halcyon days of the Isthmian, Corinthian, Spartan etc, we really need more sponsorship and advertising don't we.

Good news. The Hudson Bay Company, dealers in furs since 1670 is closing down its doors in Britain in September. Not a day too soon. Well done lynx, the anti-fur organisation for any pressure they have created, farewell you perpetrators of torture and vanity. Long may your vile trade diminish.

Woman of the month this time. Brenda Cochrane who won Opportunity Knocks earlier this month deserves the accolade. It was the first time we'd ever rung to register a vote, and yes, I appreciate a lot of people consider the programme naff, but I thought she was great. I look forwards to seeing her records on sale. Well done BBC.

July

We start this month in the most desperate of financial situations. In the last couple of weeks we've played host to two separate 'tourists' who, having lifted our spirits in the hope of selling our house, have plunged us back into the abyss of the unsold being only seven weeks away from handing over the last payment to the builders. We could rent out our present place but we cannot cope with a £100,000 plus mortgage on the new one. I honestly thought that by now we would have found a buyer. Having reduced the price at the five estate agents we're with, advertised privately etc, we are still no further forward than we were sixteen weeks ago. Both these 'tourists' were women. The first spent one and a half hours here stating that she wanted an investment to house her mother currently living in Shropshire. Could she have all the details? A photo perhaps to send to her aged relative. 'Will ring you during the week, is it OK to bring mother down over the weekend?' A week later and the cop out line 'We can't really afford it' The second time waster was so captivated on her visit at 4 pm that by 6 pm she'd returned with family friend to inspect structurally and make an offer. Even the estate agent must have smelt something as he suggested she sat on it overnight and considered properly, before discussing money. That was Thursday, by Monday still no phone call. Now we come to the rub. House OK, friend's opinion of the structural condition, OK. Failure? The name Ash Vale does not have the same social standing as Wrecclesham, Rowledge or Frensham Heights. Believe me, there's just as many yobs on the council estates in Farnham as Ash. Then again, the postal address is Aldershot, Hants, not nr Farnham, Surrey. Still, as the estate agent said 'If she wants your house in a private road

148

in Farnham, she'll have to pay another forty odd thousand pounds'. I wouldn't mind but she's living on a busy main road in a terraced house with no off-street parking so she can really afford to be funny about addresses can't she – bloody waste of time these people.

What concerns me about these rail strikes in particular is that the government cannot understand what is really needed. It's all very well stating publicly that the fare paying passengers should not have to put up with it, and that more legislation will be passed to outlaw such strikes, but it doesn't get to the heart of the trouble. Some couple of years ago, I went, by courtesy of the Rotary Club, as a guest, to visit a BR Signal Control Box and listen to a short speech by one of the South East's Line Managers. When we were chatting afterwards, he said that BR had asked more and more of its workforce and promised honey in the future. 'If we don't give it, then there will be trouble' He claimed. It's like every other service industry – no-one knows what the position is going to be tomorrow. There's no continuity, no morale. You've only got to speak to railway staff, they have no faith in management. Having seen that pompous, arrogant N.S.E. Manager Chris Green being interviewed on TV last week my suspicions are confirmed. I can't imagine anyone working for someone with such an ego. Talk about a them and an us situation, until we all consider ourselves as a team working for the same company, with the same goals, we have not got a cat in hells chance of improving our industrial relations – and provide a stable base for staff to feel content and *needed*. You can pass all the legislation in the world, but it won't alter people's feelings or views, only strengthen them. That though is this government's way. If you can't cut-back, you throw money at it, if that doesn't work you legislate.

Glyn's just completed his first full week's work. The results of his exams are fairly immaterial now. I think he at last appreciates that if he's going to work in an art studio or an advertising agency he has got to go to night school and knuckle down to some hard work. In the meantime he at least is earning a wage in the takeaway place. Hope he's

149

remembered that he's got to pay his mum for his keep out of his first fortnight's money.

Please, please Mr Ridley, for the sake of the people who care, ie the vast majority of British subjects, as opposed to those who seek profit out of your decisions, step down and let someone, anyone, take over a post that is vital to our nations well being. Go back to big business, make your next fortune, but be honest about it. If you want to be involved in building in the green belt, at least you will be be on the 'right' side of the fence, not sitting on it, only to shun public opinion for the sake of profit. Anyone who can say they need more proof that the dolphins off the west coast in Wales are in danger and are not prepared to give them sanctuary must be oblivious to all the warnings and evidence, but then, that's never mattered much or come into your reckoning has it?

Feel better for saying that, not less angry, just better. Mind you, they're all the same, aren't they? I listened on Tuesday to an interview with Kenneth Clark, the Health Minister. When asked for his response to a survey which concluded that three out of four people believed that his measures or reforms for the NHS would end up with a cut in services, longer queues and waiting lists etc, he calmly stated that three out of four people were wrong. It's so easy, isn't it, You just brush aside the fact that the public prefer to believe their doctor rather than a politician. He added, I thought humorously, that if there was a survey conducted in which three out of four people thought that the world was square, he would be one of the one in four who was right. How pious. It's not as if this government has a good track record. Short term cash injections to reap short term benefits, or cutbacks. If they want cutbacks, start with the Office of Fair Trading and go back to Buyer Beware, cut out the Commission for Racial Equality, who receive £100 million a year from the government, and the Equal Opportunities Commission. Another bunch of self opinionated, self righteous humanists who take no account of life as it is, only a Utopia they will never achieve with all the legislation in the world.

I see that from a leaked document it appears that the government is trying to sell shares in the water industry to

150

more companies outside Britain. Not just Europe, where the French now have considerable financial stakes in it, but to North America and – perish the thought – Japan. I cannot put into words the reasons why I feel so sceptical and suspicious about its privatisation over and above the expressed concerns one has heard and read about over the past month, but I feel that time will prove for reasons not yet considered that this particular act will be looked on as one of the biggest errors of our recent history.

Tell me, why do we continue to import Europe's waste, besides profit, no I can't think of a reason either. It really is preposterous that children in different areas of the country living near these disposal sites are suffering from various sicknesses. We apparently have only five inspectors. Still if you can make a profit . . .

It's Wednesday evening, my cousin and I have just finished a game of squash that he has roundly won five–one. How could I play so badly against someone who wears contact lens. I'm too bloody fat and too bloody slow, that's how. Anyway we've joined Maureen, Tony and Valerie, all of whom have been swimming with the masses. Now it's time for a drink. Yes, they have white wine this week, but only sweet wine. Yes, there's only one girl serving, although another has sauntered out to get herself a drink. I'm not sure whether there is an art to this or whether she's thick, I do know really, because managing to come to the front of the bar, pour yourself a drink, ignore eye to eye contact with any prospective punter and shuffle back to the staff room takes a bit of doing, but then practise makes perfect. The older woman who's always playing with the till has just appeared. Yes, more change in and more change out, Funny cove.

I finished the above 'bit' just as the drinks were coming, I'm now home and waiting for Maureen to bring through some sarnies and tea before we go to bed. It never ceases to amaze me the views some people have on McEnroe. Tonight it was three–two in favour of never allowing the oik to set foot in Britain. Maureen, my cousin Simon and I against Tony and Valerie. They're nice, respectable people, well they must be, I speak to them, so how can they consider him the main attraction at Wimbledon. Both endorse his tantrums, stating that he is right to question decisions and calls, both consider his action 'entertainment' and both believe that the majority of fans are behind him. I could not get through to them that at the end of the day it's a game and I'm sure you get as much good luck as you do bad from the umpire's decisions. No-one else whines and whinges on like him. We considered him a bad influence on the youngsters starting up in the game (Britain isn't included in this as we don't seem to have any up and coming players). Which reminds me, whatever happened to Sue Barker. We also disputed their claim that the majority of Brits welcome him here every Wimbledon. I cannot stand the intimidation that's shown to all officials. Valerie seems to feel that his rebellious attitude is fresh and worthy, but what can you expect from an Australian living in Hampshire, albeit near the Surrey Border, who would prefer to live in a New York high rise block if given the choice – nuff said.

Feel let down now. While we were out, Jehovah's Witnesses called, but my daughter didn't tell them to call back, I could have just coped with them. A lovely lady we know, Mary, quite one of the liveliest and colourful people you could have the pleasure of meeting has a stock answer for any religion, cult or sect that appears on her doorstep. Bearing in mind she is a pensioner. She says 'I'm sorry my religion forbids me to discuss the matter with you'. They leave open mouthed before a foot can be put in her door.

Sandwich spread and tomato sarnies – lovely. I shall devour these and then it's off to bed. You know, I said to Maureen on the way home, 'When we go to bed do you fancy playing "hunt the sausage"'. She said 'Do you mean "let's look for a chipolata"?' Can't some women be hurtful? Just my way of bringing a little variation into the 'let's see if she's going to have a headache' game.

Night- Night.

It's been a busy couple of days since Wednesday. I've been down to a little village near Marlborough to buy a couple of cars. There are another couple I'd buy if I can get them underwritten. The chap I've bought them from is someone I used to work with some years ago. His forte was the h.p.

and leasing of vehicles, so when our company packed up he, like me, went out by himself and I'm glad to say seems to be enjoying his life and running a nice little business in a very pretty area.

A few years ago we went off for a long weekend to Amsterdam for the Dutch 'Grand Prix'. It was basically 'boys weekend away' John had purchased, to sell on his return, a Morgan in British Racing Green with spoked wheels. What a posing machine. I can say that sort of thing as I was much younger then! Believe me, it was as they say, the business. We left Ash Vale around midnight and despite the cold, but being British, we drove to Dover with the top down and arrived as the light was just poking through in the extreme distance. A cup of tea and a hot dog or two were very welcome. An uneventful voyage and landing preceeded our racing through Northern France towards the Flemish border. The sun shone brightly and I remember as we left the French customs the radio played Bonnie Tyler's 'Lost in France'. Good omen. Belgium came and went. We held our breaths from border to border and tipped the cigarette tray and everything else we didn't want out during that period of the journey. Well that's what Belgium is for, isn't it? We stayed the first night in a hotel. The doorman suggested we lock our car up safely as they could not be held responsible for theft and damage. After several forays up and down the steps leading to our rooms with the tonnou, covers, suitcases, spare wheel, tools and various accessories, the doorman was in two minds whether to believe us when John commented 'the engine's the hardest part to get upstairs!'.

An evening spent looking around the red light district and the following day's Grand Prix were without incident . . . , except when John, having waited ages to be served in a bar, held his blue passport aloft and exclaimed 'Excuse me, we're British, two pints of your bitter please, stout German' Now they don't like being called that in Amsterdam, do they? John's saving grace is that he's tall and well-built. I'm not and I didn't say it. It was just that the sight of this arm with passport above a sea of heads did go down well with me. Got served though.

The afternoon's racing over, we were invited to a little village to join some friends of his wife's, she being Dutch. The sun was still blazing. They welcomed us warmly and showed us to our rooms, saying they were going to have a bar-be-cue and lots of people would be coming, so it should be a good evening. A shower and a change of clothing being had, I ventured out to the garden to be greeted by the host. Needlesss to say a blue sky, blazing sun and general ambience of a bar-be-cue determined slacks and casual shirts – besides it was all I had to change into. More guests arrived, John made his entrance – Dinner suit, highly polished black shoes, bow tie – the lot. 'We always dress for dinner in Surrey' he said to the hoots of laughter from some and quaint looks of amazement from others. 'Why is it we all speak English but you refuse to learn any other European language' asked one guest 'You need only to have a working knowledge of English to get by in life if you're a foreigner' replied John coarsely. 'We're all Europeans now' someone else chimed in. My turn now 'How dare you' I said 'Being British does not mean being European, We are an island. If we have to have a common market it should be between English speaking nations plus Germany' 'Yes' agreed John, 'the ideal common market would be Britain, Australia, New Zealand, Canada, South Africa and West Germany' He refrained from his usual comment that the rest of Europe wasn't worth a light. Not surprising really as the tables set out looked really inviting and the charcoal burner slowly cooking the fish emanated mouth watering smells.

No, we had not got off to a good start but I feel it's important to stand up for your corner and educate those Euros that despite political propaganda, the majority of people in this country do not consider themselves Europeans and would prefer to remain an island race. Anyway, John went over to the chap who was smoking these fish on this vertical contraption. 'How do you get the fire going' enquired John 'Ve use zer kindling vood' came the reply. 'Really' said John 'In Britain we use immigrants' Peels of laughter. 'Ve make ze jokes of ze Belgians' he added 'Don't care whether they're black, white, Scottish, Welsh or Irish' John continued 'We just take the piss out of them, anyone's fair game – as long as they're not English you understand'. The last bit was added with mock severity. That was it, the break through. Once they'd realised we all knew the same jokes, only the nationality had changed we got on like a house on fire. Good food was savoured, fine wine was quaffed, well you can't drink the beer it's so bloody gassy, and a convivial evening was had by all. I remember a single lady there by herself. I believe her boyfriend was English and came from Manchester, but I didn't hold it against her. She got better looking by the glass and I asked her is she would like me to take her home. I added that nothing of a sexual nature was in my thoughts, I just wanted to curl up on her bed and be her mascot. Pathetic this, isn't it. Anyway, amazingly she stood firm and resisted my overtures, going home alone by taxi!

About 2 am though it was still extremely warm, in the distance thunder started to bellow forth. It was at this point that John voiced his all time classic 'Should we change the record to Marching Music?' He enquired 'It looks as if the Germans are invading again. Hope your army's not like Norway's – day off when being walked through!' Funny he is, diplomat he ain't. Glad to say, probably through drink and an acceptance of English eccentricity everyone fell about laughing, although I think they were relieved when the lightening started, just in case . . .

A pleasant journey, well as pleasant as it could be through what must be some of the most boring, flattest countryside around ended on the boat in Calais, where having sat down for dinner the anchor was raised and John exclaimed loudly to all 'frogs' sitting near us 'The great thing about untying a boat is that you're then in England' Not a view shared by those around us I suppose but I concured with his opinion that British Territory extends to the shores of all foreign lands. Clutching straws it might be, but then there is little to hold on to nowadays.

I've skipped a bit and I'm not re-writing it now. At the French customs in Calais, our luggage, being covered by the tonnou which swept around behind our seats encompassing all and sundry, also housed the top end of a large umbrella, which ran parallel to the car ending up by the hand brake between the two seats. While John was answering the questions the customs official was asking, paying special attention to the one about rabies, I looked the other way, pushing down

155

the bottom of the umbrella with my hand, thus raising the top that pushed the stretched tonnou into a small peak. At the same time I gave several 'yelps' or 'barks' much to the irritation of the said frog who offered to rip the car apart if we didn't take it seriously. How can you take being French seriously?

That weekend still ends up in conversations and is looked back on with fond memories. As far as John's concerned he hasn't changed. He's traded in the current model – wife, not car – for a new blonde version and has added another two children to the country's population. When telling me about the best way back to the A303 from his place he mentioned going through Ludgershall. 'What's that like' I asked 'Awful place, full of council houses with young tarts pushing prams' He hasn't changed.

Glyn's just had his first driving lesson in a Peugeot 205 Diesel. Pratt that I am, I agreed on his last birthday to pay for ten lessons. Shows how out of touch you get. I thought they would be about £5–£6 each – they're £12.50 and that was one of the cheaper quotes. Having waited almost six months to get his licence (it arrived on Wednesday) I can see why he's so eager to get started.

Without trying to be boring about 'trains', but on a serious note. There's a steam locomotive that's been preserved since being withdrawn in the mid-sixties called 'Union of South Africa'. Now it's owner, so I have heard in the railway press is seeking sponsorship to repair and return her to working condition. She has worked on many occasions since being withdrawn from BR but with costs of £100,000 being involved, outside help is required. A large international oil company have expressed interest in sponsoring this work but are unhappy about the locomotive name. That was the name given to it in the thirties, that is the only name it's carried and that is what it is. You can't change these things. What sort of world is it when the name of a loco determines whether a company helps a project or not. Mustn't mention South Africa. Why is everyone so paranoid about it. Personally I won't go into the Co-op because they *don't* sell South African foods. I'm not going to be told what country's produce I should and shouldn't buy, because of political or racial pressures. These lefties don't go on and on about Japan or South American countries whose atrocities to humans and animals are well scripted, but then they're white.

When push comes to shove you certainly see people in their true colours. Mrs Thatcher has ignored all the pleadings and advice from those who care and gone along with those wishing to exploit Antartica for minerals, sorry profit. Didn't she say something about caring for our environment, and she still has Mr Ridley in charge. Can't trust any of them. I heard a programme on Radio 4 discussing 'Sites of Special Scientific Interest' (S.S.S.I.) where a comment had been made by a Minister proclaiming 'no S.S.S.I.'s have been adversely affected in a major way for the past three years!' – or words to that effect. Now the programme dealt with those associations on the ground who take issue with Government Ministers and can actually tell you and I the truth which is a completely different story altogether. Tales of roads bulldozed through woodlands, heathlands, last vestiges of green land on the outside of towns etc. Tarmacing of sandy areas for car parking on previously unspoilt dunes, barriers across estuaries disturbing the homes of hundreds of thousands of birds. But no, the man from the ministry pompously sticks to his guns and says 'What a good boy am I'.

I see that the Pay Research Unit conclude in a survey about working mums that a large number of international companies are without creche facilities and that with the increasing problem of staff recruitment the companies are lagging behind in wooing women workers. Less that thirty-three per cent of the British mothers with children under five go out to work as against Denmark's seventy-five per cent. They seem to want women to go out to work. Personally I would prefer it if women with small children were dissuaded from returning to work. One hears so much of latch-key children left to fend for themselves, it is surely better that mums stay as long as possible with their offspring, especially the under fives. Let's educate those at school better so that they can achieve higher paid jobs, Christ, there's enough unemployed morons around. Mothers should be at home looking after children. If they want a career, don't have children. Another small, but distinctive, sop to the left wing are creches. The spiky haired, boobless brigade whose vocabulary centres on words like 'community', 'meaningful', 'executive', 'poverty', 'action', 'wants' and 'needs'; and the all time favourite 'Rights'. And they'll all be union members. No wonder these companies are keeping their heads down.

Well Mr Dodd's reasons for not declaring monies earned, to the Inland Revenue, make funnier reading than his jokes. Be interesting to see how it goes.

After a weekend watching the deadly German duo win Wimbers, how proud Mr Hitler would have been. I received this Monday morning a pleasant call from my man in Bracknell informing me that we've sold two metros and a panda over the weekend. Although they have yet to be paid for and collected, substantial deposits have been taken so it augers quite well for the start of the week. I feel as if I've taken someone else's luck. No doubt I'll be giving it back before the week's out.

The builders tell us that completion of the new home is only about six weeks away. Had to pay out another £10,000 on Friday, up to £45,000 in total. Good old Midland Bank. Why am I saying 'good old', they're making a fortune out of me. No punters on our place over the weekend. We're now considering renting out our present house if we can't sell it, moving into the new place and panicking.

Awash with money to invest in business outside their normal spheres, I see the Japanese have been granted licences to drill for oil only 120 miles off our shores. French owned water and Japanese owned oil, where on earth is this country going. On the subject of petrol, it was on my recent soirée to South Wales that I reminded Dad of the trips to visit the seaside, relatives etc as a youngster, when armed with paper and pencil I would write down all petrol companies I knew and have a league table of the makes and names used. In those days there was no Elf, Burmah, Jet, Amoco or Texaco. The latter was 'Regent', I still have a Dinky tanker bearing that name. Once again there was a ruggedness about the pumps. Solid, house coloured and with a globe on top with lights displaying the producers name, reminding me of railway station gas lamps with the station's name proudly displayed in the pre-grouping companies colours, but then they would, wouldn't they. Regent, with one of its grades called 'TT' was always my favourite. Usually coming third in the table behind Shell, purveyors of 'Super Shell with ICA', and Esso, long associated with tigers whose grades included 'extra' and 'golden'. Was there a 'Golden Extra', maybe, the memory does play tricks. The names were friendly and warm. So much more so than the two, three and four star, although as I write it appears that only four star and the newly introduced unleaded will be available soon. There was a five star but that disappeared about a decade ago, along with British Sports cars. I also liked the pumps displayed by the smaller companies. 'Dominion' was blue with a three-cornered globe, 'Power' was green with a diamond globe 'National, mustard pumps with globe portraying winged head or helmet, the precise details elude my memory. Another one was 'Cleveland' whose advertising always contained reference to their petrol including alcohol in its make up. Mustn't forget BP of course, green pumps with cream shield shaped globe, quite attractive. Diesel pumps were always on their own lurking in a corner looking decidedly embarrassed with their lot.

A long journey home in the dark was made all the more homely by the illuminated globes sitting comfortably on the tall, individual pumps, some of which in more rural areas were handcranked. Sodium lighting was another new facet of the late fifties that we take for granted today. Orbital roads and dual carriageways brought with them the feeling that the lonely country part was over and here you were, safe, back in civilisation, and nearly home.

'The Government hopes to persuade the City that huge profits can be made by the water industry once meters are installed in all homes'. What a statement. Ask the good residents of the Isle of Wight if they will vote Tory again in the next elections. You know, I saw a water chappie being interviewed and he said we got our water cut price when compared with what the French and Germans pay. Is that comment supposed to be relevant. Compare the various nations wages before coming up with such statements is my line of thought.

Not only will we be expected to cut down and re-use water, there is the additional insult of having to pay an estimated £100 per meter for the privilege of being ripped off, for make no mistake, that is what we are talking about. No doubt as the bill goes through the Lords, we shall see headlines about more Soviet spies being found and sent home to camouflage the excesses of the legislation.

It's interesting about the rings appearing all over Wiltshire isn't it, I expect scientists will prove the 'phenomenon' to be logically explained but when you read of the circles appearing whilst tests and readings are taking place, it makes you yearn for an unknown druid curse or an outer planet's inhabitants to be responsible. Add a bit of excitement. The fact that these rings appear on the courses of laylines and that we're talking of areas around ancient settlements in deepest Wiltshire adds to the flavour. It's probably down to dear Nicholas Ridley laying the metaphorical foundation for building to commence. Talking of that despicable moron, despite local and County Council opposition, he has sanctioned the destruction of acre upon acre of woodland, meadow and ponds in the Bramshill area. This is the development I mentioned earlier in the year that Barratts have been trying to get underway for three years in conjunction with Wimpey and Bovis. It was only a question of time. Words cannot express the contempt and disgust I feel for that cove.

Not that I am for one moment an admirer of this man, but Dr Runcie's comments concerning religious fanatics of all faiths should not go unheeded. Whilst I'm heartily sick of these Muslims in Bradford, London and elsewhere continually maligning our country and the opinion of others I look in disbelief at the hatred shown by Glasgow Rangers supporters on learning of the signing of Mo Johnson, a Catholic. I don't like Catholism, and an awful lot of my family are Catholic. I don't dislike or think any differently about them because of this fact. It doesn't matter, it is not important. As long as they don't try to convert me I'm happy, people can follow whatever faith they want to. The look on the faces of those Protestants in Scotland will stay with me for a long time. Mr Johnson is, I believe, currently in a 'safe' house having received various threats to his person. If we can't accept different religions on a football field there is little hope for a peaceful solution in Ulster.

I know it's generalising, but my respect for the Spanish is about as low as my respect for those in charge of Windscale (sorry Sellafield) or Nicholas Ridley, so you can see it *really* is low. A picture in the Today newspaper shows a bull being driven into the sea only to be driven back out again by more drunken oiks. In this one photograph I counted about 40 heads. Was no-one prepared to stop this obscenity? Was everybody genuinely enjoying themselves? The caption enlightened readers as to the purpose of this torture adding that it is 'supposed to show the bravery of the young men of Denia on the Costa Blanca'. Where does this bravery bit come into play. I cannot comprehend a situation like this when no-one wants to stand up and be counted. I sincerely hope that those involved die a slow and lingering death, they have no place in society.

The Inland Revenue case against Mr Dodd seems to be travelling along a predictable path. We're now hearing about him always wanting to be a father. Can you point out to me the relevance – other than public sympathy by way of some aah's and ooh's and the hoped for softening of attitudes when all this is taken into account.

Another reason for taking guns away from all and sundry is highlighted when you read that hen harriers nests have been destroyed presumably by game keepers so that the grouse season can get 'orf to a successful start. Hen harriers feed on grouse chicks, but the natural cycle of the food chain makes little impact on the greed of these trusty stalwarts of society – bastards.

I accept he was a good actor but I've never witnessed anything so 'OTT' as the comments and homage which followed the news of Lawrence Olivier's death. They were all doing it. In Britain and America actors and actresses were giving performances of a lifetime. Sir Richard Attenborough publicly declared that he 'loved' him. Now I fully accept and understand the context in which the phrase was used, but it made me feel queasy. Every news bulletin was awash with new (or rather) old faces gloomily accepting his passing and adding their 'different' account of his career. Having said all that, coupled with the comedians who testified in Liverpool court about the attributes, generosity and general well-being of Mr Dodd, I couldn't quite remember which one was dead and which one was being given an accolade, sorry Inland Revenue grilling.

Doesn't Julian Lloyd-Webber remind you of the chap who played the incredible hulk? He does me.

People like Maxwell Hutchinson, the president of the Royal Institute of British Architects are hard to fathom out in my eyes. He accuses Prince Charles of promoting 'cowardly' 'Old Fashioned' architecture. He obviously isn't thick, he cannot be that out of touch with the real world and the opinion of the majority of its inhabitants, so I can only assume there is a great deal of arrogance about the man. I don't know him so I could well be mistaken, but why is it that you know the vast majority of people are dismayed by the sight of these monstrosities, glass and concrete, that appear almost overnight, and yet when brick is used creating a traditional structure we warm to it. These people are there to build what is acceptable and required by the man in the street, not an elite clique hell bent on erecting yet another blot on the landscape so awful and bland that it will receive an award watched with amazed incredulity by the rest of the population.

One's resolve never to get involved in a European holiday that includes leaving from an airport during the free for all, and risking being branded a hooligan, just because you happen to be British, stands the test of time at least. I listened to the Monty Python 'Travel Agent' sketch over the weekend and his comments about being at the airport, not knowing that the plane you're waiting for is still in Iceland and has to take a party of Swedes to Yugoslavia before it can come back and collect you, is still applicable, and has been since the sketch was first recorded all those years ago, and it never changes, they still queue, accepting the handouts of sarnies and the 'comfort' of a bench surrounded by sweaty bodies. My accountant went to Gatport Airwick recently to pick up his son from holiday in the dead of night to find that the flight has been delayed. Having tried to find space for himself and his wife amongst the sleeping wrecks and the space machines played with relentless fortitude by the moron fraternity, they found peace and serenity in the Chapel. What a good idea. In two hours, only one other soul entered. As he said, it wasn't the most comfortable of chairs, but the dimmed lighting provided a quiet and peaceful sanctuary for the pair of them.

Here we are in the middle of July, not even the football season, and fifty youths are fighting in Tenerife. What must the locals think of the British. It wouldn't be so bad but half of these yobs wear Union Jack shorts and trunks. The last thing we want is this lot advertising their nationality. We never flaunted our birthplace when I was young, but then we, and life in general, was more sedate, being British was to be a member of an exclusive club. Not anymore, all you need is alleged refugee status and a little help from the church and bingo – another country member, fees paid for out of the nation's coffers.

In Rushmoor, Yes I agree with you, nobody would know where it was unless they paid rates to it – an authority covering Aldershot and Farnborough – residents in a suburb called Cove have been rightly angered by the Council's plan to build on the only children's playground in the area. A compromise has now been found whereby only ten instead of seventeen houses are to be built and 'over' half the playground can stay. What a magnamimous gesture this is. The houses are needed to ease the plight of the homeless , ie those who are unmarried with hoards of sprogs, no money but all essentials in life, video and disc player. Frankly I'd have preferred the whole area to have been left a playground.

There was a programme, one of those after 6 pm local news programmes, I can't remember which channel, on the other night, and one article dealt with poverty. They interviewed this woman with five children who lived in Croydon. She was either separated or divorced. When asked if the children ever went hungry she replied – No. Asked if she ever went hungry, she hesitated and faltered – Y-Yes. Cynic that I am, I doubted this. To be fair to the interviewer she pointed out that the house

163

contained a TV, I think a video, and a telephone. 'A telephone is a necessity' She stated. No it isn't. The TV had been bought for the kids by her ex. I somehow got the impression that if in all their research this is the best example of poverty they could find, life can't be so bad for the have-nots. Why have five children anyway.

My local paper informs us that Rushmoor Council has managed to 'seal' another twinning. A deal that's taken eight months of negotiations to achieve. The good residents of the area must no doubt be ecstatic.

You'll like this. The following are names of children living in the Aldershot area. I'll only put the christian names to save embarrassment on the estates in which they live. One reason possibly why Farnham has several good eating houses and this area is packed with takeaways the remnants of which fill the streets and gutters. Here we go. Kerrie-Marie, Romilly, Jade, Sonara, Brett, Shelley, Toni-Dee (Nice One), Sadie, Alvin, Lee, Tania, Sunny!, Cora, Curtis, Happy!, Dean, Julene, Faire, Shirley-Jo (How transatlantic). This is besides a whole lot of Kellys, Donnas, Traceys, Darrens, and Zoes. Still the tattoo and earring shops should do well. A neighbour of ours who left the lane last year had her eldest daughter's ears pierced when she was about three years old, and the younger ones done when she was still a baby. Their names were Kelly-Anne and Rozanne, so you can see what I mean.

In a side road locally , there used to be a nice bungalow called Paradise Cottage. The site was bought by a developer who sought and gained planning permission for two semi-detached houses. The first one was sold and within minutes of their arrival a gnome holding a wheelbarrow appeared in the porch. The surrounding houses must have had £10,000 knocked off the value in an instant. Fair enough, the garden and path were tidy but a bloody gnome.

I was discussing with my cousin after squash last night, which the blind dwarf won again by four games to two, the news that Sir Lawrence Olivier's ashes are to be buried in Westminster Abbey. I just wonder if Simon could be right when he says that in his opinion these things gather momentum. Laymen's feeling that a good actor has died are elevated out of all proportion by the media's coverage in both time and tribute into almost royal hysteria. Helped along by a knighthood we now see this honour of burial bequeathed upon him. Yes he was good at his job, but then so are nurses, surgeons, policemen, explorers etc.

Ironic isn't it, seven policemen are injured whilst controlling a march in East London where Bangladeshi immigrants are protesting about the lack of policing, meaning the lack of policing their nationals. Talk about bite the hand that feeds you. The sad side of this tawdry little scene is that it only received a few lines on the inside pages of the nationals. Wasn't long ago that a place on the front page would have been appropriate.

It gets worse doesn't it. Even the Benson and Hedges Cup Final is marred by rival hooligans brawling in front of the main pavilion at Lords. Please come down off the 'societies fault fence', ignore European yobs rights and birch the bastards. For once in your political careers do something popular and enforce justice.

Never having had a great deal of faith in those producing and compiling our TV viewing, any sympathies with the view that those involved listen to the punter have never rubbed off on me. Coronation Street is, I see, to be included in the Friday schedule as well. All this in an effort to win viewers from Wogan. Conceding that in the five years of Wogan, ITV have failed to find an alternative to steal the audience away, you read of a spokesman stating that the introduction of Coronation Street will 'wipe him off the face of the earth'. Just like a take over announcement. They hate competition. You win some, you lose some, not anymore.

On the subject of Wogan, I rarely watch the programme, preferring an interview situation where the interviewee gets a chance to speak and where the audience is courteous and not made to sound like a pub at turning out time. Anyway, Maureen asked me to watch one part last week where the actress who plays Dot Cotton in Eastenders was going to appear. Anyone who comes on to the clapping of the audience holding a half full glass of liquid (presumably alcohol) is suspect in my mind. Anyone who continues to ride

165

roughshod over other guests and pleads for the chance to sing should never be invited back again. Apparently Maureen had seen her being interviewed before and her ego was larger than Tesco's then. What comes over these people. It is pathetic when an actor or actress whose role in a successful soap makes them a household name, then spoils their image by having such a high opinion of themselves. The same could be said for the actress who played Gloria in Coronation Street, I saw her on a charity quiz game last year. Talk about full of her own importance. Bees knees or what. A little bit of success and Hey Presto they're the greatest thing since pop up toast – to themselves anyway. You see people who have survived the circuits for years making films enjoyed by generations, acting their way into the history books and remaining unaffected by it all. I suppose it's to do with breeding.

Well I've just picked Debbie up from school, listened to the news and been gob-smacked to hear that Mr Dodd has been found not-guilty on all eight charges. I don't know whether he was guilty or not, actually I don't care, what annoys me is that the previous weeks testimonies from fellow professionals, tales of courageous deeds in charitable work and the general back slapping that has flavoured the proceedings throughout cannot have done him any harm at all. If he wasn't so famous and such a household name, if the public gallery hadn't been so overcrowded with well wishers and those seeking to get their own fizzoggs on the box, would the jury have come to the same verdict I wonder . . .

With the period for qualification being cut from one year to one term, teachers from the European continent will be seen in ever increasing numbers. Now I can understand teachers coming here, as they have done in small numbers previously from Australia and New Zealand, but how are those from Germany, France, Belgium etc where the standard of living is presumably higher, going to cope with the price of housing, be it purchase or let, when salaries are insufficient to attract home-grown teachers in large areas of our country. I haven't read of any new initiatives for salary increases. I'd like to be a fly on the wall when these teachers have got together after a week or so to discuss their situation. They probably won't have witnessed such arrogance, disorder, lack of respect or so many children of single parent families in one school in their entire working life before, but then we have the do-gooders to thank for that once again.

There was a letter in one of the dailies from a reader extolling the virtues of water meters and defending the inevitable price rises. It makes me suspect that a 'Sir Humphrey' has summoned one of his underlings to write a letter in the cause of public enlightenment using a name and address of a chappie who cannot be traced to any government department. A sort of literary safe house. I can't accept that anyone in his right mind could possibly believe the proposed water situation to be 'fair' and you wonder whether other letters that you've read in times past concerning the defence of this government, Mrs Thatcher herself, fox hunting etc have been the work of the 'grey ones'. Phone calls to sops telling them to look out for their name and address being used and the direction to the posting box where their brown envelope will be awaiting them. This phone call being then followed by another to the Inland Revenue to anonymously announce that you have information of someone earning cash doing a 'spare time' job and not declaring it. They wouldn't worry that the poor cove might 'squeal', if he got heavy he'd probably end up as a 'statistic'. Pure Fantasy? Yes, but it makes you think.

I have read that the Broadcasting Complaints Committee have upheld a complaint from the daughter of Dickie Valentine about a programme on Channel Four called Club X in which the singer is shown as a drunken doll crashing his car. He died nearly twenty years ago. The same programme was recently castigated for a sketch about Eric Morecombe that was apparently as sick and unfunny. Having accepted that what makes one person laugh would leave another po-faced, I find it worrying that there is not only a script writer or writers that find this sort of thing humorous enough to warrant a slot on TV, but there is a production and editorial team that have made it and OK'd it. Another ingredient in the trough of bad taste. Another example of allowing disrespect to become acceptable to the young, let's face it, this programme is not aimed at the middle aged couple

167

with a three-bedroomed semi-detached, well kept garden, B reg Fiesta and 2.2 children is it? Still as long as they can cause suffering to the family of someone held dearly in the hearts of thousands and continue to earn a packet then it's OK – Morons!

I think Tony Jacklin's taken over the mantle from Mr Edwards and that upstart Pamela Bordes as the biggest bore in the newspapers. Not since Anne Diamond was sprog-coughing have I seen so many lines written about scans and scans, and dinner parties where pictures of scans are being bandied about like holiday snaps. Good luck, but it's bloody boring.

I remember a Conservative Minister commenting that where as in the old days (meaning Labour rule) the public looked anxiously and nervously at the prospect of a budget with the annual increase in the price of cigarettes, beer and petrol, they could now relax and look forward to greater financial freedom. Probably so, but it appears we now have privatisation to take its place instead, plus of course the change from rates to poll tax.

I was sad to hear of Harry Worth's death. He was a clever and amiable comic. His bungling escapades had me in stitches as a youngster, and having watched a sliver of film on the one o'clock news, his material was good and still wears well today. Not for him the bad language, innuendos and witless dirge we are subjected to by so many 'alternative' comedians these days. Ah well.

There was an advert in a national daily last Friday placed by the I.F.A.W. (International Fund for Animal Welfare) pleading for funds to stop the South Koreans from hanging dogs and bar-be-cuing them. The picture was heart rending. These dogs are apparently taken on picnics and slowly hanged as this process makes the meat tastier. How can a government, any government, allow such barbarity to continue. Why do our leaders not take action through trade sanctions to pressurise South Korea and all other countries who perpetrate such atrocities. Probably because they would counter that they will not trade with us unless we stop deer hunting (soon to return for another season's fun), badger baiting and

168

fox hunting. Something about living in glass houses springs to mind, doesn't it? and we're supposed to be a civilised country.

On the subject of wildlife it is a pity when a charity closes amid complaints and has to be investigated by the charities commission. It makes everyone think twice about giving, and that can be the difference between life and death for an animal, and one dead is one too many.

Well, Malaysia had stood its ground and hung the Briton, Derek Gregory, imprisoned since 1982 for drug smuggling. Letters of outrage at Malaysia's capital punishment have naturally appeared, but no mention has been made of the suffering caused to those living on a diet of drugs and the harm they have inflicted on others through their own action. One cannot begin to imagine the feelings of Mr Gregory's family, but if it means people are going to think twice about bringing drugs through border controls then perhaps he didn't die in vain. Mind you, it makes you hold up your hands in despair when you learn that the European Court of Human Rights (I think they mean lefts) has ruled that a West German currently in a British jail cannot be sent back to America where he is wanted for murder because he may face 'degrading' years on death row. Poor love. Why oh why do we put up with this continually wimpish attitude from those non-elected faceless souls across the water. Why, because at the end of the day this country is run by gutless leaders who cannot conceive a Britain in charge of its own destiny. We have to belong to a club. We have to be part of a ruling body. The trouble is that we play the part of the masochist in the Madam's parlour. Not for us the thumping on the table, the calls of independence. Our place is at the foot of the table, to look up to Europe as 'Spitting Image' portrayed the likeable Mr Steel looking up to Mr Owen with restrained reverence.

The bad news. It was sad to read that Mr Jacklin's wife, Astrid, has lost the baby, even if the report took up nine-tenths of a page in 'Today'. The good news. Mr Ridley is to go at last, mind you only to another ministry. Still there's not much industry left to ruin. Most of the contractions have preceeded his appointment.

We have sown the seeds of an idea about the house. The nitty-gritty is still to be worked out. Basically, we are going to sell our present home to my parents after all, move into our new house in a few weeks time and buy their home up in London which we will rent out until such time as the market picks up and then sell it. What galled me was the thought of having to accept a knock-down price and someone else making capital later. This is likely to be the one and only chance we ever have of a new house based on our own ideas, so the last thing we want is to have to sell it. This way my parents get to move next to the grandchildren in a house they like, Mum gives up full-time work to enjoy a well earned retirement and our buying their house means we will have greater income to support the horrendous mortgage on the new house.

The builders are cracking on with it. All the pipes feeding radiators etc have been laid, all the walls plastered and we're told that next week the artexers will arrive and the screeding will be laid. Since the scaffolding has been removed, the reclaimed bricks really come into their own. Coupled with the use of red tiles the place looks quite farm-housish.

Apparently the results of a survey concluded that the number of Britains who consider the EEC an advantage has risen to sixty per cent since the last poll and that more people welcome decisions being made in Brussels. Who on earth was asked? I have yet to meet anyone quizzed about Europe. Another survey with 'safe names' being used I wonder?

With Mr Lenny Henry complaining of police behaviour towards coloured people in this country, he is probably doing everybody a favour by opting out of the public eye and joining the 'overseas aid' set.

Here we go again. There is now a booklet available which will 'help' shoppers to familiarise themselves with companies who have connections with anything unsavoury. Now I go along with the 'animal' bit. I personally would love to know which companies experiment on animals so that I could avoid their products. The problem is that like all good intentions, it gets carried away by the radicals delving into areas that are of interest only to those bent on anarchy and personal

170

power. It would be interesting to see how many 'ordinary' shoppers would like to know the names of companies with military links, charitable donations, community service and the inevitable South African connection, let alone change brands because of it! As for anyone not buying a soap powder because the company concerned does not have any women on the board defies belief. Who, besides those mentioned, gives a toss. Let's hope the perpetrators of this latest waste of trees loses a packet.

So Risley Remand Centre is to close. Well done Mr Hurd, another shot in the foot. If those convicted went to prisons with conditions like those considered so inhumane as this particular place perhaps the re-offending percentage would be lower. This comment is all the more appropriate when one considers that we are approaching the end of the month with the greeting that one hundred youths have attacked police whilst they are making a drugs raid in Notting Hill. There really is bitter confrontation at these 'do's' isn't there? The sides are clearly labelled. Police and local residents who have complained about the drug dealing in the area, and the 'National Black Caucus' and the 'Mangrove Community Centre' on the other condemning the police for bothering at all. The only answer is to arrest 'white' citizens in deepest Surrey, perhaps that will allay fears of racism. No. I don't think so either.

Last night I lost again. The blind, syphilitic, dwarf won four games to two – and the wine had run out again by 10 pm. I see that at Luton Airport, delayed passengers will be able to play board games, free of charge. How do holiday makers put up with it. Still it's entertaining reading.

Although we're only half way through the year, the 'Biggest Waste of Time' award has got to go to the dockers. I can't see management being beaten by the end of December.

The Whale and Dolphin Preservation Society is to visit Peru's capital Lima in an attempt to persuade the government to end the killing of Dolphins for the local food markets. The depletion is reckoned to be so severe that they could well become extinct in the area by the end of the century. Wasn't anything about Peru in the shoppers manual

I mentioned earlier, you probably have to look under South Africa.

By the time this is read, the name Donald Kell will be forgotten by most. He's the chap who died 'having a go' against raiders holding up a London bank. John Smith in his column in the 'People' described him as 'old fashioned' adding that it wasn't a bad epitaph. Actually, he hit the nail on the head. If we were a bit more 'old fashioned' in our meeting out of justice, perhaps the perpetrators of those cowardly acts would think twice.

August

Well Glyn's still working at the takeaway. He appears to be enjoying himself. They're all about the same age there, so the social life's not too bad either. Debbie's got herself an application form so with a bit of luck she'll be earning some holiday money. She's very independent and can't wait to have a regular income to buy bits of furniture for her bedroom and extra clothing etc, whereas Glyn finishes on Friday afternoon and cannot be bothered with overtime when it's offered for the weekend. They obviously pay too much.

Business hasn't started off too badly. There's a lot of organising going on re the house and moving, but it's quite exciting really. A bit of light at the end of the tunnel. My mate John who lives near Marlborough has supplied me with another couple of cars. He's bought an Audi from me for a customer who's just starting out on his own and wants a quality used car – and they came to me!

Last week therefore was taken up with a lot of travelling to and from darkest Wiltshire. During one of our round robin journeys, John had to go to his bank in Marlborough, a very pretty, bustling, country town. 'Lot of newcomers moved in' he remarked 'You can tell them from the locals, the Surrey lot are rich, fit and well dressed, the native Marlborough cove is fat, ugly and has no teeth!' Now there's a generalisation if ever I heard one. Just before the infamous Ludgeshall there's an 'area' or village called 'Faberstown'! Not only does it sound pretty unpleasant, but the nameplate announcing ones arrival is in blue with white lettering. It looks very continental, most tasteless.

John had picked me up at Salisbury station. 'You OK' I enquired on entering the car 'Fine' Replied John 'You?' 'Got a bloody awful headache' I said. 'Suppose a fucks out of the question then' He countered. Didn't cure the headache, but it did bring a smile to my face. It was while we were driving north that we encountered legions of cars towing caravans. I uttered annoyance, commenting that I'd have them banned between the hours of 6 am and 10 pm daily including weekends. After a moment's thought I added that actually I was being too generous. There should be a complete ban on caravans. When you think of the fields and views completely spoiled by those too tight fisted to stay in B & B I feel my arguments are completely justified. John said he was going to buy one. 'You're joking' I retorted 'Yes' he said 'A large chrome one which I can hitch to an untaxed limo I've fleeced a hire purchase company for and park it in a layby doing away with the need to pay tax or community charge. I can live off the backs of others and when I move on the Council will move free of charge all the mess I've made' 'Sounds fine to me' I said 'with aims in life like these, you could find yourself settling in very quickly to a life enjoyed by thousands who find the club fees of a responsible society overbearing' I mean, why pay when threatening someone with a smack in the face can save you a fortune.

We were chatting about the old days at Heath and Wiltshire and a story came to mind that had us in stitches all over again. It was 1979 and the Sales Manager had taken on a new salesman. Very enthusiastic but a bit green. Anyway, this salesman sells a new car to a Chinaman who runs a local takeaway. What he doesn't do is to ask to see the customer's log book for the Maxi he's trading in. If the owner of the car that's being part exchanged can't find it or has lost it, you can always ring Swansea D.V.L.C. to verify the date of registration. Now this Maxi was on an R plate. Yes I know it was a Leyland car, but it still had some value. The difference between a 1976 and 1977 model was in the region of £200–£300. Bearing in mind that it was only two or three years old at the time, it was very important to make sure both parties new the position. Come the morning of the changeover and the log book is produced. Said salesman challenges customer pointing out that when they first discussed the sale he was told the Maxi was registered in 1977 not 1976. 'No I tell you 1976' responded the Chinaman. A little perplexed and harassed the salesman showed the new car to our man. 'Where is wadio' he enquires. 'You didn't ask for a radio, they're not standard' 'You tell me I can have wadio'. The long and the short of it is that the salesman agrees to work out a new price for the part exchange and fit a radio which will cost him an extra £50. A time is set for later that day and a conversation with the Sales Manager about the deal ends in the salesman being told how to play the next meeting. The Sales Manager is going to stay in his office next door shuffling paperwork and eavesdropping to make sure everything is sorted out, the last thing he wants to do is de-register a brand new car and lose a sale.

The Chinaman reappears at the appointed time and the salesman runs down the invoice spelling out all the items individually and ending at the bottom line with the cash figure they have agreed on. Silence – the Chinaman then says 'I would like finance'. Poor frustrated salesman exclaimed loudly – 'You cunt' 'Yes I can' Chinaman says softly, but with insistence.'I've had finance with Mercantile Credit before'. Peter, the Sales Manager collapsed clutching the floor safe for support. He was bought many a pint of beer in various pubs for quite a time on the strength of that story.

A wry smile was brought to my face yesterday. No, Maureen didn't agreed to play 'hunt the sausage'. I was in a waiting room twiddling my thumbs (do you know a cure for spots on the willy) when my attention was drawn towards a publication called 'The Sixer Annual' Published in the mid-sixties by Purnell. A quick flick through its pages gave an insight into how society viewed youngsters both in speech and deed in these days not so long past, and yet light years away from current standards of acceptability. Basically it was a cub and scouts annual and some of the drawings were definitely good value. There was an illustration of a cub leader with an arm around a youngster. Nowadays this would be interpreted as a prelude to sexual abuse. Another picture showed an old lady standing outside her picturesque bungalow in her well stocked garden looking on lovingly at the couple of youngsters doing good deeds. The present day scenario would have them casing the joint. The corker was an example of a sixers 'skill'. No, not giving akela a seeing to, but a park where a cub was bending down, facing away from a tree and looking through his legs at it. The caption stated that this was the method practised by tribes in remote areas of the world to estimate the height of a tree. Apparently when you can see the top between your legs, you straighten up and pace back to the tree for the approximation to be made. Can you imagine a youngster trying to practise this today. The second he'd bent down there would be a vicar or child welfare officer with 'those leanings' trying to score a hole in one. I make no apologies for mentioning certain 'trades'. After all, being a motor trader I am expected to clock cars. The fact that I don't doesn't redeem me from these assumptions at all.

Whereas Debbie's taste in music is very much of my own – Chris Rea, Supertramp; Glyn's is definitely of a different ilk. There are LPs and cassettes sprawled around the home. All this hip hop with its scratching and unintelligible dirge. There's no tune, just aggressive diatribe. The covers are no better. Titles like 'Pumping up the Jam', 'Jack to the Sound of the Underground', 'My D.J. (Pump it up Some)', 'Bongo to the Batmobile'. It's like a different world. Apparently it's 'house music' and 'street sounds'. One mixes and scratches. The names of the groups and individuals are no better. I noticed Joe Smooth, Daddy Kane, Black Riot, Wee Papa Girl Rappers, Sugar Bear and Fast Eddie. Here this morning, gone by teatime. Yes I know it's bimbo music, but the tunes penned by Stock Aitken and Waterman are sung by youngsters who look clean and tidy and appear to be enjoying themselves. At least there's a melody. Short term hits they may be, but the lyrics are about love as opposed to the anti-establishment, anarchistic rhetoric that accompanies the sort of clothing and style of the hip-hoppers. Now Glyn's not an aggressive sort at all, but he buys all these baggy trousers and wears trainers with the tongues standing up outside the trouser bottoms. His tops are all right, but he has a medallion with an outline of Africa on it, slung about his neck. Not for him a fifteenth century map of Surrey. The whole ensemble is topped off, so to speak, with a cap the like of which are sported in Inner City areas, sitting on

176

his head with the peak pointing to one side. Ah well, I used to like the Hollies, Billy J Kramer and the Kinks. I can remember my Mum's face when I appeared in a black corduroy 'beatle' suit. She was not impressed.

Having seen some of ITV's celebratory programmes, and compared some of them with today's offerings, I'd be quite happy to watch a re-run of a complete series of 'Public Eye' and 'Van de Valk'. Why do both independent companies and BBC not show their better productions again. Some definitely stand the test of time.

I see that Dad's Army is to be screened again, but what about 'It Aint Half hot Mum', 'Shoestring', 'Callan', 'The Sweeney' etc. There are quite a number I can't think of at the moment, but when I do, rest assured I shall bore you with them. I was just going to write that I had a wry smile, when I realised that I'd had one of those a couple of pages ago, so we'll assume I had a grin, when I read of a Baroness, who, being found not guilty of murdering her ex husband had orchids thrown into the dock. Being ice cool throughout the trial she was asked whether her indifference was callousness. Her reply was that it was due to her breeding. Isn't that lovely. In a lot of lesser countries she would have been found guilty, but I'm sure that these attributes serve positively here. We need a bit more class about the place anyway.

I've just returned from Bracknell. The whole station has been daubed in graffiti. Every wall, poster, nameboard and most panes of glass. One reads of moves afoot in government circles for more parental responsibility in financial terms, but it's no good pontificating over future legislation, it's needed now. Seven year olds are responsible for setting fire to five coaches in sidings at Stormstown nr Aberdare these last few days. What on earth were the parents doing letting them play on railway lines. If they were made to pay for the damage – running into thousands of pounds, they might look after them a bit better.

Is it me? Teachers draw up a list of programmes they consider suitable for children, including Blue Peter, HartBeat and Newsround, various wildlife and classic period pieces considered educationally suitable. I couldn't agree more with their choice. They slate Eastenders with its portrayal of homosexual behaviour as a norm and presumably the awful diction. I also agree, but then they go and spoil the guide by citing Tom and Jerry and Yogi Bear as too violent. I have yet to hear a yob in court blaming his latest attack of an elderly citizen on a diet of Tom and Jerry as a youngster.

Having read a synopsis of the Hillsborough report, it comes as no surprise to note that the police have come in for the greatest criticism. Of course mistakes were made and it comes across strongly that senior officers in charge were the ones who failed at a time when strong leadership was required. Pictures of those castigated have flooded the papers, but the judges comments about yobs spitting and abusing all the services have taken up little space. Sad.

Interesting to read that two members of the great train robbery have been sentenced to jail again. One for seven years the other for ten. When they were sent to prison for the train robbery, the sentence was thirty years. That was in 1964. If the full sentence had been completed, neither would have been out yet. As their latest crime was dealing in drugs, it's a sobering thought to consider that if only one person has become an addict through their involvement, it's one too many, and one case which might not have happened if thirty years imprisonment meant thirty years. Let's not forget the driver, Mr Mills, who never recovered from his battering and died prematurely. Then they make the film 'Buster'. Ah well.

There's a chappie mentioned in today's paper who has reluctantly applied for permission to develop half his farm for a new town. Developers have for years tried to get him to part with his property. Planners have threatened to seize land to make a road. It's not on is it? It's his land. There should be no such thing as a compulsory purchase order. An Englishman's home should be his castle. No-one should force the sale of property for development, road improvement or any other modern day 'necessity'. When you sit back and think, it's a bloody cheek.

It's come to a pretty pass when residents living near to the lido in Aldershot are afraid to go out for the evening because of thugs, male and female, who try to break in for free swims, then they abuse, harass and hit people who make a stand when turned away. Recently they've assaulted pensioners and overturned a police car. The trouble continues, and this is Aldershot remember. Someone had better get a grip of this anarchy before it's too late. Perhaps it is even now. How do you retrain morons when you have so many social workers of the same ilk and judges who hand out 'community sentences'.

Well, here we are, it's the 9th August and the third anniversary of my being taken for the proverbial ride. I received a phone call from the Sales Manager of a large Talbot-Peugeot dealership late in the afternoon. It was a Friday, the 9th August 1986. He said that a car I sold them in June of that year was still listed as being on finance. This surprised and bothered me. He gave me the details, I tried unsuccessfully to contact the finance house concerned and had a very unhappy weekend. Basically what happened was that a motor trader whom I had known and dealt with for a number of years did not pay off the finance on some hire cars that I bought from him, leaving me to pick up the tab. The amount being some twenty thousand pounds. I first became involved with this man, who I will call Pat Connolly, in 1978 when working for Heath and Wiltshire. He ran a small car hire firm in Farnborough and traded cars from his home in Ash Vale. We got to know his wife and children. We never went out socially with them, although if a car was being dropped off at one another's home a cup of tea or coffee was always consumed while a deal was struck. As a family, they were always very close and if Pat and his wife were leaving our place late, she often rang home to check that the kids were in, both son and daughter being teenagers. They were always happy to help and I remember Maureen breaking down and being unable to get hold of me. A phone call to the Connolly's saw them hot footing over as soon as they could. They moved in late '84 early '85 to Alton but Pat continued with the car hire with his son now helping him in Farnborough. Over the years I purchased a fair number of cars including his hire cars when they came up for replacement. He had quite a few contacts in car hire and he mentioned how some of the Spanish hire companies were concerned about the amount of time it took for bodywork to be repaired and that he would get a lot of business if he started a bodyshop over there. This was not a secretive matter and by late 1985 he was enthusing about being able to leave his son in charge of the Farnborough car hire side while he and his wife started up the repair side in Majorca. The daughter by this time had a steady boyfriend and was about to fly from the nest.

During May 1986 we discussed my purchasing the current fleet, some eight vehicles, and a month later he announced that the bodyshop was now available in Majorca, all formalities had been completed with the Spanish authorities and he was now in a position to dispose of the said cars and replace them with newer vehicles so his son wouldn't have any trouble with them mechanically. I had never had any problems with his cheques or his finalising payment of his hire vehicles so I made the age old mistake of trusting someone once too often. I collected or had delivered the eight cars, and I sold them on, five going to my main customer, the previously mentioned Talbot-Peugeot dealer. Three years I had spent building up the business with them. From buying and selling them the odd few cars in 1983 the number of transactions had exceeded 200 a year by 1985, a third of my business.

9 am 11th August 1986 saw me champing the bit at the car hire depot in Farnborough. I had been down there over the weekend but no-one was about. What concerned me was that the business name of the firm had been removed. About 9.30 am on that Monday morning the son arrived. No, his father had not replaced the cars I bought, and he'd closed down the hire company. The son was just doing the odd spray job for people. I told him the situation and went home to contact the finance company and advise my bank. It took the finance company a lot of convincing that there was a problem. 'Mr Connolly always pays and he's asked for a settlement figure on these cars', said the lady at the other end of the phone. 'But has he paid off these eight vehicles?' I enquired. 'No, but I'm sure there's nothing wrong' she added. I commented that his Rolls Royce was now in Majorca, a move that these people knew nothing about. She brought the manager to the phone. They didn't know he was in Spain, they

weren't aware that these vehicles had been sold. They wanted all the details from me. Now we both panicked. I made an early appointment at the bank. My man in the cupboard listened, he asked me about Connolly's bank. I knew his bank's name and branch. My man rang and spoke to the branch manager. He asked various questions and had the phone put down on him. 'That's the first time that's happened to me', he said 'We're usually on the same side.'

I got myself a solicitor, kept in touch with my customers and the finance company. Short of beating it out of him, the son refused to give me his parent's address in Majorca.

Within a couple of days the finance company had issued a winding up order on Talbot-Peugeot and they in turn were suing me. Negotiations with the bank ended in a larger overdraft being extended to me in order to pay off my people. I still lost the business. All of a sudden I was bad news. It took a couple of days before I could tell Maureen. She cried. To date I've never told our kids. A long interview with Farnborough CID and trips to London with solicitors and barristers for advice saw me getting nowhere fast. A chance chat with a friend produced the address in Majorca. It so happened that this friend of mine had a cousin in Palma who worked at a bank and could find out for me. Early in January 1987 I found myself at Heathrow Airport about to board a plane for Palma. After a miserable four months, my business suffering, my wife suffering, the letters, phone calls and visits to the police had produced nothing. Harmonisation of ice cream products, consistencies of marmalade and weights and measures is fine if that's what turns you on, but when you really need the EEC, when it can actually do some good, when the continuity of laws regarding those who have committed a crime would really be appreciated – it can't help me. As the chappie in Farnborough CID said. If we can't get Ronnie Knight out, we've got no chance over twenty odd thousand pounds. The implication being that although it's a fortune to you, it's a pee in the ocean to the Spaniards, who don't appear to give a toss anyway.

I had taken the train on this Saturday afternoon to Woking and boarded the Heathrow shuttle coach, taking an overnight bag and my briefcase full of correspondence – and his address. It's funny you know, but I still felt shell-shocked that a friend could have done this to me. It had been cold and calculated, but very effective. The police had asked me if I knew of anyone else who was owed money. Despite a few rumours from sources I didn't trust, nothing concrete came to light. Apparently it helps your case if there's more than one of you owed money when it comes to extradition.

I kept thinking of all the signs I should have seen, but hindsight's won wars, and looking back it seemed genuine enough. I consoled myself that it wasn't a case of trusting someone I'd met only the day before. I'd seen them with their puppy 'Benjy', shortly before they left. Yes given the same situation, I'd probably be 'done' again.

Once airborne, I stiffened, going over and over in my mind the lines I would use on being greeted. 'Greeted?' Perhaps I'd have the door slammed in my face, perhaps they'd refuse to answer, seeing me approach from an upstairs window. There might be 'friends' around. I'm no Schwartziniger anyway. There might be no-one in . . . A lady sat next to me on the plane. It had been snowing that week in Britain and it was bloody freezing. She commented on the weather as we flew over some mountains and enquired if I was going on holiday. I told her I'd rather be in Merthyr Tydfil given the choice, but I was on business and would be returning home the following afternoon. This made me smile. She asked if I was a 'yuppie'. That's rich. I didn't know they made them thirty-nine years of age and overweight, but I took it as a compliment, well there was nothing else to do. Whilst on the subject of egos, I was once described as resembling Robert Redford. To be fair the girl who said it was a sandwich short of a picnic, but they all count.

The engine of the plane finally stopped, everyone was standing up. The door opened and I felt very alone. Only having hand luggage meant a quick exit and the bus outside said 'town centre' or words to that effect. Finding someone who spoke English, I'd assumed they all did, was not as easy as I first thought. Anyway a good class hotel was pointed out to me and I walked up a couple of streets and checked in for

182

the night. Still not hungry, I changed, picked up my briefcase, went outside and hailed a taxi. The driver seemed to know where I wanted to go. The address being near a casino in Magalluf. We drove slowly as we approached the area. It was about 8 pm, warmer than England, but dark, very dark. These houses all appeared to be the wrong way round. Back doors only it looked like. I paid off the taxi and walked around the corner. House numbers on the wall to my left and car parking spaces to my right. My heart missed a beat (I just spelt missed – mist, what a pratt). There, in one of the parking spaces was Connolly's Rolls Royce. Ironical really. With all the financial problems we were having, my car had to be sold. I was now running a £500 Solara and Maureen a £100 banger. Not that we have ever been into flashy cars, but it doesn't seem much for six years self employment does it?

I checked to make sure I'd got the right place. The houses either side of Connolly's had the numbers by the door, his was missing. I was sweating like a pig. My clenched fist raised in mid air, I paused, then knocked. Footsteps grew louder, female's, the locks were off and Mrs C unlocked the door and stood there open mouthed. 'Hello, Gerry' I said, 'Hello' she replied 'you'd better come in' I felt slightly better. 'Pat' She called 'We've got a visitor' He was sitting in an armchair watching TV. Here we go I thought as I approached the end of the corridor following his wife. This was it. He looked round saw me, muttered a surprised 'Aah' and turned towards the TV again. Although he was looking at it I sensed he was not watching it. I remembered all the sales training courses I'd been on. The emphasis on making your point first, establishing your position, remembering the order of things. I stood there with a million and one things to say. The puppy, now a dog, flew in, and not being too conversant I suppose, with this financial problem, he wagged his tail and greeted me. Weeks of working out my opening gambit should I get across the threshold came out as 'Gosh Benjy, You've grown' What a dickhead. It never happens this way in movies. Gerry offered me some tea and Dundee cake from 'home' and suggested I sat down. She went to the kitchen. I walked over to the TV and stood by it. I felt slightly easier. Much as my instinct told me to smack the hell out of him, a phone call to the police would have had me thrown in prison, not him. At the end of the day I wanted my money, not revenge. 'I've come a long way and I need to speak to you!' I said.

I honestly cannot remember much about the conversation, but two hours went by, a lot of embarrassed excuses were offered and the end result was a promise that he would telephone his solicitors on Monday to ensure my bank were given the deeds of his one remaining asset in England, his house in Alton. I accepted his offer of a lift back to the hotel in the car, at least I saved on the taxi fare. I didn't sleep much that night, coming home the following midday. It was still bloody snowing. Maureen was on tenterhooks to hear some news. In the cold light of day I was still unsure about the outcome.

About a fortnight later a conversation with my solicitor confirmed that some papers had been passed to them, but that Connolly's people were dragging their feet and were making excuses when asked for the nitty-gritty. The 'it's in the post' and the 'We're awaiting instructions' bit was prevalent.

Three months elapsed before I finally abandoned hope that it could be solved amicably. On the advice of a leading barrister at The Temple, London, a charge at the land registry was recorded stopping the sale of his house. His solicitor had commented that when sold, sufficient funds would be available to reimburse me and help out with the interest I'd paid on my extended overdraft. Letters to and from Connolly's bank and only in February 1988 – how slow legal wheels turn – did his bank, through their solicitors write to my people stating that the amount Connolly had borrowed from them was in excess of the sale price of the house. Therefore nothing was going to be gained by my continuing with the charge, and they added that the house had suffered vandalism, and asked me to pay the £600 odd for damage caused. I rang the solicitor. After a year and a half we had finally got an answer from his bank, but not the answer we were looking for. I instructed the solicitor to tell Connolly's people that they could take me to court for the £600 as I had no intention of paying it. Having paid the solicitors and taken all the other expenses into consideration I was now some £25,000 down. I asked my solicitor if they had to prove there was no money left in his house as it all seemed strange that with the value of property increasing all the time and Connolly having tenants in the home for the first year paying £600 per month, that's another £7,200, there was no equity left. The £600 by the way was being paid into his bank in this country, still headed by the bank manager who slammed the phone down on my man all those months ago. My solicitor added that he'd dealt with this major bank for eighteen years and wouldn't trust them as far as he could throw them, adding that it was up to me to prove that they were not telling the truth, but that it would cost me another £4,000 to take them to court. I couldn't afford it and subsequently removed the charge on the property so that it could be sold. The bank never pursued the £600 and I've never heard from that day to this from my solicitors, strange that.

Some months later I heard that a car auction who had also dealt with and trusted him for a number of years had been taken for £30,000 the same week as me. Armed with that news, I contacted Farnborough CID and they are currently seeking extradition on the bastard. If I can't have my money I want him behind bars. Keep you posted.

A club I belong to lets its hall for functions, the income from which greatly helps to maintain the premises in a pleasant manner. Like all things there's a membership of about ninety people and the majority of work done by a few. One of the stalwarts is moving further south and lack of manpower to honour our lettings has meant more people having to join in the running of the bar, something which a lot of people, me included, have managed to escape for a number of years. But if push comes to shove, you've got to do your bit. Anyway the booking for last Saturday was an all day wedding. I was asked to cover between 5 pm and 8 pm. Apparently there was going to be a disco in the evening and more experienced bar staff would be covering from my departure time. When I arrived at 5 pm I could see someone was going to be in for a pleasant evening. It was a council house do. Very few people, eleven in all. Six on one side of the hall, five on the other. I learned that the bride and groom's families had quarrelled at the church and only these few people had turned up so far. There was a lot of food laid out opposite the disco including sandwiches which curled unceremoniously as the evening progressed. The bride looked attractive – second time around I guessed. The groom was half cut, standing unsteadily at the bar announcing the fact that although it wasn't busy now, we'd be rushed off our feet later on. During the period of my stay, one 'customer' I can't imagine anyone having him as a 'guest' – consumed eight vodka and oranges. He was mentally on his way out as I arrived but was apparently still going strong at the end, although by that time he'd wanted to fight all those assembled. The groom was an ignorant cuss whose language became worse by the round, the decibel level rising to match. 'You're gonna be rushed off your fucking feet' he told me whilst looking over my head at the optics, well not actually looking at them but it was obviously the closest we were going to get to eye to eye contact. He actually disappeared to a local working men's club with some other 'people' leaving his new wife altogether. She held up well, as even to the untrained eye 'eleven' doesn't constitute a disco. She got up once or twice and danced with a couple of children, one of whom, a boy, was continually sparring with the groom, when he was there of course, and ended up crying due to the ferocity of some of the slaps. Social workers are never around when you need them are they? One of the local wide boys tried to pull a stunt with a fellow barman by handing over a £5 note and querying the change stating that he'd tendered a £20 note. Guess what. He actually had a corner of a £20 note between his fingers and if we'd like to marry that portion up with the one in the till it would prove him right. One of the oldest tricks in the book. What happens is that an accomplice hands over a £20 note to another barman a couple of rounds previously having taken the corner off first. Then you assume everyone's stupid and will accept that you're right because you're a bruiser, have tattoos and are intimidating by nature. I offered my four pennyworth by saying that if by the end of the evening we were £15 over, we would refund the following day. This of course was not acceptable and the fellow was still winging when I left at 8 pm. A trip to the loo before I went found me up to the ankles in cigarette ends.

Pointing percy at the porcelain produced the same effect. A bowl clogged with butts. This probably explained why there were so many puddles of urine the following morning. As the American's would say, 'What a bunch of assholes' personally I prefer the term arseholes. Well I live in Arsh Vale don't I. With Sandy Gall its 'plarstic' not plastic. If it's good enough for him, it's good enough for me.

The upshot of all this was that indeed more undesirables did appear as the evening wore on and the star performance was reserved for the bride's husband, for whom the term 'groom' would have constituted a breach of the trades description act. He came up to the bar and placed himself between the two bridesmaids whilst they were ordering drinks, then caught them unawares and somewhat embarrassed, by stuffing both hands up their dresses and pulling down their pants. The 'audience's' reaction is not recorded, but knowing their mentality it probably made their evening. The bride, even allowing for her commonness, definitely deserved better. Still some women like the coarser element. Digressing, there's a girl I know who works in a local garage, beautiful body, very acceptable nose, well groomed hair, well dressed, well-spoken. You've got the picture haven't you, everyone would like to hand out a portion as they say. Anyway, she gets a lift with some incomprehensible oik at nights and apparently lives with him. I expect she's secretly waiting for me to ask her out. Look, there's a flying pig.

Now on Friday I worked in the bar again. This time it was a singles club disco. It had not been a 'good' Friday. It was the day after we'd learned from my Father that my parents were not going to proceed with the purchase of our home. To say it was a shock would be an understatement. I won't go into the boring details which is no doubt something you'll be pleased about anyway, but it meant that we'd lost six weeks for finding a buyer and we were only five weeks away from moving into our new place. Within an hour of receiving the call from dad I'd phoned an estate agent and decided to let our current house on a six months let. It wouldn't pay the mortgage, now a hefty £130,000, but it would at least subsidise it. A long chat with the bank would be required, but not until

187

the financial considerations were finally determined. Maureen was very upset and burst into tears. 'We're back where we were six weeks ago' She said. 'I know, I know' I replied cringingly as it was my parents not hers. The estate agent rang on the Friday to say that a couple would like to come and see the house with a view to letting. Unfortunately it was to be that night when I was serving at the club. Our two eldest were going to Majorca with my parents on the Saturday and I'd agreed to buy a car from a local dealer that was taxed and MOT'd and able to travel to Gatwick. Yes it came in, and yes, it was as described, the trouble was no-one could find the keys. Maureen took me up to the club and said she would collect me at 11.30 pm when the disco ended. At least this way I could indulge in the odd bevvy or two, safe in the knowledge that I wasn't driving. Although the disco started at 8 pm, very few people arrived much before 9 pm. As the evening wore on the lights were dimmed and the smoke hung lazily in the air. It was amazing just how many people were smoking. There were, by 10 pm, quite a few couples arriving together joining friends already there and making for a nice atmosphere. Frankly, it could have been a birthday disco. It was sometime after 11 pm when the bar was shut but before the last song (Lady in Red) that I felt it got a bit sleazy. Couples were dancing to slow music, with male hands caressing female posteriors and female hands moving up and down the partner's back and shoulders. It seemed false somehow, as it it were expected. The bonhomie of earlier was gone, play was being made in different quarters for what was presumably the main reason for being there, a bedmate. Some of the women who came by themselves were very presentable and well spoken, some attractive, some less so, but one or two were complete dogs, making their moves towards their quarry after sufficient dutch courage had been raised. Ah well, it all contributed towards club funds.

We've had the kitchen fitted and a very good job has been made. William made us laugh. He announced that as he knew it cost a lot of money and was new he wouldn't kick it. I felt this to be a very magnaminous gesture on his part.

I spotted another couple of house names that intrigued me. One is 'Bonjour' – the occupants obviously went on a day trip to Calais, and the other one, wait for it, is called 'The White House of Happiness'. It's a large house, could be private or could be a rest home. Pretentious or what!

The train derailment at West Ealing by vandals may be remembered by the time anyone reads this, if they read this, but it is an example that is more sensational and newsworthy than many cases of smashed windows and inconvenience. What concerns me is that despite all government rhetoric, nothing substantial is being done to combat this problem, one which is getting worse.

I remember mentioning earlier how close I thought we were to complete anarchy. I don't mean in the 'coup' sense, but one whereby lawlessness cannot be countered effectively. With regard to the railways we have fires being started on trains, signalling equipment being stolen as well as the mindless vandalism that costs lives.

I would like to see a sentencing system for potential deaths. Recently two men in Wakefield were jailed for five and four years for stealing signalling equipment. I believe they were charged with 'endangering the safety of passengers'. To my mind that's not enough. I would have them locked up for twenty years with no remission, no parole and any compensation to be paid out of what they earn breaking rocks. It might just deter somebody else. A video should be produced showing these people working hard instead of watching TV and playing snooker at our expense. We have twelve year olds being given absolute discharges and made to pay £12 costs after ripping up signalling equipment and placing it on the track. Three months detention was meted out to a fourteen year old who caused around £30,000 of damage by placing a manhole cover on the track derailing a high speed train and obstructing another. I'd make the little sod pay back every penny plus compensation, and if it took him the rest of his life, so be it. I'd place ads on a regular basis telling the public how much more he, and others like him had to pay and when they were likely to be free citizens again. A sort of on-going humiliation.

Mind you BR don't help much by leaving so many materials lying around. The days have gone whereby equipment left would remain untouched. In the 'old days' trains were run to recover equipment almost immediately. Nowadays we don't have the locos or wagons available, all so susceptible to the accountant's knife.

Just a quickie. What a dreadful state for our country to be in when thirteen per cent of all children have only one parent, and don't tell me there's no connection between that figure and the rising crime rate among the young.

The good news. A hefty pat on the back for the Nature Conservation Council. It looks at last as if they have successfully reintroduced the Sea Eagle back into Britain as a nesting bird once again. A project that started in 1975 and has seen many ups and downs now looks to be establishing itself with pairs into double figures around the Scottish coasts. Terrific news.

What annoys me about these D.I.Y. shops being open on Sundays is that when they are taken to court and fined, heavily I'm glad to say in some cases, they continue to stay open and flout the law. In most other walks of life a prison sentence would follow in cases of continual law breaking. Now I know that's not really practicable but surely some form of instant closure order could be enforced. If the law is unfair in their view, tough, but fight it through the courts, not by disregarding the laws of the land. What makes Texas, Payless, Homebane and B & Q so special anyway.

I've read of a call from the Atlantic Salmon Trust for the seals to be given contraception. Without delving into the practicalities of such a move, I see it as yet another example of the nibbling away at Mother Nature's balance. We keep on, don't we? Believe you me, the earth will get its own back on the human race, you can only push it so far.

Over the last few months, I've been cutting out articles and letters to the press about the rugby and cricketing parties that are shortly to play in South Africa. Now I'm not a fanatic of rugby, I back Wales to the end on TV but that's as far as it goes. With cricket I have to look and see if Glamorgan have moved out of seventeenth place in the championship league and whether they have progressed the first round in any competition, and being British I feel a certain guilt at not getting excited. I'm afraid I cannot bring myself to work up any enthusiasm, my mind wanders. The adrenalin flows, however, reading comments from former England players or past 'rebels' who decry such tours. So what if they're going there purely for the money. It's been said many times by many people, business booms between Europe and South Africa, why is sport any different? Is it going to help the black population if nobody visits their country to play a sport? I would like to know how there can be so much written about the fact that a small number of sportsmen are playing matches in S.A. It's continuous headlines when players are named and headlines again when two coloured cricketers resign from the proposed tour because of pressure. That's the bit that pigs me off. If someone wants to go, it's their choice, or should be. Turning up at English Cricket grounds to protest and hopefully put a cricketer out of his stride is not only childish, but moronic. I would like to see the boot on the other foot. I wonder how many of these protesters, being offered jobs there for a short time with a good financial incentive, would still say no themselves. Who are they to stop a perfectly legal situation occurring. Let's face it, if the South African Cricket Union had been allowed to put its case to the Cricketing Authorities, opposition to these tours may have been seen in a different light, but to many people, any sympathy with the anti-apartheid brigade goes out of the window when sportsmen are pressurised, blackmailed and threatened. Trying to ban England from the Commonwealth games in Auckland is another arm twist. If those cricketers are performing or plying their trade overseas in any country, it is their choice. It is legal to go to South Africa, so why should labour councillors decide to lobby cricketers during matches. Why should the South African Non-Racial Olympics Committee (SANROC) approach our Prime Minister and ask her to try to stop the cricket tour. We can't win. Even if we do not include in future matches those players who have just signed up, it doesn't end there. The anti-apartheid lot will still be complaining about Gooch and anyone else who represents an official England team abroad. It's the old, old story. If we're talking about a tour of a country where the discrimination was between two white races, no-one would even stir.

Getting back to the International Cricket Conference meeting at Lords, why, when New Zealand and Australia voted in favour of hearing South Africa's case did England lead the vote against. I can see nothing being gained by this act, we'll still be considered racially bias whatever our decision.

Never one to cease being amazed, there's a chap I've just read about who was involved in a fracas outside a restaurant during which he broke a window and squeezed a W.P.C.'s left breast. His sentence was one month jail for smashing the window and four month's for indecent assault. Causing countless thousands of damage by vandalism would be a far lesser sin. This W.P.C. has been in the Police force for five years and commented that she was offended and embarrassed by the incident. If that causes her to feel so shocked she shouldn't be in the force. Perhaps a convent would be more appropriate.

There's a fisherman chappie in Wales who recently caught an Ocean Sun Fish, no I'd never heard of one either. Anyway, it weighed 88lb and took half an hour to reel in. It apparently comes from the Gulf of Mexico which is some six thousand miles away. The picture in the newspaper seemed to convey a feeling of pride about the catch. All that way just to be killed off for a 'bit of sport'. Pity it hadn't pulled him in instead.

You may remember I mentioned that an area called Bramshill has been given the go-ahead by Mr Ridley to be built upon by a consortium of builders, well there is a lot of local support against this move and directions from the Environment Minister, Mr Patton will be eagerly awaited. It was a nice touch, I thought, that my local paper, the Aldershot News ended the story on this topic by using the words of William Blake 'The tree which moves some to tears of joy is, in the eyes of others, merely a green thing which stands in the way'. How apt.

Talking of the countryside, my cousin, Simon, who is on holiday at the moment, and I went for a wander by car around the Whitchurch (Hants), Fordingbridge and Romsey area yesterday, seeking out old railway stations. Out of the sixteen we visited exactly half were inhabited and only one

192

was in a run down condition. Curiously the vast majority of these stations – turned - residences were on lines that closed thirty or so years ago. The closures around the Beeching era are usually associated with complete destruction. It was as if they had to lay waste, as soon as was practicable, the area upon which the stations were built. Luckily, more reasoned (if purely financial) judgements now prevail, and owning a closed station is a revered pastime, almost a quest in some eyes. The effort which has gone into one or two of those encountered yesterday were to be praised. An old ordnance survey map is a must for seeking out some of these sites. The odd one or two nestling in or close to the village from where they got their name, others literally miles from their namesake. The clue to distance is sometimes aided by the addition of 'road' after the place name, but not always. It is however an excellent way of perusing charming English villages and supping bitter in small local hostelries.

On the way back, the radio announcer, when commenting on forthcoming events stated that a certain boys choir from somewhere in Western Europe was on tour and then pro-ceeded to whet the appetite of those interested by playing an excerpt from a classical piece featuring a young boy a very high pitch voice. The mind conjured up the classical scene of a fresh faced boy with brylcreemed hair in red and white gown holding his hymn book aloft. The innocence of it all disappeared when I mentioned to Simon that there would be a lot of perverts jumping with joy having heard the news. Choirmasters and choirboys abroad on holiday, huh. Nudge, nudge, wink, wink.

A few sniggers at the situation developed in a down-ward trend when I suggested locations for 'gay' communities to live. Those that readily sprung to mind were – Pratts Bottom, Anerley, Nether Wallop, with Whipps Cross, and Whippingham (for the sado/masochists) Queen Camel, for those with bestial tendencies and Brown Edge – there's a subtle one. I suppose that if your average poof has a mental problem he'd go to an analyst, if he has a headache he'd only take a remedy that contained analgesic, and if he were a spaceman he'd make for Uranus, well it's better than them

193

making for my anus. It's surprising what fun you can have when you're trapped on the Winchester by-pass.

I never thought the day would dawn when dockers and I had anything in common, but I'm extremely pleased they have the commitment to turn away the dangerous PCB cargoes that head this way from Canada. It's no good those responsible for trade stating that Britain has the expertise for its disposal, that doesn't allay fears, not on any local or national scale. No-one, except those who will financially gain from these deals wants this country to be the dumping ground it is.

Our family, like everyone else's in the country, listened intently to the news that a Thames pleasure boat had sunk and many people had drowned. With the number of disasters this country has suffered this past twelve months one knows the script already. On Breakfast Time, the following morning we had analysts (that word again) trauma experts, council leaders, and solicitors all ready to enhance their reputations, and in many cases egos and bank balances. We've heard it all before, and I've commented on it before. Why do we have such in-depth discussions in the media before the boat has even been recovered and without the necessary investigations able to commence.

One aspect that does hit home is the difference in our river boat quality. If you go on the canals in Amsterdam, or on the Rhine in Germany the boats are modern with good facilities, glass clad bottoms for maximum viewing and clean in appearance. Having seen the disco area of the Marchioness with the free standing seats reminiscent of a Lyon Corner House in the fifties it makes you realise how far we are behind in our river transport. I've seen many pictures of European and American tourist pleasure craft and the standard looks superb. Us? We keep building additions to the structure of the vessels, some of which formed part of the 'little boats' flotilla that sailed to Dunkirk nearly fifty years ago and resemble the worst examples of houseboats. We never seem to be able to get it right, do we?

Well that's August. Not a very good month made worse by the news that George Adamson had been murdered. A man, who with his wife, Joy, has made such an impact on animal welfare and shown the viewing public just what trust and understanding can be achieved between the icing of the jungle and 'mere' human beings.

September

The mobile phones have produced a new breed of pratt, or is it the same pratt showing himself in a new light. Yesterday, as on most Wednesdays, I played squash at Guildford (and yes, they had dry white wine available, but not smokey bacon crisps). Anyway, while we're in the changing room, in comes a chappie with a bag full of clothes from the lockers and takes out his mobile phone which he switches on and continues looking at all the time he's getting changed out of his bermuda shorts, which speak volumes about him. I suppose by looking at it, the thing will start ringing. Glad to say it didn't.

Upstairs to the bar and after what seems like an eternity we were served. Who should sit next to us but our friend with the phone, laid out on the table so that all around can admire his star qualities. To most people, the last thing they would want is to be disturbed while out enjoying themselves. I expect he's waiting for the introduction of the under-water model so that he can show off even more.

We've just been to Aldershot to have a look at a new tumble dryer. While Maureen was asking the assistant in the electricity board shop the technical questions that are an anathema to most males when I spotted a girl about twenty with a baby in the showroom. She was just standing there and an assistant who asked if she could help was informed that she was being looked after. It transpired that the young girl was with an older, white haired man twice her age, and dressed rather gaudily. He was obviously not her father by the way he fondled her bum on the way out. The other hand was clutching the mobile phone which the assistant informed me was switched on and off, tested, extended, held out aloft, shaken and stared at all the time she was describing the actions of various washing machines – but it still didn't ring. These people must be lacking an awful lot to even consider that anyone would be impressed by their activities.

Third time lucky with renting the house. It looks OK. A chap came Monday evening and wanted to rent a place for himself, his sister and her fiance. The sister is apparently a social worker, but I wont hold that against her if she's paying rent, currently taking some children on a holiday to Weymouth. Its ninety-nine per cent certain but they're coming together on Sunday so that she can see for herself. Its fingers crossed till then. We've had this before though, haven't we. All the 'Its just what we're looking for', 'I've always wanted a farmhouse kitchen, with a sink that's not under a window' 'I'll be back on to the Estate Agents in the morning'. We've had it all. Then we've suffered the 'Can you put the wall lights on' 'Can you put the outside lights on' 'Can you close the doors' 'Can you put your head up my arse! Its no different selling a house than selling a car. Everyone wants something for nothing.

On the home front things are not much different. Glyn and Debbie are on holiday in Majorca with my parents for a week, so we've only got William to contend with. The milk and biscuits seem to be going a lot further, the kitchen is generally tidier, there's no butter, jam, sandwich spread or branston left on the table. One of Glyn's most annoying habits despite all the ear bending is to stick his finger through the milk bottle top instead of pulling it off completely. He seems to be gaining confidence at the burger bar where he works, which is good. He still assumes you're expected to know everything without being taught, but is quite pleasantly surprised when he finds he can cope as well as anyone given a bit of tuition. Its all down to confidence, which is definitely enhanced by working with a group of people his own age. Debbie has been earning herself some pocket money for her holiday by working during the school summer break at the same place as Glyn, entailing us picking her up at 11.15pm, which is the close of play. You know, as I sit there in the car park waiting for her to finish, there is constant shouting from a nearby public house. I'm surrounded by the litter thrown out of the cars previously

197

parked while the occupants stuff their fizzoggs in the troughs. Only the odd car is left in the now unlit car park.

When you need the police to be around, there's more chance of discovering rocking horse shit. The screeching of brakes as youngsters zoom in and out of the burger place is continual. Night after night, endless hordes of Mk II Escorts, XR3's (where do they get the money) and Cortinas race around the perimeter of its circuit, spin around the exit bollards and turn left into the main road. No stopping at the junction, no looking left and right, no bloody concern for anyone else at all. And where are the police? Who knows. I rang Farnborough CID the other day to see if there was any news about Conolly's extradition order. 'Sorry, there's no reply from CID' Said the switchboard chappie 'Can you ring back'. Lucky its not an emergency I thought.

Here we go again, that dreadful commission for racial equality lot are still at it. As you've probably gathered by now, my sympathies with any religious order are somewhat slight but if an employer wishes to advertise for christians only, why shouldn't he. If I was looking for a job in the paper and came across his ad. I'd consider that this particular position was outside my sphere as an atheist, but I wouldn't whinge on and on, or complain. If that's what the man wants, fair enough. Its that bloody neurosis again.

I'm not blind to the fact that charities, when successful, become big business, but I have reservations when I read the go ahead has been given to advertise on TV. Apparently with an increase in the number of organisations wishing to advertise at peak periods the cost could be over a quarter of a million pounds per minute. I wonder if the income generated will ever cover these costs which are horrendous. My other concern is that big business will support well known charities on the box. Once charities start colluding with household name companies, their independence must be called into question. There have been several derogatory comments concerning supermarket chains with 'green' labels extolling their concern about the environment on the one hand, while happily building out of town stores in green fields, on the other. Is it me being cynical, or am I right to think that the day is not far off when a large food retailer 'does a deal' to back a particular charity if it doesn't highlight some aspect that would jeopordise their public image as a caring company.

Oh the way of commerce is a mucky one.

Well our fans in Sweden lived up to their unenviable reputations once again. Having seen the pictures in the papers and the films on the TV news it makes you want to throw up. Why did the Swedes release them without charge to run amok once again I fail to understand. The Swedish authorities appear to have caved in completely by letting ticketless louts in the stadium. Mind you, it brings a smile to your face hearing our 'outrage' at the Swedes soft option by our own dignitories when they have been so 'successful' in combating this violence in British football grounds. We're still going to issue passports to these people though. Why wash our dirty linen abroad? Lets make these bastards pay with sweat and tears. If we don't, the shaking of heads and holding up of arms in despair will continue year in year out.

Its very true that beauty is in the eye of the beholder. Some photographs of the winning entry in the 'Crown Country Home of the Year' contest have just been published in 'Today'. Yes, it was a 'box' and yes, it's now palatial but extremely tasteless. The 'box' picture shows an oversized up-market council abode. The refurbished finished article encompasses everything that is associated with the mafia. You can tell the differences between the Italian influence and the English fraudsters in Spain by the interior. Its full of statues and columns, objets d'art and expensive drapes. It really is awful. The outside has pillars and beams around which ivy and creepers ascend relentlessly and a balcony complete with wrought iron pailing (they could be plastic I suppose). The interior photo shows the happy couple sitting contentedly on their settee. If this was the winning entry out of some three hundred other hopefuls I shudder to think what some must have been like. Then again, maybe its the judges who have no taste. Talk about O.T.T. Still as long as they're happy.

Handed over another £20,000 to the builders this morning. Just £10,000 left to pay, plus a yet to be determined amount for some extras, namely, portholes in the garage wall ends, extra tiling, and patio. It all mounts up, plus of course some of the furniture we would have been taking has now either got to stay or be replaced. You can't let your house as furnished if it's not, can you. Across the road in the new place they are certainly cracking on. It looks as if we're going to move in when we return from our weeks holiday. I don't know whether I've mentioned that we're going to Southern Ireland, if I have, tough. Not very convenient, but if all goes well with these latest punters and they do signal the go ahead, we'll be coming home from our hols on Saturday the 30th , moving across the road on Sunday the 1st October and they will move into our old place on Monday. Couldn't be worse timing but then if we'd picked August or November, no doubt something would have cropped up then to demolish our orderly and planned move. All the doors are on, the painter's in and staining the woodwork, the outside is being tidied up and the patio and front paths are being built. The brickies have made a good job of the garden wall so its coming together nicely now. Its just the continual financial climate that worries me. I shall see the Bank Manager before we go away and brief him, but I don't want to do this until I'm sure of renting the place out. At least that will be some money coming in to off-set the horrendous mortgage and bridging loan.

On reflection, I think I did mention the holiday, because I remember pointing out that the couple we are going with are the same ones we spent four days with in Yorkshire last year. Definitely looking forward to a break, I've been warned not to mention the 'troubles', 'catholism', the IRA or British Rule, and I'm still expected to enjoy myself!

I'm still not at all happy about ITV having sponsored progrmmes and weather forecasts. I see that the newly created faceless wonder. Powergen, is to sponsor the weather. It is of some concern that its Chief Executive, a certain E. Wallis, comments that having paid two million pounds for this priviledge (at our expense) they expect to have some influence on the forecasts. Mark my words, time will prove just how dreadful this government's been in creating a society so money conscious that greed is to be expected as the norm. It's the same with takeovers. No-one can stand the competition. It's all a questiuon of how much is required to buy out another company. Household names are with us in many cases because that's what they are. Its only when you look at the small print you discover that the beloved name revered by generations is owned by a conglomerate, and you have naively assumed it has remained independant.

The takeovers in the brewing industry are some of the most appalling. I have absolutely no time at all for the big wigs in the licenced bandit trade. I and many others have listened to the hollow justifications for increases in beer prices by the pompous and arrogant directors and executives who have appeared on newsrounds dismissing another four penny rise as essential to their continued striving for 'bar excellance'. I particularly enjoy the way they almost cry in their beer when announcing their latest rip off. Next week the half yearly figures are disclosed and once again record profits will have been achieved, a swap of pubs for hotels with another group is completed and the merry go round continues.

I was sad to see Ruddles come under Watneys clutches. Being part of 'Grand Met Brewing' has about as much face as a traffic warden. Years ago a company was a company. It's no good big business boasting their latest aquisition as 'necessary to maintain their standing in the market place; it isn't right. Every time an aquisition is made, despite all the promises, a brewery closes. The big guns have made more inroads in the brewing industry than poachers have with elephants in the African National Parks.

It's all such a farce as well isn't it. In the days of some honesty, Friary Meux beer was brewed in Guildford using local water. Allied Breweries, having realised that the name Ind Coope was no longer a show stopper decided to break up the South East a bit by re-introducing names associated with the geographical areas. Benskins for the home counties, North, (sounds like Come Dancing), Taylor Walker for London and Friary Meux for the Surrey Area. All the beers are brewed in Romford. You see an ABC house (Aylesbury Brewery Company) and supp a pint of their ale. No, you're not in a time warp, its just the name. ABC has not been a brewery for over fifty years. The beer is brewed in Burton.

Now these are just a couple of examples from the Allied Breweries story, the same is true of Watneys, Whitbread, Courage, Scottish and Newcastle and Bass. Its seems such a shame that Shepherd Neame are the sole remaining brewer in Kent, with all due respect to a few home breweries that have sprung up.

Reference to the Monopolies and Mergers people only seem to prolong the agony. Its a bit like planning applications by a major builder, if you've got the financial muscle or are a regular contributor to the Tory coffers there shouldn't be too much of a problem.

I see our ablility to be all things to all persons, thats the equality version, is being severly tested once again. It makes my blood boil to read that the Chairman of the Springfield School Parents Action Group (doesn't he sound important) has demanded that a teacher with twenty-two years experience be stopped from taking a 'Home Liaison' teachers post because she doesn't speak Urdu or Punjabi. These people should consider themselves lucky that such a post be created at the taxpayers expense. I know it sounds arrogant but it isn't every country that goes to such lengths to accommodate the wishes of immigrants. I wouldn't mind if they made an effort to integrate into our way of life. If the roles were reversed the commission for racial equality would have a field day. I do hope the relevant authorities resist such pressure from the 'action' groups. If it were up to me I'd tell them that the post was being withdrawn on economic grounds. Christ, they've cut everything else, but then we're not talking about a native white school are we.

Names and initials introducing some new profit making scheme continue their advance into agricultural technology. The latest is BST, no not British Summer Time, but a genetically engineered drug that is injected into cows in an effort to increase profit, sorry yield. It appears that the government has secretly been testing cows and now looks certain to approve its use in commercial production. One ray of hope is that all the big food chains, aware of increasing pressure re natural produce are likely to oppose its introduction and not sell it anyway. When will the powers that be wake up to the fact that unknown additives are not what is required by the consumer.

Drugs used to boost milk yields by up to twenty per cent are unnatural and dangerous. The crack is that while American stores are refusing to sell the milk, two of its major companies are seeking licences to sell the stuff in Britain. Providing the licence fee covers the admin costs I'm sure our wondrous leaders will oblige.

I'm very much a pro-royalist, but I can find little to endear me to the Duchess of York. For me, things didn't start off on a good footing by her being labelled Fergie and appearing not to mind it. Much as I feel it shows a lack of respect by the press its seems to suit her. I'ver never admired her apparant lack of concern, re her child, her penchant for holidays and latterly her involvement with childrens books that will be sold primarily because of who she is. Then of course we have the PR experts who appear on the scene to modify her image. What a dreadful way to exist, its so bloody plastic. Just as I'm writing this, shes announced her latest pregnancy. The PR chappies will have their work cut out fostering the 'golden Mum' aspect now I suppose.

Thursday 14th September has not started off with the best of. When one reads that seventy-nine beagles destined to become laboratory experiments have died in transit on their journey by ferry across to Sweden it hits home just how awful this world is. There is absolutely no difference between the train carrying Jews to destinations in Poland and this latest sickening experience. Its obviously going on all the time, but you only hear about it when something goes wrong.

The fact that we allow kennels, in this case Perrycroft Farm Kennels near Malvern in Worcestershire to continue this sickening trade is beyond all reason.

There is no justification whatsoever, even for heart or cancer research for causing pain to an animal. Nobody has the right to injure and ultimately kill an animal in this way. The perpetrators, be they the kennel owners who breed the animals or the so-called scientists who experiment on them are no different from Nazi interrogators and doctors. Its just that there is no war.

The final heart-rending footnote is coming to terms with the fact that beagles are used because thay are so placid.

On a lighter note its strange how people react to adverts. Playtex launched a new campaign a couple of months ago. One advert showed a judge looking startled as two nubile young ladies stood seductively in front of him wearing, in one case, bra and pants, and in the other, a one piece contraption. Both had gowns, wigs and glasses. A number, of women, I know not how many, including one barrister objected strongly to this and complained to the Advertising Standards Authority and won their case. What happened about the thousands of women who must have seen the ad and took no notice of the so called 'feminist' angle at all. This barrister woman, when interviewed, stated that she didn't want people to think that the law did not have a sense of humour but considered this ad beyond the pale. I'm convinced there is a deficiency in these people.

I genuinely hope my going on about animals is not boring. I know its been said before, and far more eloquently put, but I do mean what I say. I feel extremely depressed about what we are doing to animals. No I'm not going to become a vegetarian either, and whilst I risk the calls of hypocrisy, if the cows, pigs or sheep are allowed a reasonable life I can see no reason to stop eating meat, besides nuts and soya beans are fairly limiting in their appeal.

Its that Bloody EEC again. All the harmonisation between these member states still doesn't seem to concern itself with stopping atrocities. How can Spanish beach photographers be allowed to continue using birds and monkeys in the way they do. Drugged and toothless, British animal sanctuaries are bringing the poor creatures to these shores in the hope of restoring some of their dignity and providing them with a happier life.

Mind you, good always seems to be chasing evil. Now that the poachers have virtually wiped out the elephant, the evil bastards are turning their attentions to Alaska where walrus tusks are being extracted instead. Nothing is sacred. It smacks of the old wild west. Bribe the local eskimo with drugs and clothes and walk away with fat profit and leave behind another statistic.

I'd like to see these poachers, the experimentors and the people who provide animals for experiments injected with the 'aids' virus. Shooting them is too quick and painless. Let them have a taste of agony for a change. They sure as hell haven't cared for their fellow creatures.

Well feelings are still running high over the proposed development at Foxley Wood near Eversley in North East Hampshire. The deadline is close for receiving objections and public meetings have been supported by many local and national groups. Even Julian Critchley, the local MP, says its nearly twenty years since he received so many letters on one subject.

It would appear that local Tory big wigs are, for once, aware of the damage development will do to their standing at the polls, so perhaps there is yet hope of a U turn by Mr Patton.

These twinning committee 'persons' are an obnoxious lot, aren't they. Our local paper has a comments column in keeping with most newspapers but the views of their chappie, one John Kaye, are rarely different from my own. He cannot understand this desire to 'twin' with some 'polyunpronounceable' any more than I can and recently commented to that effect. The letters column this week holds one from a Mr Terry Davies, none other than Chairman of Rushmoor Borough Council's Management Committee (There's posh isn't it)

His letter includes comments that 'invaluable links' will be forged with businessmen, sportsmen, and students because of this twinning and justifies this complete waste of time by adding that those going on these foreign trips pay all or most of their expenses themselves. You'll like this bit, its a hoot. He goes on to say that 'the twinning budget is set aside to maximise the benefits to be gained by our residents and these benefits will be felt for years to come', he doesn't say how. Mind you, anyone who starts their letter exclaiming that they are, quote 'absolutely horrified to read the asinine comments' about their waste of ratepayers money has got to be treated with suspicion and not a little sympathy.

205

Just had a butchers through the property section of the 'News'. It only makes you more depressed when reading the prices (how they've fallen) but there are one or two items worthy of comment.

One that holds pride of place is a Spanish style property called 'La Cuesta' in Camberley on sale at £325,000. The comments include mention that it was designed and built for the present owners and that the Spanish influence has been reflected in most rooms – how unfortunate, I just hope that they're selling because they're emigrating to Majorca or somewhere else of that ilk.

What I like are the descriptions used by building development concerns to sell their wares. Its not the houses quite honestly, I think the standard of finish and imagination is far higher than a few years ago. The comeback in chimneys, the use of flintstone, traditional tiling and hipped roofs all add to the quality of a house. No its the names used for the development and the subtle 'green' touches that are added.

For instance 'Badgers Copse' in Camberley. I doubt if there are any badgers left, come to that any copse either, but it sounds rural. There is a large development in Fleet at a place called Ancell's Farm. This is a particularly sad case as I knew it when it was lush arable fields and ramshackled out buildings. Now its another boring mini town with no heart, just the name as a legacy. Another building company has thoughtfully provided a small map of their development near Basingstoke. If you didn't know the area it would appear that the village of Basing is the same size as Basingstoke. It has grown considerably, but not that much, little circles with dots denote trees which cover just about everywhere except the town centre. Twelve roundabouts are shown and a little arrow pointing to the site near the end of a cul de sac. The whole scene is one of rural tranquility, so far removed from the truth.

There is an Estate Agents offering a house 'close to farm-land', for how long I wonder.

Charles Church offers houses in small 'beautiful villages' and provides a picture of a boat, moored in delightful surroundings with not a house in sight. Perhaps this is the location for their next battle with the authorities. Here's another good one. Higgs and Hill are extolling the virtues of their development in Frimley. Amongst the attractions are 'beautiful countryside, wooded surroundings, picnic spots and woodland walks'. They're not lying, but its a bit like the Brazilian forests. They are there its just that there are fewer of them by the day. In our case its because *some bastard keeps building on them.*

Talking of bastards, glad that I am to hear that he took his life, a convicted rapist and armed robber killed a police inspector first and left another policeman injured. Back came the calls for hanging. The trouble is that two days later everything appears to be history. Mrs Thatcher once again called for the death penalty to be reinstated, but only for the murder of a policeman. I agree, but as so many people have commented on in the past, why make any difference between the police and a grocer or pensioner. The police should not be treated as more worthy when it comes to a sentence being metred out.

Having read this mans record, there isn't any reason at all why he should ever have been released. Everytime he's come out he's reoffended within a short space of time. Still this will be tomorrow's chip paper and there will be another to worry about in a week or so, except for the grieving relatives and friends who will still be asking 'why' in years to come.

Another example of what I said about the brewing industry, this time though its confectionery. Having absorbed Bassetts earlier this year, Cadburys have now bought out Trebor.

Back to the beagles. The sad eyes in the picture published in 'Today' will haunt me for a long time. One picture shows a Swede described ironically as a 'Chief Vet'. That's a joke. Tell me honestly the difference between him and a Nazi. I really do wish them every ill in life.

I see that Harry Worth left just over half a million pounds to his wife and that he was five months old when his father was killed in a pit accident. The youngest of eleven children, times must have been very hard. How did they manage without trauma experts and solicitors. With pride and dignity I'd imagine.

I see that Linford Christie is asking for an enquiry into Police victimisation of black athletes. Why not, they've had inquiries into everything else. Just amazed its taken so long for someone to demand one.

Only a few more days before we go on our hols. Not only are we looking forward to the break, but it will be a rest (hopefully) for Maureen, who's been living on a knife edge for the last few months. We can at least leave our financial worries behind us for a week before the move begins. Maureen's Mum and Dad are coming to look after the kids. The 'Gang of Three' sent from the Estate Agents have been and gone, confirming their intention to rent and I've seen the man in the cupboard. He appears happy about the house, considering it well built and good value. Mind, he is a bit more concerned about my ability to pay for it. The recent interest and mortgage rate rises are just stifling business. Every facet of life seems to be suffering, but the 'grey ones' carry on regardless. And what options are there.

Dr Owen seems to be as far removed from political clout as Ben Elton is from visual acceptability. Paddy's lot are unfortunately no further up the credibility scale despite being 'nice people'. Only the greens seem fresh (excuse the pun). At least its not the same boring rhetoric. To me the main let down is seeing discredited lefties in the form of Peter Tatchell riding on the backs of conferences. Doesn't inspire at all.

Hot on the heals of Rushmoor twinning with some German town, the good bergers are aiming to twin with a Tunisian town as well. Besides disease, what else will be offered. The funny thing (well, it would be funny if it didn't cost so much) is that these twinning committee persons seem to think its a good idea.

Here's a few more names for the kiddies birthday list published weekly. There's a Cheri, Ricardo, Reka, Kerina, Marsha, Leila, Jake and a Lara

One bad year and the predators are out in force, After Leyland (sorry, Rover Cars) marriage to Honda, every car they produce is a bastard, our last bastion of independence, in the shape of Jaguar, now looks like going the same way.

So Stockport is to be blessed with a glass pyramid monstrosity that owes more to Star Wars than Lancashire Hot Pot. Inevitably the seal of approval has been given by that loathsome oik, Max Hutchinson the president of the Royal Institute of British Architects, whose photograph appears beside the monstrosity. Didn't know what he looked like until today, but I don't think I'd have liked him anywhere. He looks smug and self assured. Still, better Stockport than Farnham.

I was surprised and saddened to learn of actor Philip Sayers death. I enjoyed immensely his roles in Bluebell and Floodtide. He was a first rate actor.

Well the Ryder Cup is with us again. I can't stand Golf, finding it extremely boring. Actually, its probably not so much the game as the people. Having read the fees at the 'top' clubs I wonder if it's actually a game or a 'one upmanship' league. Perhaps I'm naive for even asking.

It's been fair pandemonium here, the dishwasher's decided to leak, the aerial company are coming while we're away and I've been scouring the pages of the local paper trying to locate someone who hasn't sold a bed by the time the prints dry. If we had a bed for sale of course, nobody would want one, but when I'm looking, they're rarer than hens' teeth.

About six hours has elapsed since the last paragraph and I've been down to the local Fiat dealer and bought some cars to be sold while I'm away. A nice mixture really, there's a C plated Fiat Uno, a Panda on a 'B', a Fiorino Van which is cheap, a four door Cavalier and a Granada 2 Litre which I'm selling to a garage in the West Country. I'm taking that down tomorrow (Friday) which will take up a good portion of the day.

I've also been over to Reading to pick up a cheque and on the way back I passed a closed grocers that's selling beds and tables etc. They had four good matching chairs and a double bed with mattress that will be ideal for the people renting our present place. The shop where I got the furniture from was a sad affair. A typical village grocers, now dingy and tawdry, but still with counters and weighing scales surrounding the tables, chairs and coffee tables from the fifties, seeking loving homes. A nice wooden cased clock still humg above the serving area.

I suspect it might have been a sub post office at some stage in its life. Shelves ready to carry tins and packets clung hopefully to the walls. The glass fronted counters that would have teased kiddies with their cakes and savouries for generations were deserted of any life save a creepie-crawlie and a fly. Another notch on the scoreboard for Sainsburys and Company.

The hope is now that we can sell some cars whilst we're away. The month started off fairly well but has sunk without trace this last week. Mind you, there's so much running about buying bits and pieces, finalising details with the builders and organising the kids for the arrival of Maureen's Mum and Dad. This of course is not including preparing the kids for a week with said grandparents, who will probably insist on half cups of drink before bedtime in case they wet themselves. I just hope William behaves himself. He's been a right little towrag this week. In Aldershot, a couple of days ago he started to play up because Maureen wouldn't buy him anything. 'You can't have things everyday, you know!' Maureen said 'Well, Debbie's getting things isn't she' He retorted. 'Yes' added Maureen 'but she does actually need a skirt for school. Anyway its nothing to do with you. You get clothes when you need them. This time its Deborah's turn' Never one to harbour a sulk for less than an hour he dived off to be found between the dummies in the window of M & S standing like a spastic with his arms and legs all akimbo staring into space and drawing an audience.

Yesterday we thought we'd keep him quiet with a video. He reckoned on coming straight home with it. Maureen had other ideas. Last minute thoughts required last minute purchases. Off from the video shop on Ash Hill and into Aldershot to the Wellington Centre. 'When am I going to be able to play my video' He kept whinging 'When we get home' was the irritated reply. 'When's that' He asked 'In ten minutes' Even more irritated. Some few minutes later he burst out 'Well ten minutes has gone. Where am I supposed to play it Smiths?, Boots?, On the floor here?, Where?, Where's the video huh huh?' He keeps on and on. He's going to be as boring as me when he gets older.

Its Saturday 23rd. A couple of lines before our hols. Maureen's Mum and Dad are here. They've been given cheques to pay for the dishwasher repair, the aerial man and a couple spare in case of emergency. William has been warned to behave, but I think it's a lost cause. Deborah we know will help out and Glyn will just be out. But then he's now eighteen and he's a free agent – well relatively.

I delivered the Granada to Yeovil yesterday and collected a cheque, so that will help the overdraft's overdraft.

I've received my second briefing about what I can say and what I can't from Maureen. She said its not funny to ask for a mirror and pole when renting the car at Cork airport. No sense of humour, some people. I've washed my hair and changed my pants so its off to Ireland and see you in a week.

Hasn't it been a short week! We're back. Mum and Dad have been driven silly by William. The GPO (Sorry BT) have cut us off two days early, not all the carpet's been laid, there's no lino in the kitchen and Charlton have lost to Nottingham Forest.

Just for a change I'll do the holiday bit on a daily basis.

Saturday 23rd

Arrived London Airport (Heathrow), checked in. For every boarding pass she handed out several were thrown away. We partook of a cup of tea in some pokey little corner of the departure area and watched the antics of a couple in their twenties (who should have known better) holding hands. The only time they stopped stroking each other was when she brought his hand to her face and kissed it. Yuk.

Having queued for the security screening – it was the day after the bombing at Deal – we collected our hand luggage and boarded the plane.

When I went through the electronic screening arch I spied an attractive woman screening female passengers. I raised my hands and spread my legs, but she ignored me and a uniformed male frisked me instead, not before I'd closed my legs though. Call me old-fashioned, but if you've got to be bored stiff with all the security there should be some compensation at the end of it. I could imagine a female searching me and asking me 'What's that' and me being able to reply ' Oh its all right its only my willy'.

The couple we went with both smoke so we split up on the plane. We had two seats over the wing by the exit door. In front of us were three Irish chaps. The seats were three per side. The plane was a Boeing 737 belonging to Aer Lingus. One of the chaps in front kept looking at his ticket then looking at the seats. A friend on seeing his worried frown said, on examining his ticket, 'You're in the middle' He replied 'It said centre' It had to be an Irish plane. Who else on landing would give the times of the buses and advertise boarding houses and hotels. Having given out all this amusing information, the stewardesses announced that we could alight when – quote 'The coast was clear'.

Having alighted, we made our way through customs and into the lounge to find our car hire company. 'Who are we with Tony' I asked 'Is it Hertz?' 'No' 'Is it Avis?' 'No' 'Is it Godfrey Davis?' 'No' 'Swan?' 'No' 'Budget?' 'No' 'Well who is it?' 'Johnson and Perritt' He replied. I'd never heard of the company either. Their young lady was pleasant and courteous. 'You've reserved a Ford Sierra' She asked 'Yes' replied Tony 'Well we've got you a Toyota Carina' She countered! We were asked about our employment 'I.T. Director' Said Tony 'I'll put down businessman' She replied (The I.T. stood for Information Technology. Impressive huh!) I don't go on holiday with rubbish you know. My details were required as I was co-driver.

We received our wallet of gumpf and set out to the long term car park to start our journey into the unknown. The map was extracted from said wallet and the route followed to our destination, a small coastal village some fifty minutes away. Having stopped for some provisions (Branston being top of my list – sold under the Chef banner there – strange) we continued to the holiday cottages. The office was closed but a notice on the door directed us to the second of the two sites. Ours being up a steep hill with magnificient views over the estuary, causeway and most of the village. The aforementioned 'notice' to late guests had the number of the chalet against ones name and a footnote added the managers name and telephone number. If however, he was not there, you were to ask in the village as everybody would know where he was! Great huh!

Having settled in and unpacked, we travelled west for a couple of miles and enjoyed a very good meal. Food was obviously expensive, as was petrol at the thick end of three pounds a gallon.

We returned to the village and having parked the car walked down the hill to the local hotel. Maureen and Valerie were the only two females in the place and after a small contra-tont with a drunk who kept grabbing my leg and bringing one of his own up around his head for a party trick we moved to some fellows from Cork who were out celebrating something and, accompanied by a chap called Timmy, who played the accordian sang continually all night. Beautiful voices they had too. Everyone had a turn, some more than others. There was much ssshhhing and fingers to mouths when a fellow singer was about to commence, and woe betide anyone who interrupted. Prior to his commencement with any song, Timmy would demand emphatically 'Simmer down now, simmer down'. Having observed that everyone was ready he would start the intro. One or two of the songs were singalongs but the majority were native self pitying dirges that belied their general well being. They know how to extract emotion throughout every bar.

One fellow, well into his late sixties or early seventies was asleep for most of this. Surprising really as he was within six feet of the accordianist. Occasionally, and to everyones annoyance as he sat slumped in his chair with his head thrown back, his eyes would open and he would start saying 'Someone up there loves me' To which there would be a lot of sshhhing. To no avail, he was gone. At one time he burst into 'Are you lonesome tonight' but was again silenced by his own nodding off after the first bar. During the whole of this period, he balanced, precariously, a glass four fifths full of guinness on his stomach at a fairly acute angle but without spilling a drop. The generosity and homeliness of the pub and its occupants matched the warmth and cosiness of its peat burning fire that greeted us on our arrival that night. A walk back up the hill to our chalet (villa in the brochure) was followed by coffee and a good nights sleep.

Sunday 24th

A friendly relaxed start to the day saw us make our way around the coast road to Bantry taking in the lovely town of

Skibbereen where they park in single file on one side of the road and are triple parked on the other. Nobody seemed to care. You have to adjust to the pace of life, summed up in the time spent waiting for the first car to proceed after the changing of the lights from red to green. We estimated that at least ten seconds elapsed before movement was made. Mind, you had to compensate for the fact that traffic coming across the lights continue for the same period of time after the change from green to red.

We turned off along the penninsula towards Dursey Head taking in most of the available harbours and jetties that came our way. Locals taking a single cow for an early morning constitutional were fairly commonplace and the signposts added to the interest.

The Irish appear to have become 'good Europeans' and obviously wish to be seen to be towing the harmony line. Our tourist map stated that all old black and white signs would show distances in miles while the new green and white signs would give kilometres. Fine, except that some of the black and white ones have been repainted showing kilometres as well. I didn't take too kindly to the number of B & B's displaying '200 metres ahead' on their signs. If I had been on a touring holiday I would have given those short shrift. Yards were seen, but not commonly.

It actually mattered not whether measurements were in miles or kilometres as neither had much relationship with that shown on the car, whose judgement, despite being Japanese, I would have preferred to trust.

The weather was wonderful, the scenery absolutely indescribable, one couldn't possibly convey the depth of beauty. I never saw a postcard that did it justice. A very happy day was had by all as we 'discovered' little coves and inlets, free from Tonibells, gift shops, silly hats and loud radios.

An excellent meal at a family run restaurant on the way back and a few quaffs at one of the local hostelries in the village found us replete and more than ready for a good nights kip.

Monday 25th

Went to Cork. Highlight of the day for me was on the main road where there is a 'Y' junction. Left to the town centre and right to the harbour (for the ferries) and also airport. Fairly important junction I would have thought, but the signs pointing right to the harbour and airport, which are separate and above each other on the post have inbetween them another sign giving directions to a B & B, lovely touch.

Cork as a town was attractive, clean, with very little graffiti and full of schoolkids wearing proper school uniforms. Very smart they were. I fact, that was one aspect repeated all over the area we travelled. They were very polite and well turned out, a bit like England in better days.

Talking of old days, do you remember that fine word 'yield' being used at main road junctions. We've replaced it with STOP, whilst saying what it means it does not convey the same warmth. Well here 'yield' is seen everywhere. Strange bedfellow for kilometres and metres I thought.

Tuesday 26th

Early start was made and an extremely pleasant ride to Dingle was enjoyed by all of us. We stopped for coffee in Killarney and arrived in Dingle at about twelve (midday). We found a pleasant craft shop cum restaurant and enquired about the possibilities of bacon, sausage and eggs – there being no mention of it on the menu.

'If you go down to the supermarket in the town and buy some bacon and sausages, I'll cook them' said the lady behind the counter 'And you get me some scones while you're there' she added. A fine breakfast was had and we went in search of the Dingle dolphin. We were not disappointed having sat down for no more than quarter of an hour we witnessed this beautiful creature performing for a passing boat no less than twelve times.

The dolphin has been in the bay since 1984 and is enjoying his well earned notoriety as a tourist attraction. The great thing is that he could leave at any time but so far has not taken up the option, preferring to play with those who dive in the bay and show off when pleasure boats are around. Made my day, did that.

Evening meal was taken in the same restaurant we had been to on the Saturday night. Unfortunately the service was awful and there was no liver in the mixed grill. Back home after a late night still feeling totally secure that you're not going to be assaulted every time you venture down an unlit path or street.

Wednesday 27th

Stayed locally and enjoyed the beautiful bays and harbours of Glendore and Union Hall. Again, no plastic developments or intrusions to spoil the area, no gimmicks, no leisure centres, just good old fashioned scenery. We toured a little in the afternoon and ate in. Tony served up custard in a way that my Mum used to, much to the annoyance of Maureen. Comments like 'Gosh I haven't had custard like this since I left home' didn't help either. (You will pronouce that as eIther not Either wont you! I cant stand Americanisms.)

Thursday 28th

Bearing in mind I'm writing this on our return I'm still not sure whether it was us or not, but by now I felt an irritation had crept in. Perhaps we had inadvertantly annoyed the other couple or perhaps they'd had an argument. Its funny, but the old adage of 'don't go on holiday with friends' is very true. We've known this couple for over five years and although disagreed on many occasions have never fallen out. Tony had, during the day, become louder and more manic in his actions. When we went into a craft or woollen shop, he came out bearing surprise gifts, as if to please his wife. Now I've never thought of Valerie as a Queen Bee, but one or two instances during the holiday had made me question this. Earlier in the week, while Maureen made breakfast, the three of us walked down to the supermarket in the village for some milk. Tony and I were walking along the pavement and Valerie was slightly behind. Now on our way down the hill I rememeber us all walking side by side, but when we crossed the square of the village to the pavement it was obviously narrower. Anyway she said 'excuse me' and pushed between us adding that she was not used to walking six feet behind a male (or in this case two). She entered the shop and we stayed outside, admiring the peace and tranquility of the place at 9am when at the same time the M3 would be blocked and activities around Aldershot would be halted by security checks. I asked if Valerie had got out of the wrong side of bed. Tony didn't answer directly, but his offering, which I cannot remember, smacked of wriggling with a brashness that thinly covered an underlying lack of confidence.

A trip to Skibbereen and Schull made a spendid day out and we purchased fresh fish and vegetables to have at 'home'. Tony, obviously pleased with my comments re his custard, decided to repeat the exercise. That evening we had our main course and afterwards sat around the coffee table playing cards. Apple pie and custard was to be eaten during a break in the games and we enjoyed the cosiness of a peat fire. Now its funny how innocent things can cause major problems, but the newspaper I used to start the fire with was the Mail from earlier that week. We did not need all the paper and the 'Femail' insert was still lying by the fire, the headline commenting on burning bras. Halfway through a hand of cards being dealt with red wine flowing nicely, Valerie made some remark, fairly innocently I think about the papers lead. Quite what happened over the next half hour was more akin to the TV play 'Abigails Party'. Marriage, feminism, divorce, children all got fair air time and Valerie got very wound up and said 'I think we should stop now'. Silence. Tony, always the soother obviously wanted to calm things down and tidy up the loose ends. Unfortunately it only refuelled the fire and it was two against two. Germaine Greer entered the argument and a complete polarisation of views could be witnessed. We were all giving our four pennyworth with no personal abuse being delivered whatsoever when Valerie exclaimed 'Don't shout at me'. I wasn't aware that I was. I obviously hadn't upset her husband as he continued arguing with Maureen. I countered again and she got up and stormed upstairs. I shouted 'If you leave you lose the argument, that's the rules' She turned on her heels and barked 'Fuck Off' 'You've lost then' I retorted. Tony got up and followed her leaving Maureen and I looking amazed.

The long and the short of it was that Tony announced they were going out for a walk and duly buggered off. After a cup of coffee we too, went out for a walk around the village, not meeting them. We returned to a darkened house and having mooched around for a while went to bed, but not to sleep. It was early morning before we heard the key in the door and them disappearing into the kitchen.

Friday 29th

Maureen and I walked downstairs to the kitchen to meet a Tony fairly glistening with enthusiasm for the day. He was whistling and la-laing extremely loudly in a sub-conscious effort to announce that everything was all right with our world.

Actually to us, it was. Having got the 'Good Mornings' over with. Tony asked if, quote 'We'd be able to resolve our differences' 'All over with' We said. 'Its a new day' Not to Valerie it wasn't. She was definitely off with us. The more noticeable her attitude became, the louder was Tony's singing. Maureen said she couldn't stand the atmosphere and Valerie said she was too 'upset' and didn't realise the discussion had been something we cared so much about. Well yes, we do have strong feelings about divorce and the well being of children after the break up of a marriage. What got my goat was Valeries complete dismissal of the effect of divorces and children turning to crime.

Valerie stated that she would need time to consider (what?) and would have to assess the situation and quote 'work at the relationship'. Maureen rightly said that she didn't know why she should be on trial, started crying and walked briskly to our bedroom. Tony tried to mediate.

'You're prepared to throw away five years friendship because of one argument' I asked adding 'because if that's all it means to you, it must have been a very shallow relationship' She replied that she felt she would be more on trial than us. No I didn't get it either. I did comment that all my views about Mrs Greer were totally vindicated if, having read and agreed with her clap-trap for years she had to 'work at a relationship' and 'consider everything'. Why not just kiss and forget. If she didn't want to risk anything nasty like aids we could have shaken hands.

I offered a few suggestions to try to fathom out her attitude. After all her other half was happy to consider the debate yesterday's news. What was so deep about it? I cant stand

218

not talking. You must know me by now. Up in the air, be abusive and make up the next day. Seems fairly simple to me.

Why all this sitting in the chair, wringing hands and making defeatist gestures?

Was it my conviction about the link between divorces and offending children? Was it my view on a judge sentencing a chap to four months prison for grabbing a WPC's breast? Was it my comment that the best favour Germaine Greer could have done the world was by being a miscarriage statistic? I still don't know.

At one time she asked to be taken to the airport where they would catch a plane home. I suggested that as we only had that day left we might as well make the best of it and it was agreed that we would use the car until early afternoon and they would have it for the rest of the day. We had previously booked a table at a restaurant on the quayside in Glendore and agreed to still go together. We spent the rest of the day pleasantly and met up in the evening. Valerie was frosty in the car on the way to, and back from the restaurant, but made an effort during the meal.

Goodnights were exchanged and Maureen and I reflected how anyone could be so neurotic. Suitable case for a trauma expert perhaps?

Saturday 30th

Bade our farewells to the manager, packed the car and made our way to the airport, where we checked in early to facilitate another hour in Cork itself. Incidentally we noticed that the Irish have picked up the awful idea of twinning. Although not to the same extent as Britain, I was curious to know why Cork is twinned with Coventry. Is it due to any republican tendencies on the part of members of Coventry's Council? Or is it because both cities begin with CO?

My lasting memories are of the sheer beauty of the place, the sparseness of those extremely friendly and endearing people, the fact that you can actually enjoy driving, despite the infuriation when someone doesn't indicate. To be fair, there is more chance of seeing Hartlepool score than witnessing indicators being used. I did ask a local why so few people indicated, he said the driver would probably think you knew them so you'd know where they were going to turn off.

The other thing about Irish drivers is that they wait till you're almost upon them and then turn slowly out of a side road in front of you. I don't think its bad manners, I just feel that to them its probably not that important. One nice feature was the number of local people standing outside their gates, thumbing a lift into town. Single women, schoolgirls, boys. With only one bus to Cork and back per day, hitching is an accepted way of life.

We had another couple of instances of Irish logic. One was when Tony and Valerie decided to buy some home made jam from a small cottage advertising such wares on the hill where we were staying. 'I've sold out' She replied when asked 'Oh your sign says homemade jam for sale' offered Tony ' Sure I'm making some more' said the housewife 'Will it be ready by the end of the week?' She looked incredulously at Tony 'I wont be making any till next summer, and I'll need the sign then' They left.

We saw a notice in the shop window advertising opening hours. Mon – Thurs 9am – 6.30pm. Friday 9am – 6.30pm. Sat 9am – 6.30pm Wonderful isn't it.

We scoured, without success, the new and second hand book shops and I was personally disappointd not to find any works on the Irish railways. The Irish history section was always good to browse through. Scores of books about the famine, Irish patriots, the British Rule, the IRA and associated subjects like the Birmingham and Guildford pub bombings. Books telling us how the British government have covered up over Gibraltar and the IRA killings. On more than one occasion this section spilled into books on Irish jokes, Kerry jokes, Limerick jokes, and limericks. they have a sense of humour.

With these memories and the question of our future relationship with the other couple, who, being smokers, did not sit with us on the return journey either, we flew back to England, grey skies. hoardes of people.

220

Back home we bade farewell to our fellow travellers and Tony restated his intention to come the following day and help us move. We were now to learn about the lack of laid carpet, the disconnected phone and other minor tales of woe. Still, it was nice to see the kids again.

October

Well, the first days over and I'm sitting down with a cup of tea. Tony did turn up all right, although he went home at 5.30 to see how Valerie was, as she apparently hasn't been too well today. Simon and my mate Den came as well and have only just gone. The chap who is renting came down during the morning, so I'm safe in the knowledge that everythings OK on his side and he's moving in tomorrow evening.

Tony and Simon busied themselves assembling beds, wardrobes, and bunks, while Den and I 'moved'. The two eldest and some of their friends helped and William hindered.

It seems sad, and an act of betryal to see the old house empty, but it will only be for one night.

The Sports Council I see are as neurotic as the rest on sexism, as opposed to rascism, a case of which will probably inflame them next month. This instance of shock, horror is due to a young lady named Martine le Moignan, the Women's World Squash Champion who posed on the front cover of the Squash Internatinal magazine wearing only underwear. One chappie from the Sports Council said it wouldn't promote women's involvement in any sport, or words to that effect. The only people I could imagine being dissuaded from a sport by that ad would be those so insecure, they wouldn't have time to participate as they'd be helping someone through a trauma anyway.

Some of these lawyers really scrape the barrel to obtain bail, don't they. An ex-boxer, arrested while working as a security 'officer' at an acid house party (drugs orgy) was remanded in jail despite an appeal because his girlfriend, who was expecting a child, tut tut, was in hospital with a dangerously high blood pressure. If things were that bad, why didn't he stay at home.

Well that's Monday over with. Maureen's Mum and Dad came down to help today. We've finished moving our stuff across to the new house, the aged relatives have been cleaning cupboards, skirting boards, and all the other things that only appear when you move furniture, or goods out of cupboards. Having taken down all the posters in Debbie's room, the walls were like pin cushions. So I've filled in holes on all sides of the room and spent two hours repainting.

Maureen's Dad made me laugh. He was commenting on our desperation at not selling the house, and how easy it had been to rent. "There's not too many people who will take dogs and allow smoking" said Maureen. "You were so desperate if Billy Smart had wanted his circus here you'd have let him" He wasn't too far from the truth either, was he.

Its all the little things you think about, bearing in mind other people are moving in. Did we clear out all the cupboards, did we hoover under the beds, did we remember to box the vibrator.

Just as I thought Aldershot were on a winning streak, they go and lose 8-0 at home to Sheffield Wednesday. The score is all the more disappointing when one considers that they drew the first leg at Hillsborough. They probably lost so as they could concentrate on the league. Flying pig time.

The good news is that the channel tunnel finances seems to be in trouble. Please, please, will somebody, anybody, put their resources to good use and save us from Europe, rabies and French policemen. Consider it as practice.

If proof were needed that throwing money at a project does not necessarily achive the required result, take a look at the Broadwater Farm Estate, or preferably don't. Since the 1985 riots, over three million pounds has been sucked in by the concrete maze. Four years on, and the police still can't raid the purveyors of drugs which abound in the area, without confrontation with residents. It doesn't help of course, when news of an impending raid is spread by all and sundry to those involved. And to think that the council bothered to plant flowers and repaint the flats. Money would have been better spent on our museums. At least the visitors would have appreciated it.

Went to the bank to see my man. He seems very happy with the situation, especially now that the tenants have moved in across the road. The problem is that whilst I've got the maximum mortgage which is tax deductable, my loan for the building work is four times the rent we're receiving. So, having calculated on a second calculator (the first one didn't work, in fact everytime I meet him, his little friend lets him down) the nett result is that if we do manage to sell the house next year, we're going to need another fifteen thousand pounds on top of this years price to break even. That interest certainly adds up doesn't it.

There was an interesting article in the Mail on Sunday this week. That well known bannerman for everything alternative, Tom Robinson, was being interviewed. Having heard him defending, nay advocating, the attributes of a poof's life, it was interesting to see that he's been living in harmony with a member of the opposite sex, and for a period of no less than four years. Mr Robinson is apparently still fighting for causes most people would consider less important than the price of eggs and it was not without some amusement when I learned that one of the tracks on his new LP deals with a friend dying of aids. True to form.

The news today is that a royal (Marina Ogilvy) is expecting a baby outside wedlock. One of the morning papers ran the lead heading 'Royal Baby Sensation'. I thought they were going to follow it by saying that Fergie's baby would be black. Now that would have been a hoot. How somebody who is twenty-fourth in line to the crown could achieve front page status is beyond me.

The greed and selfishness goes on, doesn't it? I see that the British Colony of the Caymen Islands is exporting Hawksbill Turtle shells so that they can be turned into ornaments. Where are they bound for – Japan. Its always that lot. They really are a nasty race of people. Thank God for Greenpeace.

Well England have just drawn 0–0 in Poland. We all know what an awful match it was from our point of view, so I'll draw a veil over that issue. Looking at the advertising hoardings

224

around the ground, its fine by me if Joe Bloggs Jeans and Mornflakes Oats want to advertise, but I do get peeved by British Gas putting up fortunes for their name to be seen. Where else can I buy my gas from. What with that and the continued unsubtle ploy to make you buy water shares, they really are immoral bastards.

I spoke to my mate who lives near Pewsey earlier this morning. He said a friend of his was telling him about his partnership going sour and how awkward the other fellow was being. He knew John had been involved in the splitting up, some years ago, of a partnership and asked if the other party was Jewish. John replied in the negative and the friend asked his surname. John told him and he said it sounded Jewish. "No, Flemish" replied John adding "Their the same really, its just that when the Germans marched in the Belgians lay down pretending to be dead while the Jews actually were. This point was proven at the end of the war when the Flems got up and the Jews didn't." Not to everybody's taste, but it amused me, I am though, easily amused.

It's the Tory Party Conference this week. The good news is that Mr Patten has overturned Nicholas Ridley's decision to approve the building of five thousand houses at Foxley Wood – The worrying thing is that Consortium Developments, who had hoped to gain permission are not about to give up and obviously consider the idea, be it there or thereabouts, is still very feasible. The bad news is that politicians in general still haven't got the message that the public are not interested in their abusing the opposition. That's been the main thrust of what I've heard so far. Still there's not much to sing about when considering their own achievements.

I watched Question Time last week. A lot of questions from the floor were naturally to do with inflation, interest and mortgage rates. The Tory's representative, Kenneth Baker, kept harping back to the Callaghan administration during the late seventies. Everyone can do that. How far do they want to go. I'm sure Mr Callaghan, if he had been there, would have cited the Heath Government for the situation they found themselves in when taking charge. It would be a sight for sore eyes to witness a politician saying publically 'We got it wrong'.

Among those children in the area whose birthdays fall this week are the unusually named Ocean, Sabine, Erin, Clay, Claud and Carey.

There was a sex shop in Aldershot which closed fairly recently. The owner of which has just been fined £2,500 for selling obscene videos and magazines. OK if that's the considered amount, fine, but how do those who mete out 'justice' compare this offence with assault or robbery resulting in much lower amounts or youth custody. There appears to be no yardstick at all.

We still haven't heard from the friends we went on holiday with. I mention this because I've just read of a case where a nineteen year old girl has been detained at Brookwood Mental Hospital for assessment after starting eighteen fires in eighteen months. The last instance by the way caused £182,000 worth of damage. The judge commented that she'd gone to pieces after the break up of her parent's marriage some two years ago. As I said earlier, in the vast majority of these cases the youngsters are from broken homes. The number of adopted children who offend is quite high as well, despite being given all the love and attention that their 'new' parents can offer. At the end of the day there is no substitute for real parents.

Its a pity Valerie doesn't look more closely at the relationship between young offenders and the break up of the family unit as we know it. A little more of the real world and a little less of Mrs Greer wouldn't go amiss I'd say.

I read with incredulity, an article in 'Today' concerning various travel companies in this country offering 'safaris'. It appears to have all the sleaze one associates with massage parlours that double up as brothels. Here we have camera wielding tourists unwittingly covering up the real operations and profit centre, that of killing 'game'. A peculiar use of the word if ever I heard one.

The article listed the various fees for wild animals killed and centered around a family who consider taking the life of a seventy to eighty year old bull elephant from twelve steps distance 'exciting'. Even worse, and enough to make you throw your hands up in the air in rage is their comment that friends and relatives back home can't wait to see the snapshots.

If there was any justice in this world, people like them would have been put down at birth. How can their 'holiday' be called fun? How can anyone consider shooting such a magnificent and harmless creature as an elephant 'exciting'? They even admitted the animal didn't stand a chance.

If it was up to me, they'd be some of the first against the wall.

You know the twinning twots in Farnborough and Aldershot (Rushmoor to them) that I've been going on about, its like topsy, it never stops. Having completed their latest success with some Teutonic town, there are now calls to twin with Pakistan and Poland as well as the previously suggested Tunisia. Apparantly if they can twin with a Tunisian sand trap it will be a first. Gosh, golly, excited oohhs and aahhs!

The serious point is made when one considers that the borough are spending £11,500 on a ceremony to officially twin themselves with the bergers of Oberursal. What a disgusting waste of money.

You might recall this incident, but I write as we're witnessing an unusual happening. Nuns are barricading themselves in their hen house in a bid to stop the slaughter of some five thousand chickens, harbouring the salmonella bug. Now whilst I think that a nun's (come to that monk's) life is a cop out and a waste of time, its their decision. Providing its not going to cost me anything to support them, fine. I thought that any religion taught its followers to respect all forms of life. If that is so, how can these people justify keeping hens in such appalling conditions as those described by visitors. Ironic isn't it, that these nuns live at 'Our Lady of Passion Monastry'. Passion, there's a word to conjure with. Doesn't seem a lot of it being shown towards those birds does it. And people wonder why I'm cynical about religion.

And now for something completely different. Actually its something entirely similiar to several other gripes. Those lovely Charles Church builders (whose namesake and founder died in a plane crash a couple of months ago) are seeking permission to build three thousand houses between Cambridge and Newmarket. The area is beautiful, but no, they cant leave it alone. Anyway, included in the three hundred and eighty acre site is a ninety acre farm owned by a seventy-four year old lady and her forty year old son. They have turned down six million pounds for the estate and hope that development of the surrounding fields will not take place either.

I clap my hands together in admiration when reading that she saw off a surveyor with her shotgun. All power to her and I hope they both succeed. For God's sake, the farmhouse is 15th Century. How far will these greedy bastards go to completely wipe out our countryside and heritage.

I see that Britain is to roll over on its back and submit to Europe again. In this instance we are to allow Euro MP's to sit in on House of Commons business. Although Mrs Thatcher is not going to like this idea any more than the proposed Euro social charter for workers rights, she will undoubtedly agree in the end.

Italian fishermen are using a fine mesh that catches virtually everything including dolphins, which are a protected species. In order to avoid heavy fines, they cut off their dorsal fins so they die a slow lingering death. Around four thousand have died so far this year it is estimated. Banned in every European country except Italy, the massacre continues unabated. Wouldn't this be a worthy cause for the grey ones in the EEC to busy themselves with. Probably take up too much time, and anyway, lunch starts at 11.00am.

Whilst I'm sure everyone applauds the government's decision to crack down on litter louts and make companies and institutes responsible for their own buildings and property, it appears that hospitals, courts and other government buildings are to be exempt under the crown immunity laws. Why is this?

Such is the fervent opposition to Mo Johnson playing for a protestant team, arsonists have tried to destroy the house he is currently living in. If these acts are typical of how religious bigotry affects people, I'm proud to be an atheist.

The world of elephant conservation appears extremely corrupt. The ban, if it is enforced, is better than nothing, but anything less than a total ban forcefully and enthusiastically worked by all countries is a hollow victory. I promise not to go on about elephants until the next time.

It's those wonderful Charles Church people again. Having got their grubby little hands on the last remaining open space in Shawfield Road, they are now attempting to build another seventy houses on nursery land in another part of Ash. There have been twelve applications so far, to build on this land. All have been refused. Both the local parish council and the Borough Planning Officer consider the proposed building as an incursion into open countryside, but those good builders are stating that low cost housing is required, and they're obviously the people to provide it. The application has been made by 'Charles Church Heritage PLC' heritage? Thats rich isn't it. They wont accept 'no' for an answer will they. Push, push and push again until an appeal wins the day. Oh how I despise these people. Its so unfair and one sided. The public cannot appeal and appeal. Once the ruling is in the builders favour thats it, but then money speaks doesn't it.

The nuns have lost and their hens have been destroyed. How could these people with supposed christian leanings allow battery principles to be used. As an animal welfare chappie stated, they're better off dead.

The Duchess of York is getting a lot of bad press. Its sad to see these 'new' royals becoming so grubby with commercialism. Surprised she isn't managed by an artiste's agency, perhaps she is. It will end in tears.

I know it was awful, but fifteen minutes of newstime about the San Francisco earthquake was definitely OTT. Didn't anything else happen that day.

Isn't it nice to know that despite a report that condemns your management as dangerous and blinkered, Sir Keith Bright, as Chairman of London Regional Transport when the Kings Cross disaster occured is to receive a pay off of £34,000, to cover loss of earnings. I'm truly pleased to hear that he is now Chairman of an electrical components company earning £132,000 per annum. He really didn't need the pay off did he?

Without a doubt, on the leisure front, for sheer relaxation and enjoyment, Michael Palin's 'Around the World in 80 Days' is going to take a lot of beating. Two episodes so far and every minute worth savouring. Not only does he appear to be a very nice person, but his ability not to overact when the very nature of his programme would entice many a lesser personality to fall into that trap is highly commendable.

Well, another act of vandalism has been perpetrated by Rushmoor Council in the name of progress. The Victorian arcade in Aldershot is to be demolished to make way for a new, upmarket version. The present traders who inhabit the shops will obviously not be able to afford the rents, but then, have development companies ever taken into account the requirements of customers, local people's feelings, or the small shop keepers ability to pay.

For those who don't know the area, it is a lovely example of faded grandeur that could easily be transformed into a really attractive area, but no, demolish it and spend four million pounds replacing it with something that you'll find in Milton Keynes, Gateshead or Basingstoke.

You won't find one like the present arcade, but by the time you read this it should be demolished.

The Councillor who was Chairman of the Planning Committee when the new development was first mooted says that he is very pleased with the outcome of the appeal, bearing in mind that between the time the original planning application was turned down and then won on appeal, the arcade was given listed building status. That has about as much effect as an SSSI or the ability of Ben Elton to shout out a complete sentence without dropping off all his 'T's.

The esteemed Councillor goes on to add that he totally agreed that the existing arcade should be demolished and that the proposed development is what Aldershot needs to meet the challenge of the future. What challenge? What future? If he means he wants to see Aldershot look like the aforementioned shopping centres I see what he means. Why build anything that will actually last and look solid and warm

They are building phase II of the Wellington Centre development at the moment. The car park, being built in some of the most boring coloured bricks you can imagine (cheap), have tubular 'bits' affixed to the walls looking like gaudily painted noughts and crosses. If this is an example of the Council's idea of quality building, then I wonder about their credentials when it comes to overseeing design work.

The present centre is bland, boring and unexceptional. Last word to the Managing Director of McKay Securities who are the company owning the arcade. "Delighted" He said at the news of the result of the appeal, So pleased.

Smile to the face time, and by heck that's a rarity these days. Those wonderful twinning people organised a trip to the French twin town of Meudon for some local children. Having initially described the visit as 'extremely successful' the real world was entered at one of their twinning committee meetings where it was revealed that the housing conditions were not dissimilar to the bastille, the kids were forced to eat out a lot of the time, nobody from the twinning town council had been there to meet them (tut, tut), and to add insult to injury the children were thought to be from difficult backgrounds.

Is that the way British offspring are seen abroad these days?

Having overspent their budget, the good ratepayers of Aldershot and Farnborough will be footing the bill. They must be delighted at the prospect.

They couldn't even get it right with the French, God knows what it would be like if they manage to twin with Tunisia.

It was very pleasing to see Sonia Sutcliffe's libel award being cut to a figure considerably lower than that first granted by a jury. Mind you, I think that anything over one pound is too much anyway.

Despite being in the motor trade, I still fail to understand the industry's logic. In 1988 Japan produced over eight million cars, the USA over seven million, West Germany four, France three, Britain were seventh in the league behind Italy and Spain with just over one million.

We don't sell that many abroad and the British buying public are not keen on the Mk II Allegro-the Maestro-now being phased out to be replaced by a joint Honda/Rover in the guise of the Rover 200 series.

Looking just like any other Honda and facing competition from the Honda counterpart, where on earth are we going.

Some chappie from the Society of Motor Manufacturers and Traders commented on Britain's 'growth' in the motor world. He said that 'Toyota, Honda, and Nissan wouldn't come here for fun'. Well obviously, but you're not talking about British cars. A Japanese car made anywhere in the world is still a Japanese car. It is back to the land of the ever-rising sun. If Rover were building factories abroad to make Montegos, Sterlings, Metros etc then to my mind that is progress. Foreign incursion into our market place cannot be hailed as a success surely. It must be looked at in the light of day as another continuing example of Britain's inability to produce its own designs, build the cars and have the confidence of its convictions to exploit the market.

You don't know what you're buying though do you. We couldn't find an English built kitchen, unless you had an awful lot of money. We cant find home produced ovens, TV's, videos. We thought we'd bought a Bendix dishwasher, only to be told by the engineers that it was built by Thompson of France and then rebadged.

Maureen's Father bought a 'Main' water heater. No its not a 'Main' is it. Its another French built item.

To my mind its a misleading trade practice. Getting back to motor manufacturers. If we are giving up as being a British competitor in the field, why don't we just be honest about it and hand it over. There seems little point in going on as we are.

You're either a British Independant producer or you're not. Its not worth badging your car with Rover labels if its a near copy of a Honda that's not only competitively priced but includes more goodies. What a farce.

Well, showbiz have had their chance to mourn publicly the passing of Lord Olivier. I watched the news, incredulously, as actors traipsed through Westminster Abbey holding cushions with Oscars, orders of merit, silver replicas of provincial theatres, crowns etc. It was almost Victorian in its symbolism. Maureen wondered when someone was going to come through carrying his first nappy. I found it all a bit gaudy and tasteless.

It makes me mad reading about a mother (divorced) whose whingeing that by working, she is twenty pounds a week worse off than if she stops at home, does not work and becomes a full time mum looking after her two children aged three and five. Her job would be better filled by an unmarried female without children, thus allowing the state to continue supporting her. At least this way the children are not farmed out to child care centres or nurseries.

She apparently doesn't get any financial support from her ex-husband. Why not? Why expect free facilities on the state.

Thank God her appeal to the Department of Social Security for child minding fees to be given to all one parent families has been turned down. Mind you, she's going to take her case to the European Courts who will probably consider us a heartless nation, slap our wrists and impose a severe fine, whilst allowing her compensation for loss of benefit, social deprivation, trauma and costs.

Her case is naturally being backed by the Child Poverty Action Group and she (also naturally) considers that existing regulations are illegal because they - wait for it – discriminate against women. I'm all for sexual equality and the quicker we men are granted it the better.

I'm glad they got shot of Kathy Taylor on Breakfast Time ITV, but the replacement is no better. Presumably they ran out of Kathy's, but the Scottish accent and the continual giggling of Lorraine Kelly, is as irritating as Kathy Taylor's incessantly looking up at her male partner (for support?) and fluffing her lines. It does seem to me that male presenters are easier to find and last longer. I don't know whether they become star struck, but whenever there is a female weather reporter on the box, they always want to 'hog' the spot and get involved with the guests. All I want to know is whats happening, not listen to a load of old claptrap. Women always seem to want to be in on things. Its as if they haven't quite adjusted to the media and being personalities, but very few progress and stay the course.

This is not sour grapes or jealousy, but to Ruth Lawrence, the child prodigy who has just become a doctor of philosophy at the age of eighteen I ask this: 'Have you really been happy with no teenage life?' If I'm wrong and she remains stable and able to cope with being so bright then all power to her elbow, but I can't help thinking that in time to come she might regret the constant beavering away to graduate and qualify, with very

233

little leisure time as enjoyed by her contempories during those very important years.

I have just read of a Yorkshire miner who has tried to take his life, being mentally tortured since the 1984 strike, because he broke ranks with his former colleagues. Many of these people have taunted him, threatened him, daubed his house with paint and sent him to Coventry. After five years of this abuse, and all because he didn't agree to a strike without a ballot, he has tried to commit suicide. I wish him and his family well, and if anything worse happens to him, there are many people, from the top of the pile to the 'salt of the earth' in the mining union concerned, who will have to live with blood on their hands for the rest of their lives. Brothers eh!

Any of you with lingering suspicions that I'm wrong about Britain being at a crossroads in direction and leadership internationally should take note. Not headlines at the weekend, but a very important point indeed was that Mrs Thatcher, when asked to vote against Hong Kong's request to continue trading in ivory decided that Britain would abstain. Why? It appears that the last thing we want to do is upset the colony while we have this little conflict of interests about the forthcoming change of ownership.

So the poor old elephant in Britain's eyes, has to suffer because we mustn't upset Hong Kong. These are two different issues altogether. Why are we so gutless and namby pamby in our ways.

I see that Mr Lenny Henry is setting up a joint project with the BBC to help black comedy writers. He appears rather upset that whereas Eddie Murphy, Richard Pryor (who I enjoy) and Bill Cosby have made it to superstar heights in America, black comedians are thin on the ground over here.

He's made it hasn't he. I assume that if you're funny you'll make it regardless of colour. Mind you, if you work on that principle, how *did* Mr Henry make it?

Will these black writers be creating comedies for black comedians only though, or will they contain – what's the phrase, oh yes – stereotyped native white people playing the role of robber or general ne'er do well. Tch Tch.

There were the thick end of 184,000 abortions throughout England and Wales in 1988. Its all very well anti-abortionists going on and on over an issue that is obviously very emotive and where very few people would be 'floating voters' but I wonder if they ever stop to consider the problems of these two countries if these pregnancies had not been terminated. Thats 184,000 children who in fifteen to twenty years would be adding to our already over burdened population. Thats besides the fact that by being unwanted in the first place, many would not have had a good start in life by being brought up in a happy and safe environment with original Mums and Dads who were married at least nine months before birth.

I can take all the brickbats by the Bohemian set, and old-fashioned as it may sound, I stand by my view.

As an aside, I wonder how many of those insisting an unborn foetus has just as many rights as a new born baby tuck in to a Sunday roast with mouth watering relish, just a thought.

Glad to see that child benefit isn't going up again. Whatever the government did was going to see them being mauled by the social do-gooders, but I still contend that despite the usual outcry that accompanies the now yearly stagnation of this handout, we actually do not know where the money is spent. I'm convinced that more goes on beer and fags than nappies and Heinz (glass or no glass).

And why should there be any handout by the government. I still contend we need incentives not to breed, not the reverse – I'll go and hide now.

There was a chappie writing to our local paper almost sneering at calls to bring back hanging, describing the act of ending a murderer's life as 'cowardly'. How is this? I doubt whether this Farnborough 'person' has ever had a member of his family raped or killed. He comments that murder isn't commonplace and that most crimes are petty. The arrogance of the man. The last part of the letter gave a clue to the coves character. he advocates the promotion of peace studies in schools banning the sale of violent toys and brings the Falklands conflict into play as well. I deduce from this that protecting citizens overseas is unnecessary in his eyes

235

whereas the protection of criminals is to be applauded. Need I say more about this poor misguided individual.

I wonder how he would feel if he were in the shoes of Mr and Mrs Benson, parents of Lorraine who was beaten, sexually assaulted and murdered by a drug taking attacker who had already served a three year sentence for rape when he was fifteen. Fancy letting him out when he was eighteen. Three years is nothing. Public stoning and castration might have made him think twice. Once the furore has died down and a few years have passed, it will be interesting to see how long it takes him to be released, despite the judge commenting that if need be he will be detained for the rest of his natural life.

Talk about one law for us and one law for others. Travelling gypsies in their usual expensive cars and caravans were seen early last week camping around the Hogs Back on the A31. Advance warning to the parish council enabled them to check that barriers to the Coronation Gardens in Ash were able to withstand a now annual invasion. Unfortunately these were dismantled. I don't know if any damage was done to them, but they were firmly ensconsed by Wednesday. Talks with the local police ended with them being allowed to stay until Sunday. If you and I wanted to pitch a tent there overnight, we'd soon be kicked off, and rightly so. But here, of course, we have a group of people, an ethnic minority who are above the laws applicable to, and abided by the majority of the public.

Not for these persecuted groups, the strong arm of the law, no equal rights for them, but preferential treatment with no rent payable and the cleaning-up bill (yes, there was one) to be paid by the rate payers. What a gutless police force we have. I suppose they would have been short of staff locally as most of them would have been re-writing confessions in Guildford (ho ho, he he)

They have an artists illustration of the new two acre site being developed at Farnborough Station on land once housing goods yards, warehouses, coal yards etc. This new conglomeration of brick and glass will totally overshadow the beautifully restored station. Nice name the developers are giving it – Spectrum Point. Has a sort of ring to it, doesn't it, a very brassy one, cheap and nasty.

The area was one of the last locally, actually looking as if it could still be in the 1960's. The red brick buildings, although derelict stood proudly and defiantly, an example of an age when space was required for merchandise to change hands, dirty work could be washed off back home and no-one thought of the effects of radiation when sitting for hours in front of a VDU in an artificially lit open plan office, (hang on, typist here, I think I know what he means) behind smoke glass walls safe in the knowledge that should you suffer pre menstrual tension while legally screwing another small independent company into submission, there would always be the trauma expert to visit on the sixth floor. (Typist here again, what a damn good idea).

Man of the month goes to a fellow I've read about in the Mail on Sunday. His name is Douglas Mills and he's fighting a one man (plus helpers) campaign to save whats left of the wildlife and heathlands of Dorset before the DOE and the local authorities finally cement over the last crack of mother nature's legacy.

Here is a *real* candidate for a medal for 'services rendered'. People like him deserve all the accolades going. Good luck to you sir.

Here's a good one. Husband dies, wife contacts funeral parlour who come along and lay him out. 'Only one problem' says the funeral director. 'He still has an erection' Wife asks what can be done. 'We usually cover it with a posie of flowers; very tasteful' She didn't want that. Seeing her naked husband lying there, percy vertical, she pinches it between her two fingers as if about to fling something cold into a frying pan and says 'cut it off'. Funeral director looks aghast 'Can't do that' he says.' Why not. I'm his next of kin and I want it off' she replies positively. Shoulders shrug and off it comes. 'Where would you like it, mounted on a plinth, drowned in vinegar and saved for posterity in an empty 'epicure' jar or buried with him?' She thought and stated that it should be inserted up his bum. Looking horrified the body was turned over and not without a little difficulty, and a lot of vaseline, the solid member was pushed out of sight. The body was placed back in its original position looking up at the ceiling. Just then a tear could be seen trickling out of the corner of his eye. 'Thats right you bastard' said the wife 'I told you it hurts' . I liked that one.

Interesting to note that this joke was relayed to me over a car phone without any interruption or loss of sound. Must be a record.

Apparently there was a chappie in the dock at Farnham courts this morning, and as the judge summed up the case, a phone rang. The defendant took a portable phone out of his pocket and answered it. The judge's comments are not known. Bloody cheek though, isn't it.

I don't really know which is worse, learning about Nigel Lawson's departure as Chancellor of the Exchequor or Myra Hindley's successful 'BA' degree ceremony. Whilst not a fan of Mr Lawson (why did he not introduce credit control) the last thing we need is instability in the government at a time of high interest rates and foreign concern at our economy.

Then you suffer the Rev Peter Timms and Lord Longford being given air time to put their case for her release. Leopards never change their spots. How insensitive these people are. A few visits to the families of those murdered might not come amiss. She should rot in jail along with all the others convicted of like crimes.

I feel, you know, like someone who is continually climbing out of a hole, only to be hit over the head again as soon as I make a move to escape. The financial situation is dreadful. I've sold four cars this month – just four. It is by far and away the worst month I've experienced in eight years of self-employment. The profit from these hasn't even paid the interest. I've cut back continually on stock. This is also the first month I've not bought a car either, all sales being vehicles purchased in August and September. It makes one very bitter to think that trade is being curtailed so much because of high interest rates. I personally do not consider this pursuance to be the answer, and I have yet to hear a reasonable argument against the introduction of credit control. As I've said all along, surely that's the area they should be targeting restraint at, not middle class families struggling with astronomical mortgages. It wouldn't be so bad if the Chancellor had stuck to his guns, but to resign and basically leave the country to it is all we need.

The only light is that Mr Hurd's departure from the Home Office and Mr Waddington's known views reflecting more of the public's concern, may be cause for celebrations in the long run. We'll have to wait and see.

It has not been a good week on two other fronts either. Farnborough's CID have told me that their hierarchy will not sanction an extradition order over Connolly as my loss wasn't enough! A twelve pound fine for parking would have been followed up at great cost no doubt. My next course of action is to write to the Chairman at the bank he was with detailing their involvement and ask his help to see if their findings were correct or if there was a cover-up. It looks as if I'm on my own now. The phrase my solicitor used about 'them' (the bank) being a bunch of shits has always stayed with me. Why didn't they inform my solicitors earlier about the assets being exceeded by the debts. How could a bank loan someone one hundred per cent of their mortgage, when I'm assured that the usual limit is two thirds or seventy per cent at most? Why did his bank manager slam down the phone on mine?

I know Connolly is no longer at the address I visited and appears to be selling mopeds near a beach according to faintly reliable sources and not doing too well either.

As a policeman said to me, they all come back.

The other bad news is that when I rang our holiday partners – Tony and Valerie – on Monday evening and spoke to Tony, he said that although he was happy to go on being friends, he couldn't 'get his wife around'. I told him not to bother on our account. I wont bore you with the details but I cannot see us ever being friendly with them again.

It is a pity as we enjoyed their company and will miss their friendship. I'll tell you how under the thumb he is. He added that Valerie was quite 'happy for him' to see us, that's nice, but couldn't bring herself to quote 'have a relationship' with a couple who had such 'closed minds'.

Now it doesn't matter to me, I accept that I can be a bit abrassive during discussions, but Maureen is the most mild mannered of people, who doesn't deserve to be treated in this way.

Tony's big mistake was not putting her over his knee years ago and giving her a thoroughly good spanking. If she wants to act like a Queen Bee, who, when not getting enough attention, sulks like a child, then she should be treated like one. Sexist? Moi?

I will finish this sorry little episode by adding that on several occasions we have met Tony's Mum and Dad, and for that matter brothers and families as well. They couldn't be nicer people. I can well understand his father falling for his mother. She is an exceptionally attractive woman with a great personality. Valerie doesn't get on with her. I once commented that despite tales about her mother-in-law, they always seemed to get on all right when she saw them and to be fair Valerie always appeared to show sincere affection. She countered that she (Valerie) was a good actress. Perhaps she was acting with us for the period of friendship, who knows!

I just stubbed a toe, the one that had roast beef.

Why don't we take the bull by the horns, or in these days of equality, the cow by the udder and get to grips with the problem of ID cards. I see there are moves afoot to issue ID cards to some youngsters over eighteen, but not looking their age so they can be served in public houses without causing staff headaches. At the same time, the government are taking the issuing of soccer ID cards one step further in a bid to implement the scheme as soon as possible.

Every person in the land should have an ID card. I fail to see the 'civil rights' argument. How can anyone in their right mind object to having a card on their person unless they have something to hide. Words fail me.

Talk about OTT, I see the Home Office has issued a pamphlet for men on how to make women feel safer on the street.

Once again we're not gettng to the heart of the matter. The possibility of re-introducing ladies compartments in trains is ludicrous. Not only would I feel peeved at having to stand on a commuter train from Waterloo when there are seats in the ladies compartment – which used to happen in the sixties – but tell me what there is to prevent a male with wrong intentions, getting in at a surburban station late evening, anytime come to that, when passengers are few and far between.

BR have stated that far more local stations are to be unmanned out of rush hours. Add the gradual withdrawal of guards to the list and you have a recipe for disaster. There is no more security in separate compartments unless they are lockable from the inside, which seems impractical.

So we're not supposed to be on the same side of the road when walking in the same direction, mustn't start up a conversation at a bus stop, mustn't give admiring glances. Call in the trauma experts.

'It was awful M'lud, there I was, a simple soul, waiting at the bus stop when this man came and stood behind me and (pause while nose is blown and composure is regained) then he asked me what time the No 6 to Heckmondwike was likely to arrive' Gasps from all and sundry.

'Am I likely to receive more compensation than Sonia Sutcliffe first time round M'lud?'

No doubt, plus own social worker for a year, trust fund, public fund where contributions will top a quarter of a million pounds of which she will see about $3/8$d and local-youth and community schemes will receive the balance over a lifetime, all of which will be squandered anyway on ethnic art. Then there will be a book, serialisation in a national paper and chat shows. Women come and go so quickly in the visual media, that she could end up an 'agony aunt' with all the experience of being a celebrity, sorry victim.

All these guidelines will do nothing to lower the assault and rape figures. It will make women more neurotic. Most females accepted PMT to be a 'monthly curse' until it was deeply analysed on Breakfast Time TV, since when it has become a subject for continued discussions with fat fees being paid to gynacologists, welfare officers, union representatives and various experts.

Its like a lot of things, people don't know they have a problem until those with a financial interest in human emotion seek to get their fizzoggs in.

A woman walking along a road and noticing a man observing the code by crossing to the other side, will now assume his move to be a ruse to allay her fears while gaining her confidence so that an attack can be made later on. All we are doing is turning alertness to neurosis.

Sponsored sentences and floggings come to mind. Those convicted of 'victim friendly' crimes (there's a novel phrase) could be accepted or adopted by big business to wear logo embossed clothing, the fees for which would be used to further their reintroduction into society.

Town squares and village greens could become venues for public floggings for instance. Stocks could also be brought into use once again. The woodwork for which would have the name of the local craftsman endorsing his work. Small side shows of local crafts would be present. Local grocers would sponsor the eggs and tomatoes to be thrown, while topless page three girls would distribute bingo cards and pose in different positions alongside the stocks, smiling brightly as the criminal receives his 'lot'.

For drink offences, breweries could do a lot worse than being seen in force extolling the strength of their latest 'yob making' brew. The permutations are endless.

November

I don't know whether its true or not, but I've read a number of 'important' people want their local boundaries changed so that they can live in Bray, Berkshire rather than Maidenhead. Isn't it dreadful how snobby some people can be. They must be very insecure to need this reassurance every time they give out their address, unless its purely for financial purposes when they come to sell their houses – to other snobs.

I put the above on a par with those 'honorary doctorates' that are given out to celebrities. When you think that actors Paul Eddington and Nigel Hawthorne have received these accolades from Sheffield University it makes you ask 'why'? Is it so that those who made the suggestion can name drop when lost for words at a dinner party, or perhaps it will get them a free day at the studios to meet their idols. Perhaps both. Its no different from those doing a job and getting a knighthood for doing it. Can't help thinking that it devalues 'proper' BA's, Ma's and 'Sir's' given to those who have worked hard to achieve their degrees or have sacrificed a large chunk of their lives to help others.

No-one is excused the wrath of the neurotic ones. Poor old Roald Dahl is being lambasted for writing childrens books about witches thought to be too 'spooky' for kids by American mothers. Must protect the litle darlings from bad dreams and distress. Time for a trauma expert I think.

Any lingering doubt about my being a cynic where disaster funds are concerned end here. Apparently only a quarter of the Lockerbie fund – over two million pounds – has been paid out, and that relatives have received just over £100,000. Mind you, local youth organisations, local community projects and the Wildlife Trust have all received a share. I'm just surprised that the Broadwater Farm Estate hasn't been the recipient of another enormous cash injection.

Here's another one of those upstarts. Having learned that the actress Gwen Taylor, who became famous in Duty Free and A Bit of A Do struggled like a lot of others to achieve success, I looked forward to seeing her on the Des O'Connor Show. On she came full of importance, hands and arms flailing in exaggerated form to make a point. I like a good personality, but it does appear that success goes to a lot of people's heads.

I don't know what people get out of surveys, but one has just been completed on 'garages attitudes to women'. The main result, inevitably, was that women considered mechanics 'sexist' and 'condescending'. Well they had to be sexist didn't they. Stand in a gents' loo pointing percy at the porcelain and its sexist. I suppose we're expected to squat to attain equality. Get up to offer a female a seat on a train or bus – sexist.

Anyway having established that mechanics do not exactly warm to volumes of technical jargon when confronting women (the apparent condescension factor) it comes as no suprise to discover that fifty per cent of those surveyed admitted they had no idea of fitting oil filters or replacing bulbs. Small wonder they earn little respect when something goes wrong. Its like all these things, its all right being equal as long as you're having things done for you.

Talking of surveys, I see that one published in the Director Magazine states that prejudice against women and ethnic minorities is still very prevalent in board rooms.

Watching the number of programmes where female names come up on credits, articles about female success in big business, the media and self employment, one wonders where all the prejudice is. I'm convinced its hyped out of all proportion to stir up trouble.

The report goes on to say, as if suprised, that people try to recruit colleagues from similiar backgrounds with similiar likes and dislikes etc. Well, whats new. This is called Human Nature. Jews are renowned for sticking together, thinking about it, I suppose that is now a racial tendency to be frowned upon.

Asians stick together, West Indiands stick together. We however, are not allowed to. Funny isn't it.

A few more birthday names now. There's a Tasma, Coralie, Kane, Severiano (guess whose Dad likes golf eh) Mara, Pascale (how Euro) Jeanna, and a Camille-Fay. There are a sprinkling of Tracey's. Leannes, Waynes etc plus a couple of Aarons. Well never mind.

Well, Ford look set to gobble up Jaguar, our last bastion of British quality in the motor industry. Even the American Jaguar distributers state publicly that it won't be the same once they become just another subsidiary to be integrated over a decade or so. No doubt, production will be transferred to some dusty Spanish outback where the leather will be cheaper and the profits higher.

Having misused his time in the 'Ministry of Destruction', our beloved Mr Ridley carries on his hatchet work by sanctioning the takeover of this previously prestigious company. Will nothing be left alone. I just need to hear that 'Perrier' have successfully bid for Youngs Brewery in Wandsworth for my week to be made a complete disaster.

Its sad to see that the RSPCA are not going to be represented at this years Crufts. When a show as renowned as this refuses to accept posters reflecting the seamier side of pet owning and the associated misery of starvation, torture and ultimate destruction, it comes home to you just how much real care and love there is by these breeders and there ilk for the good old mongrel. Talk about bury your head in the sand. How can people purporting to be animal lovers dismiss those attempting to save lives so readily. How? It doesn't look good for them, does it. Goes against their pedigree grain. Might affect the value of the continually in-bred offspring. With their selfish attitude I'm surprised Mrs Thatcher hasn't offered them a Ministry.

Everything is so complicated these days isn't it. A couple of advertisments by Benetton are causing ructions in the neurotic circles. Doesn't the fact that their advertising agency have to consult the Advertising Standards Authority, the Commission for Racial Equality and London Regional Transport before an ad can be placed besides an escalator

– say something about the way we tread so warily these days. You'll never please all of the people all of the time. The two ads in question show a black hand and a white hand cuffed together, bringing cries and complaints of rascism, sex and bondage, while the other portrays a black woman breast feeding a white baby. This shows up black women as being wet nurses to white babies according to the ads critics.

To be fair, without reading the furore over the handcuffs ad, it didn't strike me as being rascist, how could it. There is one white hand and one black hand. An equal amount of hands. Even I didn't see it as an off duty white policeman leading away a black chappie suspected of something or other in beautiful down town Tottenham. I just saw it as a symbol of their slogan "United Colors of Benetton". Even if they don't spell colour properly.

I do take exception to the second ad as I'm not in favour of pictures portraying white babies being breast fed by black women. Mind you, I'm not overly keen on black babies being fed by white women either. A view shared, I'd imagine by many people of both colours. I'd have to be pretty annoyed about it to complain tough, I feel it's another example of the current trend to force equality on you by brain-washing.

How does anyone read bondage into handcuffs. All it does is to confirm in one's minds-eye the sort of people that exist at the CRE. They get so uptight and misled by something thats fairly innocuous. But then that's why they work there, helping to fuel a fire that could be controlled far more easily by their being made redundant and coping with something more in line with their mentality – sweeping gutters. No, there's nothing wrong with being a street cleaner either – dear oh dear.

I'm so glad to be able to report that the twinning committee seem to be at the final hurdle now, in its bid to seal the bond as it were – as opposed to sealing the bondage, see they've got me at it now.

Last month thirty-eight people from Rushmoor (remember its Aldershot and Farnborough to you and me) went to Germany. This week the German delegation are to be welcomed here. Isn't that nice. After the ceremony, all those hangers-on will attend a banquet at Farnborough's dreadful Recreation centre. I say dreadful because it represent everything that's nasty in grey concrete. This little lot's going to cost the ratepayers a fortune, as there are to be two hundred and ten people to dinner.

Afterwards there will be tours of the local beauty spots and sites of interest. These include the convent, the Royal Aircraft Establishment, the Lido (used by yobs as a focal point to rob and injure) the West End centre in Aldershot (frequented by a continuous stream of fringe theatre and other obscure productions) and the Princes Hall. This is another concrete building, backing on to the Police Station and currently undergoing various changes in order to make it look more like a theatre and less like a secondary modern school.

At the end of the day this wondrous weekend will have cost the ratepayers over £11,000 as I mentioned earlier. Good value isn't it!

Another milestone in the area's history happened this week. On a site where once stood a cricket pavilion, a new centre has been built. To be run by the 'West Indian Association', it will cater for all ethnic minorities. This is apparently a long standing ambition of this group and has been financially supported by TVS who have given one thousand pounds as part of their community project service.

An interesting point I noted was that a former Mayor of Lambeth attended the opening ceremony. He – wait for it – was representing the present Mayor of Lambeth who couldn't make it as he was away in Russia! Still, it makes a change from swanning off to play in Mrs Mandela's football team.

The ex-Mayor chappie said that he 'extended the congratulations of the people of Lambeth to all those who will use the premises'. I wonder if *they* know.

The president of the association commented that this was 'not just for West Indians, but for all ethnic minorities regardless of colour or creed'. Well there's no excuse for gypsies to cause thousands of pounds worth of damage to recreation grounds and municipal gardens in the area now, they've got a new 'ethnic' centre of their own, haven't they.

Pity it isn't still a cricket pavilion though.

Getting back to junkets and being serious about it, I have learned that unless someone has £2,000 in readies, a woman can be left worrying for the thick end of a year over whether she may have breast cancer or not. In Birmingham I see the waiting time is forty weeks. So much for this government's committment to a National Health Service. It is iniquitous that anyone should be reduced to having to pay privately for tests of this nature. Add to this the fact that in some cases it could be too late for some women to be treated, it surely must come home to those who wield the power that this is false economy.

It just strikes me that if all the money used in back-slapping foreigners and saying 'what good boys we are' were to be used on more vital issues such as screening tests, the country's power base would receive a tad more respect from its citizens. Then of course you'd be asking those good 'bergers' to miss a free meal and a chance to go toadying.

One thing I look forward to on a Saturday night is the timeless 'All Creatures Great and Small.' Actually early evening Saturday viewing is quite good with Blind Date and Beadles About. The only irritating thing about the latter is Beadle himself. On more than one occasion the wind-up could have been continued but he has to get his fizzyogg in by coming on as the bearded policeman. He never looks convincing, but I expect it boosts his ego. I still wish we could wrap up Saturday viewing with Match of the Day and a good chat show. I like Sue Lawley, but its still not 'right' somehow.

I see there's to be a new wartime series called the Free Frenchman. I'm looking forward to that, hope my enthusiasm is justified.

Looking back to past TV triumphs about the last war, it never ceases to amaze me as to why series like Enemy at the Door, Secret Army amd Manhunt aren't re-shown. I'd watch Manhunt again just to see Cyd Hayman being inquisitioned in the nude by Robert Hardy. Down boy, down!

A lot of those wartime dramas are worth repeating, but I suppose I'll have to be content watching weather sponsored by Powergen (who? – exactly)

I was amused, if that's the right word, to hear that Trevor Evans, friend of the kiddies cartoon character 'Fireman Sam' is actually black. A lot of people will be under a misapprehension, as despite his Welsh name and the quintessential appearance of an English Colonel he is more than tanned. According to the production people, they made him black to give 'broader appeal'. They also comment that by having a Welsh accent, preconceptions about the way coloured people speak would be broken down. I thought it was fairly obvious that accents are picked up regardless of race and colour.

A touring company want to bring the characters to life, but may have to abandon the idea because they can't find a black actor with a Welsh accent between the ages of thirty-five and fifty. So hundreds, maybe thousands, of children could be denied the chance of seeing some of their favourite characters because of the licencing people's hang ups. Don't suppose you can have a white actor 'made up' any more, far too rascist.

So our children are to be led down a technological path at school in order to take on the 21st century as they will know it. They are likely to be taught how to use a computer as soon as they sit down in Primary School, learn advertising, research and marketing skills at eleven, and make up their own business companies and understand the machinations of the financial world by the time they're fourteen. Great, but will they be able to take £3.02 from £5 without resorting to a calculator? and will they know where to use a comma, or what words warrant a capital letter? No, I don't suppose so either. They will, however, be greedier than our present generation and more ruthless in business and in the home – and you thought it was bad now.

William has just come home full of the news that Father Christmas is visiting their school in a couple of weeks. He's informed us that its not 'his' Father Christmas but a pretend one. At nearly seven William's still convinced of his existence. I don't want it to end in tears by telling him that he doesn't exist so I'll have to be a bit diplomatic. I know, I'll tell him that Mrs Thatcher considered the reindeer too expensive to keep so they're being butchered

by Dewhursts and sent to Japan as a gourmet dish. No –
oh well.

While I think of it, that miserable woman that owns the cat
who still tries to get in for a little bit of TLC and then craps
on our front garden, never ever kept up the myth about Father
Christmas for her boy. I suppose she must have saved a few
bob not taking him to Debenhams Christmas Grotto etc, but
she can't be happy. The boy has on more than one occasion
told William he's a baby for believing in him. This nastiness
rubs off doesn't it.

One of Maureen's sisters was saying that a certain section of
people are calling for the word 'snowman' to be discontinued
and 'snowperson' to be substituted in its place. I won't say
anymore.

Maureen's Mum and Dad looked after William a little while
ago – when we were on holiday in fact. Anyway he kept
talking when they were watching TV. Sshh, sshh Mum kept
telling him. 'I know' he exclaimed after the last outburst of
sshh's. 'If you say sshh, and I say 'it', we've made a swear
word' Doesn't miss a trick that one.

While watching Blind Date last night, it occured to me that
Cilla Black used to be Priscilla White. I suppose going from
White to Black was OK, its the other way around that would
be rascist.

We sat and watched the British Legion Remembrance fes-
tival on BBC later on and its still very moving, watching the
old boys walking across the floor holding aloft flags bearing
names of long disbanded, but not forgotten regiments. The war
widows with the lady and little boy representing those lost in
the Falklands brought a lump to the throat, because you realise
how recent the event was, and how many young lives are still
affected by it.

I always enjoy the lighter side of the show when the new
recruits perform their exercises and the re-enactments take
place. One point I did note was the reference to the logs,
used during the exercises, as being 150lb in weight. I would
have thought that metric measures would have been used.
Actually Wiliam's teacher told us last week that they have
been informed that both metric and imperial are to be taught in

250

school now, not just metric by itself. We don't want to let go of the past do we. Its just a shame to see our measurements, like our distances and currency dying a slow, lingering death.

While I was up at the local railway club the other day, browsing through the library, I came across a company magazine dated Spring 1962. A quick flick through brought only tenuous links between this Liverpool manufacturer and railways. It was the 'gossip' that was so interesting. Pictures of the 1961 employees children's christmas party showing five to ten year olds with short, neat hair. The boys in pullovers, sleeveless jumpers, sporting ties. Girls with hair pulled in by slides, white knee-length socks and flared skirts. Not an earring amongst any member of either sex. In the photo, two children are sitting on Father Christmas' lap. The thoughts of sexism over his title are farther away than landing on the moon. Mind you, in a little over a year, the Beatles were to descend on upon the world!

Turning the pages, there was an account of a 'Stag Night' held at the Court Restaurant, Harlesdon, London on the evening of the 5th January 1962 where thirty-four members of their London office sat down for what was described as an excellent dinner, followed by singing and a race meeting. Not for them sealed boxes of American horse races, but 'Mr Michies clockwork variety'. Wasn't life tame in those days. Mind you, after the evening was over, the workforce could have happily taken a bus ride home without being assaulted. Actually they could have walked home, couldn't they. Can you imagine that now.

On page five appears an article about a visit from ABC Television to Broadcast live a programme called 'Sing Along with Joe'. This apparently was a televised 'Workers Playtime' type of offering with a spot called the 'Pretty Girl' competition. That would also be frowned upon now, wouldn't it. There are pictures showing the six selected girls from Wages, Cash Office, Power, Packing Room and the Icing Room.

There's another article about an employee from their Birmingham Depot whose spare time is taken up as a Special Constable, something to be proud of then.

Towards the end of this biscuit manufacturers magazine, there are lists of those employees who are still with the

251

Company and have completed so many years services. I've just counted them, and there are nineteen who have served over twenty years, ten over thirty years and nineteen over forty years. Going over the page an amazing sixty-seven have just finished their tenth year. There are a list of retirements that concern ten more employees. The lowest is twelve years. The rest range from twenty-three to forty-nine years. Oh that we could inject that sort of stability in todays workforce. The company name is still with us, but I believe as part of a large conglomerate, and I bet a pound to a penny its not like it was then.

No-one working in that era would have thought that the inside pages of the national dailies would contain a story where a blind epileptic girl waiting at a bus stop outside Waterloo station, would be attacked by thugs chanting 'We hate blindies'. This was the work of two women and a man who punched and kicked her. On the same day another girl suffering from cerebral palsy was thrown out of her wheelchair and into the road because she refused to hand over her handbag to two men in The Old Kent Road, South London. What a slippery path we've come down.

I watched that 'Free Frenchman' programme during the week. Although it was the 'introduction to characters' episode all neatly packaged at a wedding, the American accents annoyed and dismayed me somewhat, but we'll watch it again to see if there's an improvement.

Those devious bastards, the development fraternity, are finding new ways to create land availability locally. They are buying up typical suburban homes in rows of five or six and then putting in planning applications time and time again until they gain approval to build blocks of flats. The end result is that no overall plan can be achieved and the area concerned becomes a horror story. To be fair to a number of councillors, they are not happy with the situation, but as it stands, the law is definitely on the side of the developer as we've seen from past experience.

A young girl is attacked and stripped by a gang of youths on a late night bus and all they get is slapped wrists. What more can one say, only that while this incident is still news, another

252

lady aged forty-two has been raped and robbed in Tottenham (used to be such a nice place) while she was closing the boot of her car. These rapists must be waiting for someone to make the smallest of moves so as to continue their evil ways. I'm just waiting for some left-wing sociologist to consider rape an art-form.

Whats amused me about the breaking down of the Berlin Wall, and the general to-ing and fro-ing past border controls to see what the other half is like, is the fact that as soon as it became general knowledge over here, all anyone could ask was how long it would be before they invaded Poland. On financial programmes and City comments the 'Mark' is used more and more as a guidleine to the pounds strength (or weakness). Never underestimate the Germans, a combined and united Germany would make it even more of a powerful influence, both financially and politically in Europe. No doubt, given a decade, they would find a reason to leave NATO and the Common Market. I view the present euphoria with mixed emotions.

There's now only one district, Dwyfor, in Wales that is 'dry' on Sundays after the latest referendum. Fourteen areas went to the polls, thirteen decided to open their pubs on a Sunday. I think it's nice for these idiosyncrasies to continue, providing its not where I live.

Besides the border situation in Germany which is now getting extremely boring, the other news seems to be about the liver transplants, actually transplants in general. A surgeon chappie was saying that it was difficult persuading more people to become donors due to the worries about prospective punters not being dead when the organs are extracted. Its not that that worries me. My concern is over offering, having accepted, and their taking an organ of mine while I'm fit and healthy. My organ is then transplanted, everyones keeping their fingers crossed and then its rejected. Knowing my luck, it would go to a solicior who would sue me under the 'trade description act'. I can see the court case being described in a tabloid now. 'Second hand car dealer 'gives' iffy organ'. They would comment about never being given anything from an Arfur Daley. A motor trader's lot is not a happy one. Still if it went to that bastard in Spain who owes me the £25,000 and it failed, would I really care? Would I buggery.

I remember when I worked in car hire, the girls who worked at the airports, Heathrow and Gatwick certainly, always considered themselves above those who worked in provincial locations. There was quite bitter rivalry between the main centre in London and the airports over who you would help out with cars if some depots were short of supply on a holiday Saturday for example. Thinking back, a lot of girls, when on rental courses, strutted. The uniform had a lot to do with it. At airports they were frustrated air stewardesses. Why they should think it so grand I don't know. I suppose its the exotic locations a lot of them fly to, like Manchester Ringway, Edinburgh Turnhouse and Bradford, that gives them dillusions of grandeur.

Men on courses do not seem to display the same bitchy tendencies about positions. I accept that you'll always get the 'Derek in Coronation Street' type where 'designate' on your business card would count for a lot, but in general we take courses in a far more level way than females.

A lot of them would gain greater respect if they were themselves and didn't hide behind a title or badge.

As I've said before, you see it a lot with actresses, who have 'made it' after so many years. You get it in 'posh' shops where the sickly-sweet well-dressed assistant does anything but assist, considering you somewhat lower down the pecking order than an estate agent, and you can't get much lower than that.

Another trait I've noticed is that these same title concious women only show off, be it subtle or bitchy, to other women. Their name dropping is also generally confined to conversations with members of the same sex. They flirt with male colleagues, more so if he is in a position of power. They have to go and introduce themselves and tell them what they do, collate statistics, make phone calls, tell some lesser oik to make tea and collate more statistics. What really makes her week is when a lesser oik in another branch has not produced her reports, so a phone call can be made

254

and a mother hen approach is taken with the underlying statement that its a 'good job' its her as she'll cover for you and then makes it known that she has one hell of a job with certain offices who are always behind with their work.

There was a contestent on a quiz show I was watching the other day who described herself as a secretary with a fashion house, adding that she had to make a lot of phone calls 'all over the world'. It was obviously important for her to get this point over.

And that's another thing, how many pushy Dads do you know? Whenever I see budding singers and actresses at talent shows or on the box, its always the Mum's that are doing the 'chatting up' of the organisers or judges.

I liken these types of females to council house owners who suddenly win the pools. They are not accustomed to money and recognition and they can't really handle it. Still it's amusing watching them.

Despite all the hope some ten years ago when the Tories returned to power that education would improve, no-one thought that, along with every other ministry, it would be subjected to cuts and shortages of staff. I was reading of a little girl last week who, since September has had nineteen teachers. Where is the stability in that? Where is the efficiency and economy come to think of it.

Past educationalists must be turning in their graves in despair as we offer softer options as the expense of the basics. Deborah has had a time of it with biology this year. Different teachers, and that's when they are lucky. Bearing in mind this is mock GCSE year its very important to get it right for the pupils.

Sometimes there are no teachers, so its a case of 'carry on revising'.

It comes to a pretty pass when West Indian families in inner London are sending their offspring back to the Caribbean so that they can receive a traditional British education. The trouble is that at the next Tory Conference, they will still be slapping each other on the backs and congratulating themselves on their achievements.

Apparently the West Indian teachers in Barbados teach things like respect, discipline, manners and the three R's. You know like we used to do here.

These left wing do-gooders have a lot to answer for.

Ironical really that some twenty years after Labour tried to make them a thing of the past, Grammar schools are still thriving and look set to expand their numbers considerably in the near future.

Well timed actually, as this week there is the case of a dyslexic boy who has had extra tuition outside of school hours stopped because of a cutback in Hampshire Education Departments funding. The lad used to receive one and a half hours teaching in the home every week because of his disability. The spokesman for the Area Education Office came out with the usual blurb about it having to stay within its budget. Well that is their God isn't it. A classic case for transferring all the financial funding from town twinning to Education I'd have thought. I mean, what at the end of the day is more important – twinning obviously.

Its sad that despite all the incidences of child abuse both sexual and physical that have ended with the poor mite dying, *no* real lessons have been learned. Though seventeen warnings were given another lad of two has died from constant beatings. All the reports include comments from the Social Services employees saying that 'lessons have been learnt and major changes are being implemented'. I thought they had before. No-one ever really carries the can though do they? Everybody's involvement seems to be as an aside, as if they're just 'passing through' a case. There's always so many people involved. Once again this was a situation where the lad's Mum was living with a boyfriend. I do hope there is a hell.

I forget to mention it, but a week after we moved into the new house, we had two unexpected visitors. Some friends that we had lost touch with over seven years ago. In fact they had missed out our last house completely, so a little detective work was undertaken to find us. Very glad they did. A date was arranged for them to come over for dinner and last Saturday was the appointed day. It was as if we hadn't seen them for two months not seven years. Besides all the catching up about each others children we talked about friendship during which the story about our holiday partners was told. They apparently had suffered the same sort of fate with a couple who they were very friendly with, still living in the same road as them. They nod acquaintance but that's it.

As Maureen said, we lost two friends on holiday, came back and regained two more, back to the status quo.

Talking of acquaintances, a chap I know was a British Telecom worker, with them for years until he took early retirement. He is one of these chaps, staunch Labour supporter and candidate in most local elections, who really has contributed to the local community over a number of years. He really can't have a lot of time to himself. He's on the board of governors of two schools, management committees for the local halls, the Citizen Advice Bureau etc, and revels in it. Even he, though was saying that the continual paperwork being churned out by the Education Authorities from Government is making a school governors job like a full time one, but without the payment.

I was a governor of a local first school for over four years and I agree that the amount of paperwork was ludicrous. While I think of it, that's another aspect about female 'power' that amuses me. On more than one occasion I have come across mothers who have either put themselves up or made it clear to friends that they would like to be put up as a 'parent/governor'. One of these Education department sops to democracy. Then they change, instead of being just a parent they are now 'in' with the staff. You'll know by the 'strut'. 'I am now a parent plus, so I must make it known'. The trouble is that so many women gossip that it becomes a 'clique' with only favoured mothers being in the know.

I'm going off at a tangent. Back to our Labour chappie, the point is that these grey paperwork churners are taking the enjoyment out of the community work done in spare time for free. I expect they'll be sponsored soon.

As I'm writing this (Tuesday 21st) Deborah is once again off school, this time its In-Set training. I've never known kids have so many days off during term time for various reasons. If its not in-service training its National Curriculum

Training. Its a pity they couldn't be trained to go in their holidays.

In Williams school Governors Report that we received in July (I'm just reading it now) there is reference to sex education in school. No they haven't gone as far as asking Samantha Fox to display her wares yet.

What does dismay one is reference to the fact that quote, 'as family groups and relationships gradually lose their clearly defined traditional characteristics, we can no longer assume that most families have two parents, and that children in the same house are related in any way. We must be very careful not to let any children feel that their own unit is in any way unusual or inferior. However, we should still be trying to encourage more stable relationships...' It goes on to state how by use of words like 'mate' and 'fertilisation' the teachers get across the basics.

If that was screed from a school in the Bronx I could understand it, but this is Surrey. Today's break up , tomorrow's delinquent.

In the same pile as this report was some gumpf from the Tories they handed out just before last May's local council elections. According to these 'gems' I possess, they have improved our Health Service by making it more efficient, providing us with a choice and giving us value for money. Ah, that phrase again. The one used by that woman who is so tight, she squeaks. They go on to tell us how they have expanded the Health Services, sorry *our* Health Service. Education Standards, have also improved apparently, giving improved standards, increased parental choice and regular assessment.

To back up these educational statements there is a full colour handout with two children posing behind desks, pens in hand, with smiling faces presumably pleased they are being educated under such a caring government. Both are in school uniform consisting of grey pullovers, white shirt and blouse (no, one is not a transvestite, there's a boy and a girl) school tie and neat hairstyles. No tramlines, earrings or other jewellery.

The little girl has got her head over to one side as if she is in a fairy liquid advert. Very beguiling, but unfortunately it doesn't represent the majority of British schools now.

Here's one that will make you smile. Another of these handouts is extolling the virtues of the poll tax. The heading reads 'If the Community Charge was unfair we would not have introduced it' Pompous bastards. The picture's amusing also. Husband (I assume) slightly taller than wife with arm around her. She's smiling, he's looking pensive, probably due to the fact that he's got to pay for the pair of them. Now of course taxpayers money is being poured down the drain in an attempt to get you to pay by direct debit for the cursed tax. What a bloody cheek. The only saving grace is that they're using music by the Walker Brothers, oh the lovely sixties.

The private phone line numbers under the agony aunt columns are becoming more hilarious. Were you aware that as a woman you can dial up and find out about 'Wind in your Vagina' I'm not quite sure if its telling you how to get it or how to get rid of it, but for 25p off peak and 38p on peak all will be revealed. There's another one on 'Tightening your Vagina'. For reasons of equality we have 'Losing your Virginity' for men and another number for women. 'Masturbation for Men and Women', but wait there's a number for 'Male Circumcision', but nothing for females. An ethnic trait that hasn't been pandered to? Must have been left out by mistake, a sure case for the race relations people.

The Radion advert on TV's bugging me. Its not the content, its the pronunciation. If its pronounced Raddion it should have 2 d's. I mean your home isn't full of raddiators is it? Mind you, thinking about it, the Roman arenas weren't full of glade-iators were they? Next.

Went to Wolverhampton by car yesterday. Not wishing to get 'one of my heads' by driving around the M25 and up to the M1, I decided on a route through Reading, Oxford (ring road), Stratford upon Avon and up through Alcester, Redditch, Bromsgrove, Stourbridge and Wombourne. It is some years since I travelled in this direction and it brought back happy memories of the train journeys in the late fifties early sixties when we would leave Paddington early Saturday morning and speed up the old Great Western Main Line to Birmingham Snow Hill and Shrewsbury where there would be an engine change. Off we would go behind vintage GW

259

Engines to either Tywyn or Portmadoc for the Tallyllyn and Ffestiniog Railway annual general meetings.

They were glorious experiences. Whichever location was applicable. The train would leave about 11.30 pm to the clicking of cameras, the roar of the whistle, the cheers of the locals and the detonators of British Railways feeling elated, cards would be played until one by one we fell asleep. Around 2.30 – 3.00 am everybody would come to life. We would be in Shrewsbury where our steeds would be unharnessed and either a Castle or King class engine would take us through the night to Paddington. Once through Reading General (beautiful name) I would lean out of the window trying to escape the smut but happy, ever so happy. I still go on steam trips occasionally now, but there's no passion, no real excitement. Steam engines are confined to certain routes and certain speeds with no late night sorties at all. Any tour that you do go on is tinged with memories of what it used to be like when every station had a goods yard, not a B&Q. The over bridges straddle empty ballast thanks to rationalisation, themselves subject to grafitti and harbouring trolleys thrown from the pavement above. No longer the semaphore signals and signal boxes worked by a servant of the operating company. No more the gangers hut, burnt out by vandals, just two lines, one sometimes, going from A to B and missing out all the places in between.

As I drove to Wolverhampton I remembered the route south of Birmingham where all the track was quadrupled and having raced through Leamington and Warwick we would knock off the stations listed on our itinerary in a very short space of time. Hatton, Lapworth, Knowle and Dorridge, Widney Manor, Solihull. There were a number of 'ands' in the area. Acocks Green and South Yardley, Small Heath and Sparkbrook. North of Birmingham Snow Hill, once a giant amongst stations, were Soho and Winson Green, Handsworth and Smethwick, Bradley and Moxley before arriving at Wolverhampton Low Level. Today, what stations that remain open are pale shadows of their former selves with the obligatory graffiti strewn 'shed' that calls itself a waiting room. Where are the sturdy red brick buildings that added strength and solidity to the system? Where are the gardeners who doubled as porters tending this years entry in the station garden competiton? Where is the quality?

I'm off Bromsgrove. Its gone and got itself twinned with Gronau or something.

Still rumaging through bits and pieces I've come across one of William's earlier school books. Glad to say they are all like this still in his school. Its full of pictures and stories of girls doing girls things and boys doing boys things. This should upset the libbers. The cover shows a boy about to break the tape in a race, while a little girl runs behind. Both appear nicely dressed. Mind you, they do throughout the water coloured paintings. A turning of the cover tells you that Yellow Book 1, Through the Rainbow was first published in 1964 having had twelve impressions up to 1977. One picture shows girls playing with dolls, another has a little girl making something with clay by a window overlooking open space and bushes. Shows the book's age doesn't it. For school playing area read future DIY. Further on into the book, the finished clay model becomes a doll. Pleased with that success, the girls go on to paint. The boys meanwhile are making aeroplanes and trains. They are also building castles out of the sand in the sandbox.

Aeroplanes to bomb people, castles from which to attack people? dear oh dear. Ah, there's a picture of a little boy making a boat with a sail suspiciously like those used by Vietnamese Boat People on the journeys to Hong Kong, before they go back again of course.

At the end of it all, they appear to be the picture of inno-cence, probably because in those days they would have been going home to a real mum and a blood related father. The end painting is one of the father with a hand on the shoulder of the young boy, expressing his praise for the work the lad has done in the book being held in the mans other hand. Yes its definitely his father. He's dressed in casual, but smart attire, looking not to dissimilar from the actor Charles Tingwall. He used to be Dr Dawson in Emergency Ward 10. That dates me doesn't it. Anyway, he's also wearing slippers and that definitely doesn't lead me to believe that he's a child molester, or mummy's boyfriend or both.

You know I said Mr Patten's refusal to allow development at Foxley Wood is seen only as an adjournment by the consortium, Well they are now crying in their Chablis and whinging that they have spent two years planning the site and now it looks as if it could be wasted – Do dums doos.

The West Surrey and North East Hampshire Health Authority are holding a competition open to anyone to design a logo. Fancy being logoless in this day and age. Obviously their name isn't enough. A decision will be made at a meeting in January 1990, Apparently its not necessary to incorporate the name in the logo. Wouldn't be would it. The end result will no doubt be bold, full of colour and indecipherable.

Some people have less taste that Bracknell has class. Going into Aldershot today I passed a mobile home with stone cladding. Mind you, that wasn't the end of it. The other day whilst at some traffic lights I spied a house (semi) that had 'stuck on' lead added in diamond form to the windows. Heavily varnished front door, front wall with brass insert containing the house name, which indeed ended in 'House'. How could they, a semi. Crowning glory was a lych gate with tiled roof. And all to no avail, it still looked like a semi-detatched council home. I mean, you could never accuse me of being a snob.

December

Well I'm very disappointed in the Free Frenchman. I'm not a prude, but the amount of time spent on love scenes detracts enormously from the seriousness and drama of the subject. If someone is having an affair, fine, tell the audience, but don't keep showing couples in the act every five minutes, its unnecessary.

I was in an office yesterday, sitting at someone's desk, and I spotted a notepad with the words 'Roy Scot Trust'. Now Freudian or not, my love of railways told me it read 'Royal Scot', until I looked again. I asked the owner what it meant and he told me that it was short for 'Royal Bank of Scotland Trust'. Everything has to be shortened, or replaced with a logo, doesn't it. 'Roy Scot Trust' sounds like a cancer fund.

There was quite a lot of reaction to the articles about beagles being used in experiments. The vast majority of people don't want it, do they. I'm pleased to note that Safeways are to ban all non-food products that are tested on animals, let's hope that they are true to their word. Over eleven thousand tortured beagles a year in this country alone, over three million animals altogether makes terrifying reading. There is no excuse.

In the local paper last week were the usual photos of weddings held in the local area, six in all plus the spiel about the young things. Interesting though was the fact that two couples were honeymooning in the USA, one couple in the USA *and* the Caribbean and another in Hawaii. Only one were staying in Britain – Norfolk, while the last pair were going to Majorca, never mind.

Have you heard the one about the dyslexic pimp – he bought a warehouse. Subtle huh!

Apart from the purely biased and unfounded reasons that they're foreign and anyway its 'human nature', ones dislike of the French, and Italians gathers credence when taking into account their love of eating horsemeat. Apparently from 1992 EEC regulations are to be relaxed so that British horses – and ponies – will be more readily available for overseas consumption. People in the know, ie the British Horse Society and the International League for the Protection of Horses are most concerned because dealers will be able to come here and buy whole herds at a time to be shipped abroad and killed in a foreign abbattoir. Alas, their standards and concerns for the welfare of animals tends to be much lower than ours, and with the draft EEC regulations currently being drawn up allowing only one break for rest and water we get a good idea of the 'standard' of bureacrat in charge of these affairs. Workers rights – yes, workers charters -yes. Basic animal needs – forget it.

Once again the civil liberties lot are backing a lost cause. Dorset Police' decision to ask members of the public to shop drink/drivers should be given all the support possible, but where are the C.L. lot? Well they're concerned about 'rights'. They cannot see the wood for the trees can they? Yes of course the Police are going to receive the odd call from someone with malicious intent, but if the 'victim' is stopped and found to be OK then no harm's been done, except wasted time. On the other hand, if someone knows a driver has been drinking, does not report it, and finds that the chappie has maimed or killed someone, then they are morally as guilty as the driver.

The Council for Civil Liberties are no better than the likes of Lord Longford, are they. I mean, why bother about the victim when you can bend over backwards to protect the guilty and blame society. There should be a place for these people, Japan's far enough away and they certainly deserve each other.

Britain's on the rack again, I see, over its decision to repatriate the Vietnamese refugees who have fled to Hong Kong. Not only is it America's legacy and their problem, but its really rich when the Vietnamese tell us they are not going to accept their own people if they are being deported from the British Colony 'forcibly'. The silence from the rest of the world, when help is asked for, remains defeaning.

I've been down to a local garage and bought five cars including an MG midget, two Maestros, a Saab and a Fiat Strada. Three of them are ready to go straight in the paper for sale, the others will need a bit of work first. I'm quietly optimistic that this month will see a slight upturn in business, by Christ it needs to. Everybody seems to be in the same boat, even the large rental companies are retaxing vehicles they would normally have sold by now, because there are just no buyers.

I started to watch that Secret Policemans Ball programme on the TV the other night and turned off after a couple of sketches. Why do popular comics have to resort to filth and innuendo to get a laugh? Perhaps that's why they are so popular. They have to shout at you, the Ben Elton syndrome seems to be spreading. I obviously didn't learn my lesson as I turned on Channel 4 to watch Hysteria 2. Having glanced at a trailer and seen John Cleese on stage with Tina Turner I thought it could be amusing. Wrong. It was just a rehash with a few changes of 'artistes' from the previous Amnesty International offering. I saw Stephen Fry and Lenny Henry trying to 'shock' the home viewers in a pathetic sketch about condoms which was just smutty, and two stand up comics, who weren't, utter the biggest load of drivel since the government declared that public ownership of the utilities need not result in larger bills.

All of a sudden, Mel Smith comes on and starts spouting about AIDS. Simple soul that I am, I was not aware until his appearance that this is what it was all for. Funny, but when the camera had swung onto the audience, I had commented to those around me that it appeared to consist of every social worker, teacher and other Brent employee with a conscience. All the male theoretical screwballs without ties, donning loud and sometimes sloppy jumpers, their female counterparts sporting loud dangly earrings and rats maze hairdos. Should impress the children though. I imagine the idea is that if you dress immaturely then your pupils will consider you to be on their wavelength and conform to your requirements and ideals more readily.

265

Talking of bottoms – there's more than a tenuous link here – I went to the doctors yesterday. Initially I'd made an appointment about my big toe which appeared to be blistering just below the nail, and not wanting to experience how a prisoner felt being tortured by the Gestapo, I felt a compunction to save the nail. No not the Whale, the nail. Anyway off I went, saw a lady doctor *on time*, and she prescribed some cream, which I could obtain from the chemists down the road for the obligatory £2.80 fee. Not for me the free handouts, supplementary benefits (sent to you by Girocheque, cashable at a post office) and free milk etc. I say etc 'cause it surely can't stop there, hang on, there's rent subsidy, rates rebates as well. Of course when the dreaded poll tax comes in they'll only be paying twenty per cent of the total bill anyway. Not for the likes of us though. We work, do not have hordes of kids and try to pay our way – well this is Surrey you know.

Having sorted out my toe, I explained the other, and to me, more serious problem. I've been suffering for the last two months or so from stabbing pains in the groin and backside. It literally is like having someone insert a spear up you. It causes me to double up, the pain coming in spasms. I've had this on and off for many years, but until recently these occasions have been rather infrequent. We were out for dinner on Saturday night when I got these shooting pains as we were eating, most uncomfortable. She examined me and stated that I definitely was not suffering from a hernia. Actually I wonder how many punters with similar pains can visit their doctors and with eye to eye contact discuss their problem. There must be a lot of decadants wondering whether they are victims due to their own preferences. Not for me though, clean living you see – smug bastard.

Anyway she diagnosed 'irritable bowel syndrome' and prescribed some peppermint tablets. Amongst the questions she asked was one about flatulence (for those in mobile homes, wind, and for those with no home, farting).

This irritable bit is an understatement. If the doctor had been in bed with Maureen and I last week when I let one go, the term 'bloody aggressive' would be more appropriate. Still, lets see if this other £2.80s worth works. Time will tell.

The young lady who is typing this up told me about a book from W H Smith, that is a directory of publishers and agents. I obtained a copy and having made a few notes on types of books published, the numbers published yearly etc I sat at my desk, stretched out my body unconciously, and picked up the phone. God was I nervous. Here I was, entering the unknown. It was at this moment that self-doubt really hit me. I know nothing about publishing, and probably even less about writing. I've spent nearly a year on this, told a lot of people about it, and now its crunch time. 'William Collins Sons and Co' it said on page 153 of the year book. They seemed a good bet to start with. I thought, I'll ring them in a minute. That minute has stretched for two days. Its the thought of somebody telling me 'thanks, but no thanks'. Anyway I've made the call, spoken to their New Manuscripts Editor and she's asked me to send in a couple of months and a synopsis. Maureen has typed up a list of subjects covered on a monthly basis with a covering letter and I'm about to go to the post.

Its all very well telling yourself that famous authors, household names even, have sometimes been turned down time and time again before getting their first work published, but it's still upsetting when it's YOU! What started out as a sideline exercise becomes a very consuming part of one's life and yes, I will be very disappointed if this is to stay collecting dust on a shelf. What am I going to do next year. Go back to selling cars full time? Start on a follow up just in case this gets published? Only time will tell.

I'm sure that if I asked the right people, I'd get an answer, but it always amazes me how ITV and BBC viewing figures are compiled. To *know* that nineteen million people watched a particular programme, putting it at number one for the week, against another contribution attracting 18.9 million and coming second would seem to require a very technical survey. Is it based on one thousand people and multiplied I wonder? No-one ever asked me what I watched.

Sad to see Trevor Francis out of a job, and Mel Machin come to that. Lets hope they go to clubs who will appreciate their talents.

You remember the trouble we encountered with 'travellers' camping on public land in the area, well the local Parish Council at last weeks meeting, discussed this problem and are now going to write to their MP about the cost and concern of these people flouting the law. That is the whole point. The law is there. By-laws exist to stop you and me but no action is taken against travellers. The Council are apparently concerned that the Police did not move the caravans on. As the Parish Clerk said, he had received letters from people successfully prosecuted under local by-laws, wondering why they were not implemented when required for these trespassers. Next year they will be writing again and asking the same question, when another invasion takes place. They're just bloody gutless, thats the problem. 36mph in a 30 area is so much easier to deal with, and it helps the statistics.

Is it me? On page two of the newspaper 'Today' a few days ago, three of the five articles dealt with people 'suing'. Out of interest the other two articles were about the Phillipines coup and the British Aerospace takeover of Rover Cars (for which we are now answerable to Europe), slapped wrists and sent to Coventry I expect, still its better than being sent to Torremolinos. The three cases of suing comprised Ferranti's attempt to sue the ex boss of the American company they took over for £127 million, Count Tolstoy's plight at being successfully libelled for £1.5 million by Lord Aldington (unbelievable sum) and lastly, one dear to all householders hearts, that of a couple selling a house which was suffering from subsidence and not declaring it. The ins and outs of the case are immaterial really, but the main issue at stake is that, like cars, prospective purchasers no longer buy on the 'buyer beware' ticket. So another stage is reached whereby a couple who did not have a house inspected before purchase successfully manage to sue, receiving £12,000 damages and £5,000 costs and interest. They had the choice, whether it was to save money or blind belief in the opinion of the sellers, I know not, but having taken the course of not bothering to have an inspection, I find it incredible that they can even be in the running, let alone win the case. What was it I said in January about the over-protection of consumers.

Well the MG Midgets gone, a Fiat Panda is about to go, and the Saab will be at the end of the week. Just got to get the fan repaired so that the heater works properly and that should placate the buyer. Interestingly enough, the Midget has done 91,000 miles and the Saab 93,000. All the media coverage of 'clocking' car dealers but never the 'clocking' public, doesn't alter the fact that if the car is what they want and cheap enough, they'll buy it regardless of mileage.

We ordered a table and six chairs, a hall table and coffee table from a well known and established furniture store. Delivery was to be six weeks. That was seven weeks ago. A phone call produced the reply that the furniture is late due to a problem with wood suppliers in Romania. Well it makes a change from the computer being at fault. The upshot of it all is that we may be without dining room furniture at Christmas. While Maureen was on the phone she asked why we could not have the table and chairs which are on display in this company's Aldershot branch. The woman at the other end of the phone told her that it was 'against the law' to sell it! Maureen asked which law this was, but she didn't know. When told that we had seen a suite of furniture with 'reserved for' tickets and the customers name on at least two occasions she was unable to say why this should be. They have promised to ring us next week and let us know what's happening.

To add insult to injury, not once during the twenty minutes we were in their shop did anyone come up and ask if they could help us. We sat down on suites, looked at colour swatches, compared designs and discussed the merits of each. But no, a Scottish chap, dressed without jacket, kept milling around, smoking, and two other non-assistants roamed aimlessly. We'll get a three piece suite elsewhere.

The afternoon had started off badly. Having parked in a side street, we made our way through to the main shopping area via the Co-op which has doors at both ends of the shop, saving you a walk around the block. There was rubbish strewn outside its entrance from the car park, the interior walls were dirty, scuffed and in dire need of a paint. I can't imagine that the floor saw a good clean daily. If it did there are an awfully large number of clumsy people who shop there. Liquid remains, large splashes dried and blackened. It was like driving through Belgium. What concerned me was the number of people shopping there oblivious to low standards, to put it mildly. There again, on observing the type of shopper, one sees a picture begin to form. A large number of prams, cries of 'Put that down, Duane' and 'Don't touch Charlene'. The perpetrators of these and other well known phrases expounded daily in the public nuisance areas known as Council estates have come shopping. Unmarried mothers with grubby faced little oiks in prams or just in tow. They are usually smoking, wearing short skirts and high-heeled shoes in gaudy colours with bleached hair (lank) to match, or not as the case may be.

Safeways, Sandhurst is like an oasis after this lot. Anyway, I digress. Having tried on several occasions to contact Toys R Us, yes I think its a silly name as well. On a par with the Pizza or MacDonalds phrase 'to go'. Not takeaway, but Pizza to go. To go where? on its holiday, for a bath, a night on the town. Another one that sounds unfinished is polyunsaturates. It doesn't sound right either. I'm sure it should be polyunsaturated something.

I'll start again. Having tried on several occasions to contact Toys R Us, without success, we drove to their Woking shop to get some transformer characters, a couple of children's games and some Tyco blocks that match with Lego, but are much cheaper. Actually that last bits not quite right. Lego seems a rip off – that's better.

Having driven across the wild and desolate terrain that's known as Pirbright, and turned right prematurely into Brookwood Hospital, only to lose our place in the queue of traffic heading for the previously named multi-cultural metropolis, we arrived to find a new ring road being built. Finding our way and bearings, the sign pronouncing 'Toys R Us Car Park' came into view. A quick right turn, up a spiral drive and into – a public car park. No signs now saying 'Toys R Us Car Park'. Dirty windstrewn concrete mass, graffiti despoiled staircases expectations of a would be mugging around every landing and the bastards expect you to pay 20p per hour until 8pm for this privilege. Any hopes that the store would have improved since

270

last year were quickly dashed. About twelve check out desks and four lights on. 'No Tyco, sold out' stated the brainless wonder. This was after having shown him the area where Lego was, and Tyco wasn't and explaining its function.

Well we got the transformers, a video, a present for our niece and a couple of bibs and bobs. Fifteen minutes queuing found us in the hands of a young lad who rang up the same item twice. As unpaid stock control measure, you can no longer be expected to witness the amount quickly being deducted from the next item. Oh no, nothing so simple. Three times he rang for a supervisor. Another five minutes with the queue building up.

Maureen eventually had to walk over and 'persuade' a supervisor to come back and play about with the computerised till. Surly bitch. I wouldn't mind being used for stock control purposes if it actually worked, but the one item we really wanted was 'out of stock' and 'we might not get any more until after Christmas'. They were only advertising it the day before on TV. The phones continually engaged, so you cant find out. I wonder if it is the same in their American branches. I doubt it.

Anyway, on Monday we're off to the nativity at William's school – he's a King with one line and Simon's coming down next Friday to help me run the bar for the single's group Christmas party. He's staying for the weekend, so no doubt we'll be visiting a railway line somewhere.

Does Chris De Burgh not remind you of Ray Davis from the Kinks? He does me.

A Lambeth resident, unemployed, strangles his 'pet' cats and is jailed for three months. One cat's died, one's survived. Why was he not disqualified from ever owning an animal again? It's no good a spokesman for the Campaign Against Drink Driving moaning that we think more of animals than we do humans. In cases like this it's not surprising, but I know what he means. He cites a case of a drunk driver who kills a young mother and is fined £160 and banned for one year from driving. To my mind, both acts were murder. Both were apparently through drink. Perhaps there should be an intelligence test before you can consume alcohol. No that wouldn't work. Intelligent people drive having got rat-arsed. Public execution for a first offence, that's more like it.

It will all be forgotten by the time you read this, but Nadia Comaneci, her lover and his ex-family are becoming tiresome in the newspapers. How on earth the Mail on Sunday can consider it worth reporting on at any great length, let alone headlines, nay, two thirds of the front page news beats me.

A lot has been made of the two finalists in the British Astronaut Competition. One young lady and one chap. There had to be a lady finalist, and I'm not saying for one moment that she isn't one of the best candidates, or even *the* best, but there had to be an Eastern European or coloured finalist in the Miss World competition. Another venue the viewer was permitted to witness in those days of ordinary pleasure, when we sat at home and could only hold our hands up in amazement, wondering how a dog (Apologies to the National Canine Defence League) like that could be in the final seven when the one we'd rooted for was knocked out at the first hurdle.

Is this the tip of the iceberg though. It surely won't be long before an unmarried mother is a must for inclusion as a finalist in any competition so that the left wing TV interviewer can record the hardships and the determination of the contestant. Having a child with a terminal illness should just tip the scales in her favour I'd have thought.

I'm getting a bit worried about Charlton Athletics league position. I hope their board of directors do keep faith with Lennie Lawrence and not take a leaf out of Queens Park, Ranger's or Manchester City's book.

Not a bit impressed with 'Today' newspaper at the moment. All the Water Share advertising and promoting is definitely making me feel sick. Is there a knighthood going spare or something?

Ah well, one bright and unexpected side effect of the current high interest rate comes from the knowledge that more women are having abortions so that they can continue working, and help with the mortgage. Every cloud has a silver lining, huh.

I was interested to note that the manslaughter charge brought against a young woman whose unborn child died after a car crash has been dropped. I know it was in America, but what sort of woman goes on a drinking session when she's eight and a half months pregnant? The person in question is of course a 'Ms' and she was represented by a leading civil rights campaigner who commented that never before had a woman been made criminally responsible for anything that happens to a foetus. Would her views be the same if by some gynaecological 'transplant' it was the male who gave birth and not the female. Cries of 'murder' would no doubt be reverberating around the court with obsessed women baying for blood and balls – if we still had them.

The above bit was written over a week ago, the nativity came and went and William's brain was unfortunately miles away when he should have delivered his line – so he didn't. Simon stayed last weekend, the Singles Club Christmas party went well and I've received a letter back from William Collins saying 'thanks, but no thanks'.

I must confess to feeling extremely depressed. Maureen commented that I didn't really expect to get a 'thumbs up' first time round, and she is, of course, right. It still saps one's confidence however.

I don't think much of these new 'comedy' first class stamps. The gold side profile of the Queen's head appears to be lost on half of these offerings, the subject itself seems to be 'clutching at straws', and the 'p' for pence is missing altogether. Yes I know its 20 pence but I would still like it to say so. This is another example, small I grant you, but a fair example none the less of how we are degrading a symbol of authority, lowering the reverence our currency should deserve and proving that it won't be long before we witness stamps portraying a single pregnant woman, a scene from war-torn Beirut and the case for the Health Department v Ambulance Workers. Come to think of it, sponsored stamps could be just around the corner too!

Our local church, the one that keeps putting on little 'dos' in support of Amnesty International has just produced its latest copy of 'The Parishoner'. In it is an article on 'War Toys'. Tanks, guns, airplanes with bombs etc. In fact anything connected with the normal healthy upbringing of a young chap. I played cowboys and indians as a lad, and I've never yearned to be Clint Eastwood. We played out many Second World War 'fights' after seeing a Saturday film, but we didn't end up mugging old ladies. Banning toys like that will not deter those who seek to injure and kill. Surprise, surprise, there's a support group called 'Play for Life' who visit trade fairs and try to persuade toy manufacturers not to make these dreadful weapons of death. Aren't they boring sods. They hold karate classes in the Church Hall. I wonder how they wrest their anti-aggression views with that of those lads and lasses grunting loudly and kicking hell out of each other? I remember, they pay the church for hiring the hall. Money talks?

I saw a Christmas card had been sent to the club I belong to the other day. Being nosey I observed that it had come from the club's solicitor. In the bottom left hand corner of the card it said 'In Aid of the Solicitors Benevolent Association'. Never did I realise that benevolence extended to that occupation.

Could you imagine anyone going out and asking to see some charity cards and picking out those over priced, blood-sucking lot. What a cheek.

With 1992 approaching as fast as the Channel Tunnel, and Nestles having to be pronounced Ness-Lay I suppose I will have to ask for Branston Pick-Lay, give William a tick-lay and play with the wife's nipp-lay.

I'm still suffering from those stabbing pains. Its the Friday before Christmas and they were so acute I was awake by 4am and could not get back to sleep, so I think another visit is inevitable. I will ask to see the same doctor again. I cannot understand these female patients who insist on women doctors examining them. Its all right if they are paying privately, but they've got a bloody cheek expecting it on the N.H.S. Another instance of a step forward for feminism that will lead to chaos if perpetrated by all females. Do they really want all patients to be examined only by someone of their own sex? I'd definitely prefer a woman doc cupping my balls while I perform a 'cough test'.

We did hear back from the furnishers, and no, we're not going to get our suite before Christmas. I spoke to their

Marketing chappie who had just arrived back from Romania having had 'exhaustive' talks with agents, manufacturers etc in an effort to placate the waiting hoards. Alas, with the country in the turmoil it is now 'enjoying' he has a cast iron case – you could say a cast iron curtain case, but you probably wouldn't. Christmas dinner on the kitchen table, should be fun. Still, my mum's given us a very useful present this year – a hostess trolley – she must have known.

'Dads Army' continues to stay as fresh as when first shown, and the film is being screened over the Christmas period, so that will be taped. I would like to see the other 'Croft & Perry' series repeated. What about 'Hi-De-Hi' from the first series again, as well as 'It Aint Half Hot Mum', as I suggested earlier.

How do ICI get away with it, nothing to do with 'big business talks', is it? I watched the Granada programme 'World In Action' a couple of weeks ago and was amazed how easy it is to dismiss claims and put case after case down to 'rare instances'. There is no smoke without fire, but they get away with it time after time.

Good to see that Harrods and all the other House of Fraser stores are to ban the sale of furs. Pressure does pay off sometimes doesn't it.

Any thoughts Paddy Ashdown has of ever being taken seriously, let alone heading a government, must surely be dismissed as laughable after his outburst over the Vietnamese. To comment that America took twenty times more refugees than Britain and assumes no retort is beyond belief. There is a tad more land available in the USA, it is their problem, not ours, and generally they are not wanted here. Still its just as well to know where the man stands, and his party for that matter, well before an election.

To retain this standard of life in Britain, we need to cut the population, not enhance it. I'm not being selfish because it helps nobody if we lower our standards to satisfy the guilt felt by certain sections who consider overseas aid as an obsession and never think of the war widow eeking out her life on a miserly pension, almost grudgingly handed to her in payment for her husband's giving of life to keep this country independent. Mr Ashdown goes on to say that 'If you're East German and you drive West, you're a hero' Yes OK, but they are not driving West to Britain are they, only another part of their own country. We wouldn't welcome 100,000 East Germans here any more than 100,000 Vietnamese so the equation is meaningless. Please don't mess about, pussy footing around trying to juggle principles with morality and common sense. Do what you know is required, say no to everyone and send them all back as quickly and painlessly as possible. As sure as eggs are eggs, whatever we do will end up in mass condemnation so we might as well do what we all know is 'right' at the start. Am I alone on this or just part of a very silent majority?

I've just remembered an instance of 'Brit Bashing' Maureen and I witnessed a few years ago when spending a weekend in Amsterdam. We visited Anne Frank's house, it was very moving contrasting the 'then and now' scenes of photos and memorabilia against the present appearance. We stayed well over an hour reading letters, getting the feel of the place and trying to relate to the horror of living on a knife's edge until betrayed. Feeling somewhat humbled we made our way back downstairs to the entrance lobby where there was a display and books available. Part of the display there was about oppression in the present time. Instances from third world countries, banana republics etc were displayed and we both sympathised as we walked around the room. All of a sudden, surprise and disgust. There were pictures of buildings burning in London and policemen and coloured people fighting in Brixton. I wish now that I had said something, I don't know why I didn't. I do remember that both of us felt fairly annoyed that Britain was represented in such an unfair way. Which country always starts a fund for this and that disaster, natural or otherwise? Which country sends relief packages, lorries with food and clothing wherever it is needed? Which country has more charity records than anyone else? We all know the answer, but we still get castigated – perhaps they're jealous of not being British, who can tell.

Its so pleasing to see that those who brought their water shares will be receiving a 'nice little earner' with instant profits being forecast. So much for a nation of shareholders, where is the stability. How many companies will be British owned at the end when shares have changed hands for the umpteenth time, the market has settled down and the big boys have cleaned up.

I see that tens of thousands of illegal immigrants are entering this country and in 1988 we deported just 2,800. Who was it said we're not a soft touch?

Another nibble at the cake of British independence occurred recently with the announcement that the good old gill is to be abandoned in the name of harmonisation, that great European cause. All it means is that spirits will be dearer, another sop to the bureaucrat, another erosion of our tradition.

These polls conducted on behalf of half-wit organisations slay me, you know. 'EPOCH', the anti smacking group are pleased with the results of a survey which confirmed that three out of four parents smacked their children. Their co-ordinator chappie, whatever that means, commented that 'the clear rejection of the more physical punishments and of smacking babies shows we are on our way'. Well whats new. Most parents don't beat their offspring. There is a vast difference between a smacking around the back of the legs as a disciplinary measure and knocking the hell out of a child. I sometimes feel that these people are looking for problems and are disappointed if they find there is not one there to correct. Perhaps that's how these crusaders get turned on. Interesting to note is the conclusion to the survey that smacking was least in favour with the eighteen to twenty-four year olds and most in favour with the over sixties. Surely the problems we have now with a lack of discipline amongst the young is greater then that encountered by the present over sixties when bringing up their offspring. Nuff said.

I was very impressed with the supermarket worker who conned his way into a top management job with Nissan and kept it for nearly four months. I know its petty, but you do feel that for once a little bit of luck and an awful lot of nerve have served to beat the system, especially when its the Japanese.

All the stars, I see, have got the fizzoggs together again to reproduce Band Aid's hit. At the expense of originality and calling themselves Band Aid 2, they should be there at the top by Christmas.

Five youngsters died this week in an Escort RS Turbo which ploughed into a wall at a speed in excess of 100 mph. The driver, a twenty-four year old, who had six passengers received the car as a present from his mother. If ever proof were needed that an 80 mph governor be fitted to all cars, then surely this is it.

Despite all the big guns in the motor manufacturing trade with their vested interest dismissing concern, this is one proposal I am sure will become mandatory within a few years.

I'm not going to say that I won't watch Smith and Jones in future, but having witnessed the pair of them kissing – I actually turned over half way through – it will take a lot to regain my confidence. Its not even funny. Having been told the punchline later on it seems to me that in order to get a laugh you have to shock. Take a leaf out of Dads Army or Blackadder or Victoria Wood. You don't have to offend, swear, shout or shock to gain an audience's laughter.

Well another one hundred and twenty-six Vietnamese refugees have been flown home, a spit in the ocean. Here we are caught between the devil and the seas they took so long to cross.

They are going down like nine pins aren't they. First its Poland, then East Germany, now its Romanias turn. What with Panama as well, the political face of the world has certainly changed this year.

Mum and Dad are staying over the Christmas period from today (Sunday) until Wednesday or Thursday. They should be down in about half an hour at 5pm. The car will no doubt be loaded to the gunwhales. William can't wait until tomorrow, but he's been quite well behaved. I've started the fire and we'll be putting out a mince pie and a glass of milk on the hearth.

Yes we are looking forward to it. There's a nice tree well decorated and lit, lots of tinsel and bunting hanging from the beams. We've put out a few presents around the tree and no doubt there will be more later. It will take the thick end of an hour to unload my parent's car and get everything packed away. Its not just presents, its the food. We buy the turkey,

Mum always buys the pork and beef, fairly traditional, what! Ah-ha, there's a knock at the door so I'm off now, see you when they've gone.

It seems like only a line ago. Its Thursday 28th December. Mum and Dad went home last night after dinner, we had the beef. There are a lot of mince pies left, the obligatory turkey pieces, some cold meats and lots of cheese, but then that's down to me, the deli's my department. Trouble is it costs twice as much as it would if Maureen shopped without me.

I have decided not to contact any more publishers until I have finished the book completely. My typist is currently in Colorado skiing down the slopes and wont be back until the New Year so providing she hasn't broken something that makes it impossible for her to type (No I didn't break anything, just a bruised rib or two – don't ask – Typist), the whole cubboodle should be in final manuscript form by the end of January.

Maureen and I made a pact not to discuss money until after Christmas. With a bit of luck we may have sold a few more cars before this month is out, time will tell. The MG Maestro looks to be on its way and we've attracted some interest in the Triumph Acclaim and the Montego.

Presents were generally less than the usual but I don't think we disappointed the children. One of my best pressies was a 'Blackadder 2' video, and knowing my love of Kylie Minogue I also received a twenty minute video tape of her swaying and miming to her hits.

I'm sure its not a record but I counted no less that sixteen of those horrid satellite dishes in one road of council houses near Farnborough. If they are not council houses then they certainly look like them. Yes they must be, the number of dishes is matched only by the number of long haired alsatians. At least three of them have got fairy lights over the porch and there are tales of a gnome with tinsel lurking on the estate somewhere. What a disincentive to buy.

I'm getting a little tired with the 'Today' newspapers obsession with the pregnant matron at a girl's school who was dismissed from her job. Having asked readers to ring in and record a 'yes' or 'no' as to whether the headmaster was right or wrong to sack her, they just keep following up the non-story. She has now coughed her sprog and will resume her battle through the courts in January. Since announcing the results of their little poll, which revealed that the vast majority of readers who phoned in thought that the head was right to sack her, the diatribe has been so one sided, you are left in no doubt of the papers stand. I also suspect that if the poll result had gone the other way it would have been headline news and not hidden away on the side of an inner page.

There is a case in the local paper of a motor trader who sold a car from home as a private sale, having wound back the speedometer, to a member of the public. He has been fined £2,400 for the offences, ordered to pay £214 compensation to the car's purchaser, plus £153 in legal costs and £150 in court costs. A total of over £2,900. It does pose the thought that if he'd ill treated or even killed an animal, assaulted an old lady, stolen goods from a house or killed someone in a car whilst drunk, his fine would have been so much lower with perhaps a community service award, sorry penance and slapped wrists. Yes he did deserve this because it does honest traders no favours at all, I just feel that having got fines in line for motor traders being out of order it would be nice to see sentences for crimes of violence reflect the same hard line pattern.

At the same time as our local paper enlightens us about 'clockers' it also reveals that Charles Church the builder who died in an aircraft crash left an estate valued at over £3.4 million. This little piece is on the front page next to a lead article about Mr Patten's refusal to allow the Foxley Wood development to go ahead.

The thought of losing too many conservative votes has obviously got to the Environment Minister. He has also vetoed the plans to build another 4,500 homes in Eversley and Hook. All of this has left one Andrew Bennett, Executive Director of Consortium Developments behaving like a spoilt little boy who hasn't got his own way. Imagine a 'man' in his position accusing the Minister of not 'going green but yellow'. Doesn't that smack of tantrums.

Well this is it, the end of the year. I still don't know whether to carry on writing notes for 1990 yet, but I'll have to decide in the next day or so. Its only when you write things down that instances you need to fall back on in an argument actually manage to be remembered.

Business wise its been a bloody disaster. House wise, yes we've managed to build and move into our new abode, but not selling the old home has soured that success. If we cant sell for the price we want early in 1990 we will definitely have to sell both and move. It wouldn't matter too much to me but it would to Maureen and the children.

I've just paid the half yearly income tax instalment, some back tax, the quarterly VAT and the motor insurance. Thats another rip-off. It was £403 last year. Now its £476. Just Maureen and I as named drivers. Over twenty-five years driving each, no claims and one speeding offence – 36 mph in a 30 area. How can it rise eighteen per cent. I'm probably paying for some finance house catching a cold over its acquisition of too many estate agencies.

Not only the end of a year but the end of a decade. One in which financial enhancement has been made the order of the day. Profit, profit and more profit. Investment only if profit in the short term can be achieved. How many people in 1979 thought that in ten years time the country would be despoiled by so much litter and graffiti, and that local authorities would be hiring teachers from Europe due to our inability to attract home grown talent to our state schools. A lot has been written and spoken about the plight of animals in the wild, but still the slaughter continues, be it in darkest Africa, less dense Brazil, the high seas or semi-rural Berkshire with hounds. On the domestic front, despite the annual pleadings, more and more unwanted dogs end up in Battersea Dogs Home.

Those who voted for a decade of law and order have been tragically let down, whereas those who have moved from one monopoly to another or from one government concern to another have been richly rewarded with vast, obscene pay-offs.

These are the days of the very rich and the poor. The rich have increased their wealth and will continue to do so with the introduction of the poll tax, those without will have all the handouts to subsidise them through to pensionable age, when they will no doubt be subsidised even further. For the tax paying, mortgage and rate paying middle class family it has been a decade of peaks and troughs with the troughs now coming home to roost with a vengeance. We are now paying the price for the Chancellors budget, where credit control, if applied firmly and early enough, would have relieved the economic anxieties, but then the power of the banks is overriding.

Who would have thought that so much effort would be put into conservation and ecology. That national papers would take on board causes, be it animal, vegetable or mineral.

Despite the environment being a vote-catcher and a genuine interest shown by the public we still witness this government's wish to dump thousands of tons of chemicals at sea in 1990. All governments appear to be the same. Some have higher priorities than others on different situations. The 'we deplore what you're doing in your sea, but we are right to kill off mile after mile of arable land for housing' syndrome still seems rife.

That sixteen per cent of all households are made up of single parents is a sobering thought.

We appear, at least, to have heard the last of Eddie Edwards, but having witnessed the Walton sextuplets again over the Christmas Season, I'd put money on watching their increasingly sponsored fizzoggs again in twelve months time.

That British Rail have to cancel trains because the accountants pen has written off too many coaches to save money, that football teams have to ground share, that pubs are no longer profitable as a good quiet evening's entertainment, that tube fares have to rise by fifty per cent to dissuade passengers from using them – these are the facts that make up the real world.

And what is in store for 1990. Will Ken Barlow be re-united with Deidrie? Will Cathy in Emmerdale Farm be bedded by Seth or Amos – or both?

Far fetched? After one channel voted Mrs Thatcher – 'Woman of the Decade' and the other voted for Kylie Minogue, the mind boggles, sorry bogg-lays.